Ending the Death Penalty

Ending the Death Penalty

The European Experience in Global Perspective

Andrew Hammel
Assistant Professor for American Law
Heinrich Heine University Düsseldorf

First published 2010 by
PALGRAVE MACMILLAN

Palgrave Macmillan in the UK is an imprint of Macmillan Publishers Limited, registered in England, company number 785998, of Houndmills, Basingstoke, Hampshire RG21 6XS.

Palgrave Macmillan in the US is a division of St Martin's Press LLC, 175 Fifth Avenue, New York, NY 10010.

Palgrave Macmillan is the global academic imprint of the above companies and has companies and representatives throughout the world.

Palgrave® and Macmillan® are registered trademarks in the United States, the United Kingdom, Europe and other countries.

ISBN 978–0–230–23198–6   hardback

This book is printed on paper suitable for recycling and made from fully managed and sustained forest sources. Logging, pulping and manufacturing processes are expected to conform to the environmental regulations of the country of origin.

A catalogue record for this book is available from the British Library.

A catalog record for this book is available from the Library of Congress.

10 9 8 7 6 5 4 3 2 1
19 18 17 16 15 14 13 12 11 10

Printed and bound in Great Britain by
CPI Antony Rowe, Chippenham and Eastbourne

To my mother, Lillian Murvine Hammel

Contents

List of Figures

Acknowledgements

This book would not have been possible without the generous assistance of the Law Faculty of Heinrich-Heine University Düsseldorf, which provided me with freedom and institutional support as I worked on the research and the manuscript. In particular, I would like to thank the former Dean of the Law Faculty, Prof. Dr. Dirk Looschelders, for his understanding. My research assistant, Agatha Frackiewicz, tracked down innumerable sources and provided me with cogent summaries and analysis that greatly strengthened my arguments and helped me avoid pitfalls. I am indebted to David Garland for comments on an earlier essay concerning the book's themes, and to the anonymous reviewer for Palgrave who subjected my book proposal to a lucid and challenging critique.

I would also like to thank the participants at the 2008 Annual Meeting of the International Institute of Sociology in Budapest, Hungary, and the 2009 Annual Meeting of the Law and Society Association in Denver, Colorado for their lively and thoughtful reactions to my presentations on the themes of this book. I am also grateful to the Open University in Milton Keynes, England, for permitting me to attend a seminar on the abolition of capital punishment held by Professor Tim Newburn of the London School of Economics. Professor Newburn also graciously permitted me to read and cite a work in progress of his on the abolition of capital punishment in Great Britain. Dr. John Carter Wood provided helpful citations, a wealth of background knowledge in the sociology and history of violence, and stimulating suggestions all along the way. Dr. Dieter Reicher of the University of Graz, whose pioneering work on the comparative sociology of punishment has strongly influenced my approach, was also generous with his time and allowed me to read some works in progress directly related to the themes in this book. Professor David Dow of the University of Houston Law Center supplied ideas and encouragement in approximately equal measure. Needless to say, despite all the help I have received from these august sources, I am completely responsible for any errors, shaky arguments or unjustified conclusions. I would like to thank The Allensbacher Institute of Allensbach, Germany and TNS/Sofres of Paris, France for permission to reproduce the graphs tracking death penalty opinion in France and Germany which appear in Chapter 7.

Finally, I would like to thank my former colleagues in the death penalty bar of Texas, among them Richard Burr, Jim Marcus, Morris Moon, Robert C. Owen, Danalynn Recer, Meredith Rountree, Mandy Welch, and

Greg Wiercioch. They brought me into the fold, taught me much about the law and even more about human nature, and continue to embody, for me, the legal profession's highest aspirations.

Andrew Hammel

Introduction

The origins of this book date to the mid-1990s, when I worked for the Texas Defender Service, a small private non-profit law firm which represented Texas death row inmates in their appeals. Representing death row inmates is vital work, not least because it regularly can and does save human lives. But most of those who do this work have an ulterior motive: they believe it will hasten the end of capital punishment in the United States. American death penalty lawyers notched remarkable victories in the early 2000s: the Supreme Court outlawed capital punishment for those who were minors at the time of the crime (*Roper* v. *Simmons*, 2005), and for the mentally retarded (*Atkins* v. *Virginia*, 2002). But if these piecemeal victories contributed to the complete abolition of capital punishment, it was hard to see how. The death penalty still enjoyed the support of about 70% of the population, and – most importantly for the subject of this book – that fact was seen, in the United States at least, as convincing proof of its legitimacy.

After moving to Europe I resolved to examine how European jurists and activists had succeeded where their American counterparts had failed. What I heard from abolitionist lawyers and activists in Western Europe was surprisingly uniform, even across different countries and cultures: the American approach was doomed to fail. To paraphrase many conversations I had, the argument went as follows: 'You cannot possibly hope to convince a majority of the population to oppose capital punishment. If you make that a precondition to abolishing the death penalty, you have lost the battle before it has begun. I don't wish to give offense, but you naïve Americans do not seem to understand that a desire to see murderers executed is a basic drive of human nature, one which only the most educated are able to overcome.' When I related these arguments to my American colleagues, they were usually greeted with suspicion.

Yet, as I delved deeper into European law and history on the subject, I began to understand what the Europeans meant. The 'European' argument, at its core, could be broken down into four basic assertions: first, there is an ingrained human desire to inflict retribution or revenge on those who

1

commit serious crimes. Second, this predisposition to seek revenge will lead a majority of ordinary citizens to favor the death penalty for murder, and it is very difficult to change their views. Third, persons with higher levels of formal education think about crime and punishment differently than members of the general public, and are thus less likely to favor the death penalty. The fourth thesis – which follows from the previous three – is that if capital punishment is to be abolished, it must be abolished by educated elites. Needless to say, these assertions are not uncontroversial, and are thus rarely stated in such blunt terms by European death penalty opponents.

This book can be considered an examination of all four theses. Part I starts with a short sketch of the divergent paths of the United States and Western Europe on the issue of capital punishment. In Europe, death penalty abolition movements prevailed, leading to the recent establishment of Europe as a truly 'death-penalty-free' zone. In the United States, the abolitionist movement made steady progress until the early 1970s, at which point a backlash set in, reversing many of the previous gains and entrenching capital punishment into the American legal landscape. This sketch sets up the remaining discussion, which focuses on why the divergence took place and what it tells us about the European world view I have outlined above. Part I continues with research from various disciplines showing a strong cross-cultural tendency for people to seek revenge against those who have violently victimized them, and to experience vicarious satisfaction when the state exacts harsh punishment in the name of the people. This impulse is not shared to an equal extent by all members of any given society, and is channeled in different ways by different cultures. It is there, however, and it is universal, as shown by the considerable popularity of capital punishment in many different cultural contexts. There is also considerable evidence that the desire for vengeance decreases with increasing levels of education. After discussing these findings, Part I concludes with an examination of why mass public opinion on capital punishment is so resistant to change.

Part II of the book is a detailed examination of the process of death penalty abolition in Germany, France, and England. In each chapter, I will first sketch the emergence of modern 'abolitionism' – defined here as a social movement calling for the complete abolition of capital punishment for all crimes committed by civilians during peacetime (and excluding the special cases of treason and crimes of military jurisdiction). In all three nations, this modern abolitionist idea first emerged in the late 18th century, was developed and expanded in the 19th century, and finally prevailed in the middle-to-late 20th century. The specific historical context leading to abolition differed from nation to nation. Nevertheless, I hope to show that each of the three abolition movements shared common traits. The idea of total abolition was pioneered by public intellectuals and philosophers, and then gradually gained in popularity among the educated upper classes, especially the liberal professions. Once support for the abolition of capital punishment reached a 'critical mass' among the educated elite, legislative proposals to abolish capital punishment were tabled, generally by lawmakers in a national assembly. In fact, the final phases of all three abolition movements were managed largely by individual lawmakers: Thomas Dehler in Germany, Sydney Silverman in Great Britain, and Robert Badinter in France. In all three countries, perhaps the chief obstacle to abolition was public support for capital punishment. These abolition movements prevailed not by changing public opinion, but rather by shielding the capital punishment issue from the vagaries of the public mood and stiffening the spines of legislators who privately disdained the death penalty but feared a public backlash if they voted to abolish it.

The first two parts of this book can thus be read as a qualified endorsement of the 'European world view' concerning capital punishment. In Part III of this book, I will propose some tentative answers to whether the European model of elite-driven, top-down abolition can succeed in those countries which have yet to abolish capital punishment. I will argue that the process of death penalty abolition fits well within the general framework of the theory of the civilizing process elaborated by the German sociologist Norbert Elias. Elias' theory helps explain why the impulse to abolition always emerged first among social elites, and why all successful abolition movements have chosen a 'top-down' model which bypasses public opinion. Although the process of change in elite opinion proceeds similarly in most societies, it is not alone sufficient to achieve abolition: there are important structural preconditions for European-style abolition movements. Many attempts to explain national differences in penal policy rely heavily on cultural explanations. I will argue that structural factors are equally important. In particular, I will argue that the process of penal change cannot be understood without careful attention to the issue of *which social groups actually influence penal policy*. I hope to demonstrate that this focus on the structural characteristics of national legal systems generates useful contrasts between Western Europe and the United States that help answer the questions raised by the U.S./Europe divergence on capital punishment.

This book is not a polemic. Arguments for and against capital punishment have changed little over the past centuries, and much more eloquent writers than I have already marshaled the arguments on both sides. This book is, rather, intended to be a comparative policy analysis: the question is not the normative one of whether the death penalty should be abolished, but rather the descriptive one of how this was achieved in the past. Nevertheless, it may be disingenuous of me to hide my perspective: I oppose capital punishment, and I would be pleased if this book helped contribute, in some small way, to its eventual worldwide abolition. A better understanding of past campaigns against capital punishment may be of use in charting the future course of the international abolition movement.

Part I
The Transatlantic Death Penalty Divide and the Psychology of Vengeance

'Revenge may be wicked, but it's natural.'
– Rebecca Sharp in *Vanity Fair*, by W. M. Thackeray

1
America and Europe Diverge on the Death Penalty

A Note on Methodology: Focusing on the U.S. and Europe

This book will concentrate mainly on the evolution of capital punishment policy in the United States, the United Kingdom, France, and Germany. This focus should, of course, not be understood as dismissing the importance of abolition movements in other parts of the globe, such as Central and South America. As Franklin Zimring and David Johnson (2008) have recently pointed out, Asia has been the main venue for executions in the modern era, and deserves far more scholarly attention than it has so far received. However, I believe my focus can be justified on several different grounds. First, and most arbitrarily, my own limitations: I can read and speak only German, French and English.

However, there are other, less arbitrary, reasons. First, the modern movement to abolish capital punishment is generally agreed to be an intellectual legacy of the European Enlightenment. To be sure, one can find arguments against capital punishment, or political orders which do not appear to have inflicted it, in some ancient and non-Western cultures, among them certain phases of Roman rule and among some Slavic tribes (Ancel 1967:5–6; Green 1967). However, until the 18th century, capital punishment was practiced in all Western justice systems, and sustained arguments against the ruler's right to take life were essentially unknown. This changed in the second half of the 18th century. In 1765, the Austrian jurist Joseph von Sonnenfels critiqued capital punishment as 'contrary to the purposes of punishment' and called for its use only when other means of 'defending common security' were insufficient (Schmidt 1995:220–1). However, the first coherent, comprehensive and sustained argument against the state's right to kill was made by Cesare Beccaria (2008), a 26-year-old Italian nobleman, in his 1764 book *On Crimes and Punishments*. Drawing especially on the ideas of Locke and Rousseau, Beccaria adumbrated a case for the complete abolition of capital punishment for all crimes. Beccaria's book quickly achieved worldwide notoriety and was translated into most major languages. Beccaria's arguments, in one form

7

or another, have furnished the rhetorical basis for abolition movements in dozens of countries and cultures far remote from his own.

I also focus my study on these nations because the abolition movements there are extremely well documented. Western European nations had high rates of literacy and political involvement during the 18th and 19th centuries. Capital punishment was always a favorite topic of debate, and remains so to this day. The U.S., U.K., France, and Germany also have highly developed legal and political systems whose operations are well understood, painstakingly documented, and influential worldwide. This fact permits capital punishment policy to be assessed against a broader background of cultural and legal development. The points of contrast I will highlight in my analyses – along the axes of centralization, bureaucratic control of policy, and the nature of political representation – are well illustrated by the nations I discuss.

Finally, these nations are influential: political systems developed in Great Britain and on the European continent have, through colonization and imitation, exercised worldwide influence. The burgeoning literature on 'law and finance' has identified dozens of statistically relevant policy and outcome differences that can be traced to what its authors call a country's 'legal origin.' According to the general scheme used by law and finance scholars, most of the legal systems in the world are marked by their origins, which were French, British, German, or Scandinavian (La Porta et al. 1998). A country's legal origin, these scholars argue, turns out to have a lasting and statistically significant effect on its entire architecture of commercial law. Japan, for instance, adopted German criminal and civil codifications, which ensures that German conceptual frameworks and legal scholarship continue to exercise a significant influence in that country's legal system. Just as legal origin helps us understand differences and patterns in the way dozens of nations structure their capital markets or regulate corporations, it may also be able to help us understand how nations across the world shape criminal justice policy.

Thus, I hope to demonstrate in this book that a careful and in-depth comparison of European and American political practice concerning capital punishment generates insights that may apply in broader contexts. In particular, I will argue that it is impossible to explain the divergence in practice between the United States and Europe without addressing two specific methodological points. First, one must carefully distinguish the opinions of educated elites toward capital punishment from those of the general population. Second, one must closely examine the question of which social actors actually wield *practical control* over the development of criminal justice policy. As I will suggest, a comparison of the European and American experiences throws both of these factors into bold relief. I hope to demonstrate that they are important to understanding death penalty abolition in different regional contexts as well.

The Current Transatlantic Divide on the Death Penalty

Currently, a large gulf exists between American and European practices toward capital punishment. Protocol 6 to the European Convention on Human Rights (ECHR), opened for signature in 1983, requires signatory states to prohibit the death penalty except for crimes committed 'in time of war or imminent threat of war.' Each of the 27 current Member States of the European Union has signed and ratified this protocol (Directorate General of Communications 2007). All 47 Member States of the Council of Europe have done so as well, with the exception of Russia. Protocol 13 to the ECHR, opened for signature in Vilnius, Lithuania in 2002, provides for a flat prohibition on capital punishment, with no exceptions. As of 2007, 22 EU Member States and 40 Council of Europe Member States had signed and ratified it. Five EU Member States (France, Italy, Latvia, Poland, and Spain) had signed but not yet ratified Protocol No. 13 (Council of Europe 2008). (In this book, 'Europe' will refer to current Member States of the European Union, unless otherwise noted.) This remarkable uniformity in practice is the product of a conscious policy. As former Eastern Bloc nations began the long process of preparing to join the EU in the early 1990s, their political leadership was informed that 'the immediate institution of a moratorium on executions with a commitment to sign and ratify Protocol No. 6 to the [ECHR] within one to three years' was a condition of further progress toward EU admission (Directorate General of Human Rights 2001:8).

Europe is thus now a 'death-penalty-free' zone – both politically and geographically, since European nations which are not EU members (such as Switzerland and Norway) have also abolished the death penalty. Further, the return of capital punishment to any EU member state is now virtually unthinkable. Formally, the death penalty is barred by the existence of the Protocols to the ECHR. But equally importantly, the past decade has seen a dramatic shift in public opinion in many EU countries away from the death penalty. Whatever the causes for this shift – which will be further explored in Chapter 7 – it has reduced the political salience of capital punishment, and largely freed Western European politicians from the task of 'educating' the public about the evils of the death penalty, or fending off serious legislative attempts to reintroduce it. European Union officials regard the continent-wide abolition of capital punishment as a significant achievement, and rarely miss an opportunity to call attention to it. Further, they are working on ways to expand the abolition model they have used to other nearby nations.

In the United States, by contrast, capital punishment continues to be the law in almost 40 American states, and is provided for by federal law as well. To be sure, American death penalty abolitionists have scored victories recently. The Supreme Court has limited the application of the death penalty, and a handful of states have recently voted to abolish capital punishment.

Although many American states have the death penalty on the books, it is far from uniformly applied. The states of Texas and Virginia together account for almost half of all executions carried out in the modern era of capital punishment (that is, since 1976); whereas many states that keep capital statutes on the books carry out executions rarely, if at all. Finally, juries seem to be getting warier of imposing capital sentences. The number of death sentences handed down has declined significantly in recent years. This development is explained by several factors: a cooling of support for capital punishment; an increase in the number of states offering true life-without-parole sentencing options; significant decreases in the crime rate; improvements in the quality of legal assistance during death penalty trials; and more careful exercise of prosecutorial discretion in charging decisions (Sundby 2006).

Despite these notable recent gains, the 'pure, simple, and definitive' abolition of capital punishment advocated by Victor Hugo in 1848 and achieved in Europe still seems unthinkable in the United States. Capital punishment continues to enjoy the support of about 70% of the U.S. population – even though that superficial number may hide weakening in the foundations of that support (Death Penalty Information Center 2007). Politicians continue to tread warily around the issue, as evidenced by the fact that no American presidential candidate since 1988 has openly opposed capital punishment. Given the highly decentralized federalist structure of the United States, the only government body that would have the definitive power to outlaw capital punishment across the entire national territory is the United States Supreme Court. Although the Court has narrowed the scope of capital punishment and increased scrutiny of the fairness of capital trials in recent years, it has shown no signs of an inclination to use its constitutional power to abolish capital punishment once and for all.

The Transatlantic Divide in Historical Perspective

The current 'transatlantic divide' on capital punishment conceals a more complex historical reality. Many European nations practiced capital punishment until relatively recently. France, the last of the three largest EU member states to abolish capital punishment, did so only in 1981. Further, as recently as the early 2000s, capital punishment enjoyed majority support in many European countries, including France and the United Kingdom. To understand whether the 'snapshot' really reveals fundamental cultural differences, we need to broaden our historical perspective. As we will see in Chapter 8, there are more similarities than differences in the historical evolution toward abolition in Europe and in the United States. For centuries, the United States and large Western European nations moved almost in lock-step on the issue of capital punishment. Cesare Beccaria's seminal 1764 condemnation of capital punishment was quickly translated into English and read by many members of the founding generation of the United

States. Jefferson, for instance, wrote in 1821 that Beccaria had 'satisfied the reasonable world of the unrightfulness and inefficiency of the punishment of crimes by death' (as quoted in Masur 1989:53–4). Earlier, Beccaria's arguments had inspired Jefferson greatly to limit the applicability of death in his 1778 draft 'Bill for Proportioning Crimes and Punishments in Cases Heretofore Capital', in which he called the death penalty a 'last melancholy resource' which should be applied sparingly, since it prevented reformation and deprived fellow citizens of a 'long continued spectacle ... to deter others from committing the like offences.' Benjamin Rush, a Philadelphia physician, was one of the first prominent American public intellectuals to openly advocate the complete abolition of the death penalty for ordinary crimes.

The early 19th century saw growing abolitionist sentiment among elites on both sides of the Atlantic. In England, the parliamentarian Samuel Romilly began his crusade against England's 'Bloody Code', which prescribed execution for hundreds of offenses. Parliament held a number of unsuccessful but close votes to completely abolish capital punishment and, in the 1830s and 1840s, enacted reforms which drastically limited its scope. Germany's *Paulskirche* Constitution, one of the results of the 1848 revolution in the German states, would have abolished capital punishment, had it stood the test of time. In France, where the influence of Beccaria and Voltaire was particularly strong, capital punishment remained a highly charged issue throughout the early 19th century. Victor Hugo's 1829 novel *The Last Day of a Condemned Man*, which portrayed the anguish and horror of an impending execution, provoked considerable debate, and was quickly translated into English. At the same time, abolition movements in the United States were gathering momentum. John O'Sullivan, a New York legislator and activist, nearly succeeded in abolishing capital punishment in that state in the early 1840s, and other abolitionist crusades succeeded in states such as Michigan and Wisconsin, which remain abolitionist to this day.

So far, the main actors in this account have been members of the educated elite on both sides of the Atlantic. In part, this is because they are the only ones who have left comprehensive written records of their activities. However, another argument of this book is that there has always been a significant gap between elite attitudes toward the death penalty and the stance of ordinary citizens. For the purposes of this book, I define elite status by education, rather than wealth. A public intellectual or high-ranking official in Austria or France would likely never become wealthy, but could directly affect penal policy in ways not available even to the richest landowner. Thus, when I refer to social elites I define them primarily in terms of education: those who, by the standards of their time, have had access to considerably greater educational opportunities than fellow members of society.

I subdivide the term 'elite' into two categories. The first is public intellectuals: activists, scholars, law reformers, and writers who enter the public sphere to shape debate on important issues of their day. The second category is the bureaucratic/policy elite: first, legislators; then come professors (in civil law countries), and high-ranking civil-service functionaries responsible for national policy development and coordination (the policy elite). Finally, we have lower ranking but still influential civil servants (the bureaucratic elite) such as prison wardens, judges, prosecutors, or police chiefs. Although their main task is carrying out public policy, they may also have some indirect influence on policy formation. Of course, there is not always a fixed border between these two elite groups. A professor at a European university, for example, may simultaneously attempt to influence public debate on a matter of penal policy as a public intellectual *and* actually shape that policy by drafting a nation's penal code.

As we will see, public intellectuals such as Benjamin Rush in the U.S., Victor Hugo in France and Jeremy Bentham and Samuel Romilly in England generally advocated outright abolition, or something very close to it. They also wrote punishment-reform polemics stressing the dignity of the offender and decrying the brutality or inutility of existing punishment regimes. These idealistic appeals gradually influenced the bureaucratic/policy elite, although rarely to the point of winning them over to the most radical proposals. However, renowned intellectuals' calls for complete abolition of capital punishment 'moved the goalposts' of what sort of reforms it was acceptable to advocate in public. Thus, on both sides of the Atlantic, the 19th century saw progressive moves in three areas: (1) restricting capital punishment to only the most serious crimes; (2) transforming executions from public spectacles with a strong religious component into private, legalized ceremonies within prison walls; and (3) introducing execution techniques believed by policy-makers to be more humane (Banner 2002:chs. 6 and 7). The dynamic unfolded roughly as follows: reformers would call for the outright abolition of capital punishment as a symbol of humanity and moral progress. Bureaucratic/policy elites – eager to don the mantle of moral progress, but unable or unwilling to abolish executions entirely – met the reformers halfway by 'civilizing' the legal and physical procedures surrounding capital punishment.

This pattern largely prevailed until after World War II. The worldwide decrease in violent crime that prevailed from the 1950s to the mid-1960s saw outright opposition to capital punishment gradually increase in popularity as a social cause among U.S. and European elites. In England, the House of Commons voted bills calling for the outright abolition of capital punishment in 1929 and 1948, but the bills were voted down in the House of Lords. Germany abolished capital punishment once and for all in its 1949 post-war Basic Law. Although France, the U.S. and the U.K. retained executions, anti-capital punishment polemics such as Albert Camus' (1957) 'Reflections on the Guillotine' (Camus 1960:174–234) and Arthur Koestler's (1957) *Reflections on Hanging* made an impact on both sides of the Atlantic. In Great Britain, the Royal Commission on Capital Punishment, which issued its report in 1953, held back from advocating outright abolition of capital punishment, but did recommend significant limits on its applicability, which were realized in the Homicide Act of 1957.

The 1960s saw an accelerating trend toward abolitionist sentiment among European and American elites, which often manifested itself as just one aspect of a bold program to completely reform criminal justice and reorient it to the exclusive goal of rehabilitating offenders with the help of the latest psychological insights. Throughout the 1960s, professors from German-speaking countries produced competing proposals for the reform of Germany's Penal Code, which stimulated a broad reform movement culminating in groundbreaking revisions to the Code. In England, Baroness Wootton and other reformers argued tirelessly for the rehabilitation of criminal offenders, and both Conservative and Labour governments drafted wide-ranging White Papers advocating comprehensive reform of criminal justice and corrections. In the United States, the President's Commission on Law Enforcement and the Administration of Justice, commissioned by President Lyndon B. Johnson, issued a 1967 report setting out a comprehensive program for modernizing the criminal justice system and building up programs of reform and rehabilitation. England, for its part, finally passed a law establishing a five-year moratorium on capital punishment in 1965, which was made permanent in 1969.

For all this ferment among the educated elite – Members of Parliament; prominent panelists on government commissions; professors of law, criminology, and sociology; and writers – the general public in all four countries remained staunchly in favor of retaining capital punishment until the mid-1960s, and sometimes beyond. Opinion polls which accompanied the 1948 debate in the British Parliament found strong support for capital punishment among all political parties and religious groups in Britain. Further, as one author observed, 'the percentage of "don't know" replies is much smaller than is customary on public policy questions. Almost everyone seemed to hold an opinion on capital punishment, and even at the beginning of a decade of controversy there were few clearly uncommitted segments of the public to be wooed by either side.' (Christoph 1962:44). On the eve of the 1969 British vote to permanently abolish capital punishment, a poll revealed that 85% of respondents were 'somewhat' or 'strongly' in favor of retaining the death penalty. The situation in Germany was similar: throughout the 1950s and early 1960s, support for capital punishment remained strong, and abolitionists were required repeatedly to fight off legislative attempts to reintroduce the death penalty (Evans 1996:789–804). Only in the United States and France did support for capital punishment decline considerably in the 1960s. Support dipped to the 30% range in France in 1969 before beginning a steady rise (Costa 2001:160). By the mid-1960s, it evenly split pro and con in the U.S. at about 45% (Banner 2002:240).

Thus, on both sides of the Atlantic, a similar pattern held until the mid-1960s: the project of completely eliminating capital punishment gained support among educated elites, while making little headway among the general population. Only after this point do we see a remarkable divergence: penal policy remained relatively stable in Europe, whereas the United States began a radical shift toward harsher sentencing and a focus on retribution instead of rehabilitation. In America, death penalty laws were upheld as constitutional after a short hiatus in the mid-1970s, and executions resumed in earnest in the 1980s. Crime victims organized into powerful political lobbies, and combating crime became a signature issue for politicians. Increasingly harsh sentencing laws led to rapid growth in the U.S. prison population. Summing up the trend, Jonathan Simon recently argued:

> Crime has become so central to the exercise of authority in America, by everyone from the president of the United States to the classroom teacher, that it will take a concerted effort by Americans themselves to dislodge it. (Simon 2007:4)

Most Western European nations, as well as Canada, also saw increases in general rates of violent crime in the 1970s and 1980s, and support for capital punishment in the UK and France remained strong during this period. However, these developments had little direct impact on criminal justice policy. Canada abolished capital punishment in 1976, France followed suit in 1981. Indeed, France's ruling Socialist party instituted a number of wide-ranging penal code reforms in the early 1980s, including the abolition of high-security prisons (Whitman 2003:84–6). Thirteen votes were held in the British Parliament between 1969 and 1994 to reintroduce capital punishment for certain types of crimes, but all were defeated, and prominent Conservative ministers and MPs came out in favor of death penalty abolition (Hood 2002:26).

Many scholars have offered explanations for this transatlantic divergence in death penalty policy. Professor Carol Steiker (2002) provided an overview of the main theories in an article entitled 'Capital Punishment and American Exceptionalism'. She noted that there is 'surprisingly little sustained commentary' on the question of why the United States has retained the death penalty, perhaps because 'people think they know why, and their (rather diverse) explanatory theories are often mentioned in passing, without support or elaboration, as if they were perfectly obvious' (ibid.:100,101). She notes ten main theories: (1) the U.S.' higher homicide rates; (2) public opinion (presumably harsher in the United States); (3) salience of crime as a political issue; (4) populism (that is, political institutions that are more responsive to the public will); (5) criminal justice populism; (6) The United States' dramatically more devolved federalist system; (7) the 'exceptionalism' of the American south; (8) European exceptionalism (that is, that it is actually

Europe which represents the exception to the global norm); (9) American cultural exceptionalism (acceptance of violence, religiosity, the frontier mentality and associated vigilantism); and (10) mere historical contingency. As Steiker notes, some commentators emphasize a certain subset of these ten explanations, others choose a different configuration. As this book progresses, the set of explanations I believe to be the most robust will become clear.

There is much to be learned from Steiker's article, and from the summaries of the literature it presents. However, many analyses of the transatlantic divergence are limited by the analyst's perspective. North American scholars, for their part, frequently lack in-depth practical knowledge of how European criminal justice policy is created. A limited focus on when the death penalty was abolished in a particular European country, or what was said in Parliament during a certain debate, provides only a snapshot of a process of social change that often developed over decades. Understanding the abolition of capital punishment in Europe, I will argue, requires an understanding of the broader context of European criminal justice policy formation: How are penal codes created? How much influence do members of the general public, or lobbying groups, have on policy outcomes? Who does the legislator turn to for advice on reforming criminal justice policy? When expert commissions recommend a penal code reform, does the legislator simply adopt it wholesale, or are significant changes made? These questions are rarely addressed by American scholars.

British and Continental European scholars who seek to explain the punitive policies of the United States, for their part, often focus on highly visible cultural contrasts between the U.S. and Europe, such as American religious attitudes or America's history of slavery and discrimination. Again, these are thought-provoking theses. However, I will argue that these cultural attitudes can only truly be appreciated when several contextual factors are taken into account. First, *whose* cultural attitudes matter? A primary focus of this book is on evidence that elites tend to think about criminal justice issues very differently than members of the general public. This large gulf in attitudes is, in fact, an essential component of any analysis of penal policy formation. If a university professor tends to think about crime and punishment differently than a bus driver, then it makes a difference whether the university professor or the bus driver has more control over exactly what criminal laws are enacted. This observation brings us to the second necessary piece of context when we think about culture: what is the mechanism – if any – by which cultural values are transformed into genuine changes in policy? The legacy of slavery and discrimination in the south-eastern United States might well help explain the current prevalence of executions in that area of the country – but, as David Garland recently argued in a thoughtful essay, many 'cultural' theories of penal policy formation remain speculative because they are 'unable to identify the mechanisms by which [a cultural] "tradition" has been transmitted over time and is translated into the decision making of legal actors in the present' (Garland 2006:438).

The fact that each American state has its own criminal code, the prominent role of crime victims' rights groups, the election of local judges and prosecutors in direct, sometimes partisan elections – these factors all determine a policy landscape that is completely alien to Continental European ways of thinking about law and policy. While we should not lose sight of cultural attitudes that distinguish different societies' ways of thinking about capital punishment, we should keep in mind that there is *always an institutional filter* between those cultural attitudes and actual, on-the-ground policy. The European filter, I will argue, insulates the process of penal policy formation from the public's will, whereas the American filter permits, and even requires, criminal justice policy to be acutely responsive to public opinion. The United States is often treated by European scholars as an outlier in which 'populist' or 'demagogic' pressure 'distorts' penal policy. But this critique itself presupposes a certain perspective. In other words, European (and, to a lesser extent, British) scholars tend to see the United States as an outlier because they are taking European ways of thinking about criminal justice policy as the 'norms' from which the United States is seen to deviate.

The European Model of Criminal Justice Policy Formation: World View

To try to broaden the perspective, I want to explore the cultural and structural factors that govern penal policy-making in Europe. I will propose that the question of how Europe actually came to abolish capital punishment is at least as interesting, and revealing, as the question of why other nations have yet to do so. As comparative law scholar James Whitman has suggested, it is often desirable to first set up a Weberian 'ideal type' of a particular legal system to draw stark contrasts and set clear parameters for comparison (Whitman 2007:353–4). By drawing such unrealistically stark contrasts, we can generate hypotheses that can then be subjected to closer investigation and, if necessary, modification. At this point, then, I will set out a brief introductory version of what I call the 'European model' of criminal justice policy formation. I will then use the term 'European model' to refer to a set of attitudes and concepts as I develop my comparative analysis. Of course, the simple, generalized portrayal of the European model here will later be qualified by more detailed observations.

The European model of criminal justice policy formation has two distinctive components. One relates to the world view of the elite actors who form criminal justice policy, the other relates to institutional structures. European penal policy-making elites believe a large gap exists between the way they think about crime and the way the 'man in the street' does. According to most policy-making and bureaucratic elites, the man in the street reacts to news of serious violent crimes with anger and a desire for more punitive sanctions. Asked for his punishment preferences, the man in the street may endorse punishments that violate human rights guarantees, such as capital punishment, life imprisonment, or summary deportation. His exaggerated fear of crime is fed by tabloid newspapers and television programs, which retail stories of violent crime and child victimization. The tabloids also deliver lurid, detail-rich coverage of sexual-murder cases, often giving the alleged wrong-doer a catchy nickname such as the 'Balcony Monster' or the 'Basement Dungeonmaster' (both genuine examples taken from the Rückert article cited immediately below). The constant drumbeat of the yellow press drives swings in public opinion, making it an unreliable lodestar for penal policy.

Against this backdrop, the quality press bears a responsibility for fostering an environment in which sophisticated, thoughtful debate and critique can take place. However, this debate goes on almost exclusively among members of the elite. In European countries, only a small fraction of the public reads the 'quality' broadsheet press. The masses instead obtain their information about the world via tabloids and television. Accordingly, European commentators routinely assume a great gap in information sources and in attitudes between the well-educated member of the elite and the average person. An example from Sabine Rückert, a prominent German crime reporter who writes primarily for the distinguished German broadsheet *Die Zeit*, illustrates this view:

> In a democratic system, the responsibility for the creation of a public consensus is not solely the task of politicians and functionaries of relevant social groups. The media must also be aware of their responsibility – especially when the subject of its reporting is themes that ... could be described as 'particularly dangerous.' We are talking about those questions which are answered by the majority not with cool reason, but rather with an access of emotion – questions which nobody would want to see answered by a plebiscite. (Rückert 2003:43)

Among European elites, criticism of the profit-driven mass media has never ceased to be a central topic of debate. Jürgen Habermas, one of the world's most prominent philosophers, recently complained of increasing financial pressure on German broadsheet newspapers. He penned an impassioned defense of the 'quality' press (Habermas 2007), going so far as to call for government assistance to prevent the closure of 'serious' German newspapers. He warned against the influence of the market on sources of news and information. In the United States, he argued, the television was regarded as nothing more than a 'toaster with pictures', rather than a vitally important communications medium. As a result, television programming was left to the free market, a fact which, in Habermas' view, inflicted a 'political and cultural catastrophe' (he uses the term *Flurschäden*, which means devastating crop damage) in the form of cheap, empty programming to satisfy the common man's needs for entertainment and distraction.

French sociologist Pierre Bourdieu joins in the denunciation of the common person's ignorance and suggestibility in his extended critical analysis *On Television*. Because 'a very high proportion of the population reads no newspapers at all,' he suggests, television 'enjoys a de facto monopoly on what goes into the heads of a significant part of the population and what they think.' Tabloid-style '[b]lood, sex, melodrama and crime' have increasingly come to dominate television news reporting, driving out a 'sense of respectability modeled on the printed press' that prevailed in the medium's early days. The stratification of the news sector creates two groups of citizens: 'those in a position to read so-called "serious" newspapers (insofar as they can remain serious in the face of competition from television) ... and, on the other hand, everyone else, who get from television news all they know about politics. That is to say, precious little ...' (Bourdieu 1998:17, 18). These are only three sources, to be sure. Yet, as anyone who has spoken to a highly educated European can confirm, the assumption of a large gap in knowledge and reasoning ability between the ordinary public and the educated elite is near universal among European elites.

Because the man-in-the-street's views of violent crime are shaped by emotional responses to lurid tales of violence, those views are simply not entitled to particular respect from elites or policy-makers. Indeed, a European policy-maker might ask, why would one accord any particular respect to the views of the common man on a subject as complex as crime control policy? Most voters have no training in law, psychology, criminology, sociology, or any of the other disciplines that would be relevant to forming a responsible approach to the problem of crime in a free society. The role of elites is not to respect public opinion on penal policy but to *guide and shape* it. Ideally elites in charge of state-sponsored media outlets (which continue to play an important role in the German, French, and British media landscapes) should try to counter the tabloids by encouraging more responsible and enlightened discourse about the problem of crime.

Capital punishment is a case in point. A 2001 pamphlet, *Death is not Justice*, produced by the Directorate General of Human Rights of the Council of Europe, encourages Member State leaders to actively proselytize among their populations against capital punishment:

> [P]ublic awareness campaigns [should] go beyond preaching abolition as an end in itself but rather focus on the educational dimension. We have to consider what type of society we, our children, and our grandchildren want to live in ... Abolishing the death penalty is a politically courageous step for politicians to take but it is also one of those fundamental societal values where political leaders have to lead and not be guided by the latest opinion poll. (Directorate General of Human Rights 2001:8, 9)

A few pages later, the point is hammered home again:

> Respect for human rights must never be dependent on the whims of public opinion. (ibid.:11)

European elites believe that the elite way of thinking about crime control is simply more rational, principled, and humane than the man-in-the-street's vengeance-driven views. They view this chasm in world view between educated elites and ordinary citizens as inevitable, and believe that it is present in some form in every society – whether that society chooses to acknowledge it or not. As the above excerpts show, European elites do not view ordinary citizens as 'uneducable', but they tend to believe the general public's views lag behind the elites' in sophistication and humanity. Nor do European elites feel the need to conceal the conviction of their own superior policy understanding and moral refinement. As we will see in Part II, European jurists and lawmakers justified their moves toward abolition with quite open condemnations of the 'brutal' or 'primitive' opinions of the 'uneducated masses.'

The European Model of Criminal Justice Policy Formation: Policy Control

The second component of the European approach, and one even more crucial to the argument of this book, is that elites have intentionally designed criminal justice systems that insulate penal policy from public opinion. A quote from Max Weber may help illustrate the connection between elite world view and institutional reality: 'Not ideas but interests – material and ideal – directly govern men's conduct. Yet very frequently the "world images" that have been created by "ideas" have, like switchmen, determined the tracks along which action has been pushed by the dynamic of interest' (quoted as modified in Brubaker 1992:17). For centuries, the ideological 'switchmen' that have directed European criminal justice policy have been the assumption that (1) criminal legislation should be the exclusive province of well-educated experts; and (2) the common man – while he has a right to enlightened penal legislation that balances security with humanity – has no right to assist in shaping it. This historical legacy endures: to this day, the European process for drafting a criminal code is expert-driven, and involves little or no input from the general public. And indeed, in this it differs little from the general pattern of European lawmaking, which stresses the 'front-loaded' comprehensive regulation of an entire area of legal relations, worked out in advance by panels of experts.

The modern European process for generating criminal legislation is, in fact, a legacy of the Enlightenment. In the 18th century, the Berne Economic Society organized a competition inviting philosophers and officials to develop a 'model' European criminal code which would do away with brutal punishments and introduce order and coherence into penal policy. The subscription invited respondents to submit a 'complete and detailed plan for legislation on criminal matters.' Voltaire enthusiastically supported the proposal, and submitted his own critical commentary on the injustices of European criminal law, in which (explicitly following Beccaria) he advocated replacing executions with lifetime penal servitude (Voltaire 1999:15–19). The 'Prize of Justice and Humanity' shows that European intellectuals were willing and eager to translate Enlightenment principles into concrete legislative proposals. And this was no idle pursuit – many reformers were able to see their proposals enacted into law. Beccaria saw many of his reforms adopted by European monarchs, and the Bavarian Penal Code drafted in 1813 under the leadership of Paul Johann Anselm von Feuerbach, abolished torture and reformed sentencing throughout much of German-speaking Europe.

Described at a very high level of generality, the European model of criminal justice policy formation runs roughly as follows. First, a ruler or legislator forms a commission of highly trained legal experts – composed largely of law professors, but perhaps also containing sociologists, criminologists, prison wardens or police chiefs. Often, the commission will be placed under the leadership of a prominent professor of criminal law. The commission will be charged with devising a comprehensive and minutely organized penal code. The penal code will feature a General Part, which contains definitions and establishes the overall conceptual structure, and a Special Part, defining specific offenses. Offenses are ranked according to (1) the overall goals of the penal code; and (2) each offense's degree of perceived wrongfulness, as determined by a rational and comprehensive ordering system.

The sessions leading to the creation of the penal code may involve lengthy, vigorous debates between experts with very different political views. Quite often a bloc of commission members may bow out of the consensus-building process and propose its own 'alternative' penal code, in whole or in part. As we will see in Chapter 4, this is precisely what happened in the German-speaking parts of Europe in the 1960s. The dissenters will then take to the pages of elite publications (such as law reviews or broadsheet newspapers) to condemn the plans of the official criminal-law reform commission. A renowned fictional account of just such a *Gelehrtenstreit* (scholars' dispute) is presented in Robert Musil's novel *The Man Without Qualities*. A chapter called 'To the Legal Mind, Insanity is an All-or-Nothing Proposition' (Musil 1995:583–8) describes the fate of a commission convoked by the Ministry of Justice in the early 20th century to update Austria's penal code, which had remained unchanged since 1852. The commission 'consisted of about twenty legal pundits who were capable of adopting several thousand different points of view among themselves, as can easily be calculated'. Everything is going reasonably well until the commission reaches the definition of insanity in Paragraph 318. Each proud scholar has his own carefully reasoned and historically validated conception of insanity, and the commission immediately breaks into at least six warring factions, including the 'and' and the 'or' factions, as well as the 'full responsibility' and 'soundness of mind' groups. They denounce each other furiously in newspaper columns, pamphlets, and law journals, and the work of the commission grinds to a halt.

Although Musil's account is amusingly overdrawn, it captures the long, weary quest for consensus on such expert commissions. Despite their bitter ideological disputes, members of such commissions usually recall themselves to their historical responsibility, and reconvene to hammer out a final draft which reflects as broad a consensus as possible. Eventually, these years of patient effort produce a universal penal code meant to define all major crimes – and govern all major questions of penal policy – throughout the national territory. Subordinate governmental units do have the prerogative to issue some criminal laws for their own particular region – but major aspects of the criminal justice system will always be defined by a unified national criminal code enforced identically over the entire national territory.

The draft code will then be presented to the legislator. It is at this point that the possibility of public influence on the actual content of criminal justice policy is at its zenith. The legislator will generally hold hearings, and certain parliamentary interest groups may propose changes. However, the number of changes actually taken up will generally be trivial, for several reasons. First, the process of hammering out the draft penal code is likely to have lasted several years, and represents thousands of person-hours of accumulated effort. Second, the code arrives at the legislature positively enshrouded in prestige. It is likely to carry the endorsement of dozens of highly respected officials and professors of several different ideological persuasions. Third, parliamentary factions who have special concerns know that those interests have already been taken into account (to the maximum extent possible) in the consensus draft. A commission member with strong ties to the Socialist party, for instance, is likely to consult with Socialist legislators or experts during the drafting process. The experts who drafted the legislation, when called to testify before the legislator, will generally declare that the draft penal code is a delicate and sophisticated legal mechanism that should not be tinkered with. Thus, they will strongly discourage individual legislators or parties from amending isolated portions of the code to satisfy particular constituent concerns.

After the penal code has been passed by the national legislature, it must, of course, be implemented. The implementation phase of penal policy is, like all the previous phases, largely insulated from the passing political desires of ordinary citizens. In virtually all European countries, the entire process of criminal-law enforcement is carried out exclusively by persons who are members of the professional civil service. Prosecutors in Germany, as well as magistrates in France, are also civil servants, as are all other officials involved in the prosecution of crime. In Germany, many law students are required to study not only criminal law, but also criminology, so that they can become familiar with the latest research into the causes and prevention of crime. The notion of electing a prosecutor or judge would be utterly foreign to the mentality of the Continental European jurist. He or she would immediately point to the risk of political influence on the decision-making process – a threat to the principle of 'neutral' and 'objective' adjudication that is a central concern in criminal cases. The only private, non-civil-servant actors who may enter into a legal case will be public defenders or private defense attorneys, should the defendant be wealthy enough to afford them. The only slight overlap with American ideas of direct popular participation in criminal adjudication would be the intermittent participation of some members of the public in adjudicating serious criminal cases. Both in Germany and in France, laypersons occasionally participate in the adjudication of particularly serious criminal cases. However, this participation is more superficial than it is in the United States.

The civil service model also extends to frontline representatives. Generally, police officers and prison guards receive extensive training and must survive a lengthy probationary period involving several traineeships. Because they are being trained for a job they will hold (or at least aspire to hold) for their entire lives, their training will usually go far beyond merely mastering the mechanics of arresting suspects or filling out paperwork. It may, for instance, include extensive instruction on the social and psychological roots of crime. Further, it will be infused with a sense of mission determined by the parameters of the penal code – which usually stress non-violent conflict resolution, rehabilitation, and reintegration of the offender into society. Once they survive this rigorous scrutiny, they become civil servants of the state. As civil servants, they enjoy considerable job security and prestige, and exhibit a strong sense of *esprit de corps*. In virtually every European country, prison guards, police officers, probation workers, and the like are also represented by strong unions.

This, then, is the 'European model' of criminal justice policy: the world view of the main actors, the formation of policy, and its implementation. The critical fact is that the traditional expert-dominated European model of criminal justice policy, while it originated under absolutism, *survived the transition of European polities into modern parliamentary democracies*. Amid the upheaval that followed World War II, no European government saw any particular reason to dismantle existing structures that insulated penal policy from the popular will. Indeed, most European elites saw such insulation as more necessary than ever. In Germany, for instance, sweeping criminal-law reforms were launched during the era of National Socialism to bring criminal legislation into line with *gesunde Volksempfinden*, roughly, 'healthy popular instincts'. Legal doctrines which limited judicial power, such as the *Analogieverbot* (which forbade judges to punish acts which were 'analogous' to existing crimes) or the principle of legality (forbidding retroactive punishment) were abolished (Lustgarten 2003:118–19). Although National Socialist legislators did not conduct polls to assess what those 'popular instincts' might be, the general population was generally content to see penalties for ordinary crimes drastically increased. The situation was, of course, much less drastic outside Germany. Yet in general, European policy elites saw the 1930s and 1940s as evidence that large portions of their populations would accede in lawlessness and brutality if given the chance. Against this backdrop, any case for radically 'democratizing' criminal justice policy was dramatically weakened, at least among elites.

This description of how the European jurists and officials view public opinion seems to conflict with American sensibilities. One American journalist, in a 2000 article tellingly subtitled 'Europe's Death-Penalty Elitism,' quoted several European politicians dismissing public opinion in favor of capital punishment and observed that '[a]n American attorney general – or any American politician, for that matter – could never get away with such condescension toward the public, at least not for attribution.' (Marshall 2000:13). As we will see in Chapter 8, there is also widespread dissatisfaction in France and Germany with the perceived laxity of the criminal justice system. However, European public officials have several responses to the charge that their criminal justice policies are out of touch with the views of their citizens. First, they argue, critics of their approach rely on a naïve and unworkable definition of 'democracy.' Every nation has recognized that certain aspects of public policy must be insulated from mass public opinion. Few would suggest, for instance, that monetary or foreign policy be made by popular referendum. European nations have simply chosen to include penal policy within the marked-off area of 'insulated delegation,' to use Franklin Zimring's term (Zimring et al. 2001:212–15).

Further, European policy-makers might argue, their approach to criminal justice simply works. Western Europe boasts some of the lowest crime rates and best-ordered societies in the world. Some citizens may resent the fact that they have no direct influence over criminal justice policy. However – as politicians often remind their constituents – they are being kept extraordinarily safe from violent crime, especially compared to the United States. Although general levels of crime do not differ significantly between Europe and the United States, levels of homicide and sexual assault in Europe are much lower than across the Atlantic (Zimring and Hawkins 1997). European elites might also argue that their approach has prevented some of the most disastrous missteps in American penal policy, such as skyrocketing incarceration rates and intrusive expansions of technologies of social control into everyday life. Of course, America's use of the death penalty – in and of itself – is also seen as a black mark. Finally, European elites may point to the history of mass political persecution in their own societies in the 20th century. The fascist movements that engulfed Europe in war and brutality in the early 20th century were usually tolerated – if not actively supported – by a majority of the population. As we will see, this argument was an important arrow in the quiver of abolitionists seeking to justify the abolition of capital punishment.

Thus, I will argue, the assumption of a dramatic gap between elite and mass public opinion – and the institutional structures that reproduce and entrench this gap – are essential to understanding why European penal policies remained surprisingly mild in the face of the general increase in crime which began on both sides of the Atlantic in the late 1960s. The mere recitation of this (admittedly exaggerated) 'European model' of policy formation should in no way imply normative endorsement. I intend to subject the assumptions underlying the European model to analysis, to determine whether they in fact adequately reflect reality. Further – and this point can hardly be emphasized sufficiently – there are significant differences between penal policy world view and formation in England and that in most European nations. Culturally as well as geographically, England lies 'between' Continental Europe and the United States, with somewhat harsher criminal justice policies, and somewhat more public influence on policy formation and implementation. Nevertheless, as I hope to show in Chapter 5, significant structural contrasts remain between the United States and Great Britain in the areas I will address, differences which contributed directly to Britain's abolition of capital punishment in 1969.

The remainder of this book will be an attempt to use the divergence on the death penalty to illustrate deeper differences in the way in which the United States and Europe create criminal justice policy. We have already seen the first stark difference: that European elites believe that waiting for public opinion to change before capital punishment is abolished is an ineffective strategy. First abolish the penalty, they say, then use public education campaigns to reduce residual public support for executions. But is this approach necessary? Is it really futile to expect large changes in opinion on capital punishment among members of the general public? Do less-educated citizens really think about capital punishment differently than members of educated elites? The next two chapters will test these assumptions.

2
What Does the Worldwide Popularity of Capital Punishment Tell Us?

Throughout recorded history, most societies have provided for and carried out some form of capital punishment, specified either by religious text or secular law. Execution for certain crimes is required, for example, in the Code of Hammurabi, the Old Testament, Hindu Law, and the Koran (Greenberg and West 2008). The *Liber Augustalis* of 1231, a codebook promulgated by King Frederick II of Sicily which was one of the first well-organized European legal codes, provided for death sentences for murder and embezzlement. Murder was punishable by death by the sword 'when the murderer is a knight or higher,' and by hanging for all others under that rank (Berman 1983:428). Until the 18th century, the existence of capital punishment – often carried out in public by torturous means – continued to be an unexceptional part of virtually all legal orders, although the zeal with which it was carried out varied dramatically by region, and many death sentences were tempered by the royal prerogative of mercy. Executions were attended by large, boisterous crowds – which sometimes felt sympathy for the condemned, but other times pressed close in to attack and mutilate unpopular convicts (Foucault 1995:5–7; Langbein 2003:154).

As noted above, the first carefully reasoned critiques of capital punishment emerged only in the 18th century. And even then, these critiques were far from sweeping, and met determined resistance. Beccaria's *On Crimes and Punishments*, for instance, was highly controversial. The book, originally published under a pseudonym, was banned by the Venetian Inquisition, and was harshly critiqued by a monk named Facchinei, who used the word 'socialist' (to insult Beccaria) apparently for the first time in Italian (Thomas 2008:xxiii–iv). Beccaria's friends, philosophers Pietro and Alessandro Verri, were forced to write a response to the monk's criticisms in which they carefully emphasized that the author of *On Crimes and Punishments* had not intended to argue against the sovereign's *right* to exact death as punishment, but only to argue that it would be politic for a wise sovereign to refrain from inflicting death, as it is not a 'just and necessary' punishment (Verri and Verri 2008). Joseph von Sonnenfels, who critiqued capital punishment at approximately the same time as Beccaria, was not an outright abolitionist. Even so, as we will see, his views on capital punishment were so controversial that he was officially prohibited from addressing his students on this subject.

But Beccaria's critique of capital punishment, however persuasive, influenced only educated elites, not least because illiteracy was still widespread in the late 18th century. Everywhere public executions were held, they continued to attract large audiences. The crowds which gathered at public executions in early 19th-century America, in fact, 'outnumbered crowds gathered for any other purpose' (Banner 2002:25). The presence of these crowds at public executions resonates on many levels. Many spectators surely attended executions solely out of boredom or curiosity, and there are also many recorded instances of crowd sentiment turning strongly in favor of the condemned, causing scenes of disorder. Indeed, reformers on both sides of the Atlantic cited the increasingly disorderly scenes at public executions – including expressions of support for the condemned – to justify privatizing executions (Masur 1989:94–5). Nevertheless, a crowd's occasional sympathy for an individual condemned criminal cannot be construed as *philosophical* opposition to capital punishment *as a practice*. For all the effective agitation against capital punishment by individual religious or social interest groups, there is apparently no evidence of a broad-based mass movement against capital punishment ever having taken root among members of the general public in any country.

Capital punishment – as an abstract proposition – remains popular among many diverse populations today. Available data show that a majority of the general public supports capital punishment in all parts of the world today except for in Western Europe and certain Anglophone nations such as Australia and Canada. A 2007 poll, for instance, found a majority 'strongly' or 'somewhat' in favor of capital punishment in countries as diverse as Mexico (71%), South Korea (72%), and the United States (69%) – although when given the option, many survey respondents endorsed life without parole as an alternative punishment (Ipsos/Public Affairs & Associated Press 2007). 'Top-line' support for capital punishment (the answer to the simple question of whether the respondent is in favor of capital punishment or against) is also 'strong' in India (Greenberg and West 2008:308) and reaches 59% in Brazil (Rötzsch 2007). Death penalty supporters have always been in the majority in Japan since World War II (Lane 2005). Even in the former Warsaw Pact nations, where capital punishment was abolished in the 1990s as a condition of EU accession, '[s]trong support for capital punishment' persists (Fijalkowski 2005:157). A poll taken in the Czech Republic 15 years after the former Czechoslovakia abolished capital punishment in 1990 showed 66% support for reintroduction of the death penalty (Schubert 2005). Gauging support for capital punishment in China is difficult, given the sensitivity of the subject. However, one recent Chinese researcher's conclusion was that over 80% of the Chinese population favors the death penalty. Virtually all of the respondents he questioned supported it implicitly as a necessary bulwark against violence and disorder (Ho 2005). For a similar reason, it is hard to find reliable data concerning public opinion in Arab nations, but two scholars recently concluded that there is little reason to assume widespread opposition to capital punishment in Islamic nations, given the Koran's endorsement of capital punishment and the pro-capital-punishment policies pursued by most majority-Muslim nations (Greenberg and West 2008:308).

These studies must be interpreted with some caution. First, there is a debate about how much we can learn from answers to the simple top-line question of whether the respondent supports or opposes capital punishment. As the results from the Ipsos poll and several American polls also show, many poll respondents say that they would prefer an alternative to capital punishment, such as imprisonment for life without parole (Death Penalty Information Center 2007:9). Some support for capital punishment is therefore likely driven either by the absence of such a definitive sentencing alternative, or by lack of confidence that the state will actually carry it out. A simple poll question likewise provides no basis for determining the *relative importance* of the issue of capital punishment in a voter's general world view. Many of the respondents in polls cited above – such as ones taken in Brazil, Mexico, and former Eastern Bloc nations – live in nations which are already either de facto or *de jure* abolitionist. Their governments are following a policy with which they disagree, but there does not seem to be significant social unrest about this fact. In abolitionist nations, many poll respondents may well endorse capital punishment as a symbol of serious crime control without having strong enough convictions to mount the sort of sustained activism which would bring it back. Finally, polls on capital punishment can be sensitive to recent real or perceived increases in violent crime rates, meaning that some of the national results may be the result of temporary circumstances inflating support for the death penalty.

Nevertheless, there is intriguing evidence that the top-line numbers may also *understate* support for capital punishment. When polls ask whether the respondent would support the death penalty for a *particular kind of serious crime*, support increases from the top-line amount. German sociologist Karl-Heinz Reuband assessed polls on capital punishment conducted from the 1950s to the 1970s in Germany. He noted that the response to the question was extremely sensitive to formulation:

> Evidence for the correctness [of this assumption] can be derived from the polls conducted by the DIVO Institute, in which, during the *same* survey, the first question asked for a 'global' assessment of the respondent's attitude toward the death penalty ('Are you for the re-introduction of the death penalty or against it?'). In a second step, the survey team attempted

to determine the number of convinced opponents among those who gave a negative answer in relation to this sanction. This was done by means of the follow-up question: 'Are you against the re-introduction of the death penalty under all circumstances, or should it be re-introduced for certain severe crimes?' The *majority* of the initial opponents supported the death penalty in response to this second question. (1980:538)

Reuband then assessed various time-series polls on capital punishment in Germany. The overall trend showed a steady decline in support for capital punishment from the 1950s to the 1970s. However, one poll simply asked whether the respondent was in favor of the death penalty 'in general' (*grundsätzlich*). The other poll asked whether the respondent would be in favor of the death penalty for murder where 'no mitigating circumstances' (*keine mildernde Umstände*) applied to the defendant's case. In any given year, the second question elicited about 20% more support for the death penalty. For instance, two separate polls conducted in the year 1978 in Germany showed a response of 31% in favor of capital punishment for the 'simple' question, as against 58% in favor for the 'no mitigating circumstances' question (ibid.:541, 542). A 1996 poll conducted in Germany found that only 37% of Germans said they favored the death penalty in general, but 50% of the very same respondents favored it for murder/kidnap cases, and 60% favored it in cases in which a young child had been sexually abused and murdered (Noelle-Neumann and Köcher 1997:767). On the morning of the parliamentary debate in which the French National Assembly debated whether to abolish capital punishment in 1981, the newspaper *Le Figaro* published a poll showing that 62% of French respondents favored the death penalty in general, but 73% favored it for 'particularly atrocious' crimes (Badinter 2008:195).

As we see, many members of the public clearly perceive a meaningful difference between the death penalty as a general philosophical question and the death penalty as a just response to a particular kind of heinous crime. Although this divergence in responses may seem irrational on the surface, we will see that it probably reflects deeply entrenched cognitive patterns.

Explaining the Popularity of Capital Punishment

Why is capital punishment popular with solid majorities across many cultural boundaries? It is surprising how little attention has been devoted to this seemingly important question. Most of the countless millions of words that have been written about capital punishment are devoted to arguing for or against it, and these arguments generally come from representatives of educated elites: lawyers, politicians, professors, doctors, religious leaders, or journalists. Whenever these polemicists do address the issue of support for capital punishment, they often resort to stereotypes. As we will see in

Part II of this book, European anti-capital-punishment activists frequently dismissed popular sentiment in favor of capital punishment in elitist terms, openly dismissing it as 'backward' or 'primitive.' Former U.S. Supreme Court Justice Thurgood Marshall took a gentler tack in a 1972 judicial opinion. He acknowledged that support for capital punishment was strong, but, in a famous passage from one of his Supreme Court opinions, suggested that death penalty supporters would change their opinion once they were made aware 'of all information presently available' concerning the injustice and immorality of capital punishment (*Furman* v. *Georgia* 1972:362). According to the 'Marshall hypothesis', as it is generally known, the public's desire for revenge will be blunted when ordinary citizens are made aware of capital punishment's grave flaws as a policy.

More thoughtful assessments of support for capital punishment do exist, although they are scattered across a number of disciplines. The field has been explored primarily by criminologists, psychologists, and sociologists – many based in the English-speaking world. These studies reveal some interesting and important points about support for capital punishment, even across cultural lines. In the following discussion, we will assess several different potential explanations for the death penalty's widespread support, starting from a more general level and moving to more culturally bound elements.

Revenge and Human Nature

The majorities who favor capital punishment are, one could say, just thinking what comes naturally. Thinkers as diverse as Samuel Butler, Adam Smith, and Charles Darwin have speculated that the impulse to seek revenge is a component of human nature (McCullough 2008:10–11). In the early 1980s, Australian philosopher John Mackie proposed that the desire for retribution may be rooted in evolution. In an essay entitled 'Morality and the Retributive Emotions,' (1985), Mackie argues that the impulse to demand 'positive retribution,' that is, the 'principle that one who is guilty ought to be punished,' cannot be satisfactorily explained by rational argument. Even were one to posit that punishment of an offender would be pointless or counterproductive, it will still be demanded. 'The paradox is that, on the one hand, a retributive principle of punishment cannot be explained or developed within a reasonable system of moral thought, while, on the other hand, such a principle cannot be eliminated from our moral thinking.'

Mackie demonstrates that arguments for the legitimacy of retribution punishment are either simply consequentialist arguments that have been mischaracterized, or – when more closely scrutinized – turn out to presuppose the desirability of positive retributivism. 'People find [these supposedly rational] accounts plausible because they are so firmly wedded to retributivist ways of thinking that they find it difficult to confront the task of justifying retributivism ... without implicitly assuming what they are setting out to explain.' Invoking David Hume, Mackie contends that arguments for retribution are simply window-dressing for a basic emotional desire for revenge that exists prior to, and independent of, any rational argument. Drawing upon then-recent theoretical advances in evolutionary theory, Mackie goes on to suggest that the desire for revenge may be so hard to explain and justify because it is part of our evolutionary conditioning.

Mackie's essay foreshadows many themes later developed by researchers in diverse fields, which converge on the idea that a predisposition toward revenge is deeply rooted in human nature. 'Human nature' is a controversial notion. The social sciences are currently host to a vigorous debate between two camps of scientists and scholars. The first camp draws insights from the field of evolutionary psychology. The starting point of these scholars and thinkers was summarized in a seminal volume in the field entitled *The Adapted Mind*:

> Culture is not causeless and disembodied. It is generated in rich and intricate ways by information-processing mechanisms situated in human minds. These mechanisms are, in turn, the elaborately sculpted product of the evolutionary process. (Cosmides et al. 1992:3)

Evolutionary thinkers believe in human nature; that is, in the idea that there are certain deeply rooted attitudes and dispositions that transcend cultural boundaries. Evolutionary psychologists contrast their perspective with what they call the Standard Social Science Model, which seeks explanations for human behavior in external factors such as culture, socialization, and local tradition. According to evolutionary scholars, the Social Science Model is little more than an ideological construct, driven by an earnest but misplaced desire to minimize the fact of human variation and to foster attitudes – such as racial tolerance and cultural relativism – that mainstream social scientists consider desirable (Cosmides et al. 1992:23–49). McCullough identifies the idea that 'revenge is a disease, and forgiveness is its cure' as one of the normatively laden assumptions of the Social Science Model of human development (McCullough 2008:8). However, evolutionary psychology has also been challenged by other scholars who argue that its claims are exaggerated and its methodology weak. The human mind, these opponents argue, continues to evolve much more rapidly than the evolutionary psychologists suggest, and many supposedly ingrained adaptations turn out, on closer inspection, to be far more influenced by cultural factors than evolutionary psychologists hypothesize (Buller 2005).

The general debate over evolutionary psychology exceeds the scope of this book. However, regardless of the overall validity of the evolutionary psychology model, scholars associated with its approach have developed a powerful explanatory framework relevant to the issue of support for capital punishment. In their classic study *Homicide* (1988), Martin Daly and Margo Wilson applied the analytical framework of evolutionary psychology to killing and vengeance. They note – in a chapter titled 'On the Cross-Cultural Ubiquity of Blood Revenge' – that their research had found one form or another of 'the idea of taking a life for a life' in '57 of ... 60' societies under study, at all levels of development, from all corners of the globe: 'We encountered either some reference to blood feud or capital punishment as an institutional practice, or specific accounts of particular cases, or at the least, some articulate expression of the desire for blood revenge.' In modern societies, Daly and Wilson note, we continue to find strong punitive sentiments awakened by 'events we never witnessed, affecting people we never even met.' (ibid.:226, 273). These sentiments, they propose, are driven by our 'vested interest in the maintenance of the social contract: a commitment to pursue our individual interests with restraint and to punish those who cheat.' Drawing on these and other studies, Daly and Wilson argue that the desire for revenge is an evolved trait: '[T]he revenge motive is effectively deterrent in function and has evolved for that reason. Vengeful urges are profoundly linked to familial solidarity, and are problematic to those who aspire to forge polities on other than familial bases. But revenge is also an onerous duty, and people have willingly relinquished their retaliatory rights to the state, in exchange for guarantees that justice will indeed be executed.' (ibid.:295). Another recent review of the literature on cross-cultural intuitions of justice found 'striking' evidence that 'across demographics, even across cultures, humans share nuanced intuitions (1) about what constitutes serious wrongdoing, (2) that serious wrongdoing should be punished, and (3) about the relative blameworthiness of offenders' (Robinson et al. 2007:1637). The authors – law professor Paul Robinson, professor of law and biological sciences Owen D. Jones, and professor of psychology Robert Kurzban – suggest that the instinct to punish, as well as intuitions about the severity of particular crimes, have a strong evolved component.

Daly and Wilson suggest that the impulse to punish criminals seems to be linked to a phenomenon evolutionary biologists and psychologists call 'cheater detection.' Among social animals who must cooperate to achieve goals (such as eluding predators or combating parasites), biologists have long observed a tendency toward 'tit for tat' behavior. Within flocks of birds, for instance, one bird will generally groom another bird it does not know, expecting that the favor will be returned. If it is not – if the second bird 'defects' from the cooperative scheme – the first bird will retaliate in kind by refusing to groom the defector. Among large colonies of social animals, 'tit for tat' establishes itself as the evolutionarily stable strategy – the mode of behavior that, in the long run, if adopted by all or nearly all of the individuals in the group, most improves the survival chances of each group member. The key feature of 'tit for tat' is that it begins with each group member cooperating with the others, but requires retaliation against those who 'cheat' on the cooperative system (Dawkins 2006:75–6).

Evolutionary psychologists have shown that most humans have developed a similar aversion to cheating which serves the evolutionary goal of fostering cooperation. To measure this impulse, psychologists developed games (Price et al. 2002) which required subjects to cooperate to achieve an important goal, but which also permitted individual group members to increase their gains by 'defecting' from the common scheme. Studies consistently find that most test subjects spend considerable time and energy monitoring fellow subjects for signs of possible defection. If a cheater is caught, other participants favor punishment. One intriguing finding is that test subjects usually set a punishment that goes beyond what would be strictly necessary to compensate the group for the cheater's defection: for instance, they will insist on punishing cheaters even on the last round of the experimental game, when punishment would not contribute to changing the cheater's future behavior (Fehr and Gächter 2000). The non-cheating participants also frequently spend more time and energy attempting to catch cheaters than is strictly 'rational': they will 'over-monitor' other group members even in situations in which cheating would cause relatively little harm to the group's overall goal.

The dynamics of cheater detection do not map one-to-one onto the desire to see retributive punishment inflicted upon criminals. Yet it is not hard to see the typical criminal as a kind of cheater: someone who obtains an advantage for himself or herself by breaking rules society has a strong interest in seeing followed. Clearly, cheater detection draws upon powerful, deeply rooted intuitions of justice – thought patterns which, as Mackie noted, seem so natural that they hardly need explanation. Further, the study findings that people will 'over-monitor' to detect cheating and 'over-punish' cheating when it is found correlate with Mackie's observation that people will still endorse punishment even in those situations where it provides no practical benefit. One is immediately reminded of Kant's famous argument that a murderer should still be executed, even if the society which had incarcerated him (and to which he could present a danger) had completely ceased to exist (Ataner 2006).

In an influential 2001 article, psychologist Jonathan Haidt sought to explore other aspects of feelings such as disgust and revenge. He asked study subjects in three different countries, for their reactions to hypothetical scenarios that, while they involved no harm to third parties, were likely to provoke aversion. One hypothetical scenario, for instance, involved a person using a national flag to clean his toilet; another asked participants to judge a family who had cooked and eaten a pet dog that had earlier been killed in a random traffic accident. Haidt found that large majorities of study respondents in all three countries registered strong aversion to the activities. However, they were usually unable to explain precisely *why* they found the activities distasteful. Haidt theorized, to paraphrase the title of his paper, that the emotional tail was wagging the rational dog – that is, that study participants felt a strong aversion to the activities on an emotional level, even though they were unable to furnish convincing rational explanations for their reactions. 'The central claim of the social intuitionist model is that moral judgment is caused by quick moral intuitions and is followed (when needed) by slow, ex post facto moral reasoning' (Haidt 2001:817). Haidt, like Mackie, argues that many of the mechanisms that drive social intuition – for instance, a tendency to try to harmonize with the opinions of family members or social groups – have evolutionary bases: 'From an evolutionary perspective, it would be strange if our moral judgment machinery was designed principally for accuracy, with no concern for the disastrous effects of periodically siding with our enemies and against our friends' (ibid.:821).

Another study, designed by two psychologists and a law professor, set out to analyze this phenomenon specifically in the context of punishment. The authors noted that the question of 'what [it is] that people in a society seek to do when they punish actors who intentionally commit known wrong actions' was surprisingly under-researched (Carlsmith et al. 2002:284). Their study posed several different hypothetical criminal scenarios to a test group of college students and asked the students to rate how severely they would punish the actors, and what factors would drive their decision. They found that, although the students often *claimed* to be using the deterrence-related factors as their guide, their actual punishment decisions ignored factors associated with the deterrence model of punishment, and instead followed a pattern that was clearly explained by social intuitions of just deserts. The authors cautioned that their results, if anything, probably underestimated the actual role of just deserts and retribution, since the study participants were all Princeton students, who were likely to have less punitive attitudes than the broader population. On a similar note, a recent study of jurors who voted for death in a capital case found that the majority of them declared that they were motivated by a desire to 'see justice done,' but that they strongly resisted a characterization of their motives as seeking revenge (Sundby 2005:127).

These analyses of punitive sentiment show that many people simply do not understand their motives for favoring capital punishment. When people are called upon to *justify* their support for capital punishment, they will often invoke socially acceptable, 'rational' arguments such as deterrence. However, at the deeper and more primal level – at the level of social intuition, to use Haidt's phrase – people who favor capital punishment do so simply because it is the best expression of their outrage at vicious murders. A recent overview by psychologist Joshua Greene of the neurological and psychological literature on the motivation for punishment came to the following conclusion:

People endorse both consequentialist and retributivist justifications for punishment in the abstract, but in practice, or when faced with more concrete hypothetical choices, people's motives appear to be predominantly retributivist. Moreover, these retributivist inclinations appear to be emotionally driven. People punish in proportion to the extent that transgressions make them angry. (Greene 2007:51)

For the majority of people, then, support for capital punishment is visceral. Hearing an account of a brutal murder makes people angry, generating a desire for vengeance which can best be satisfied by the killer's forfeit of his own life. For many people, taking the killer's life enacts a kind of symmetry of retribution in a way that no lesser penalty can. As William Ian Miller (2006) recently argued in a cross-cultural survey of vengeance and retribution, the trope of balancing or 'evening out' the harm done by imposing a penalty on the wrongdoer equal to the harm inflicted by his wrong is deeply rooted in dozens of diverse cultures. For millennia, Miller reports, it has been regarded as one of the primary duties of the state to enact just such a symmetry of retribution – often by physical mutilation. These accounts of the roots of retribution harbor an important lesson: because the sources of support for capital punishment are themselves not rational, we should expect that rational argument against capital punishment will have only a limited prospect of success. Drawing on many of these sources, Susan Bandes (2007) has recently argued that abolitionists should simply embrace the reality that debate on the death penalty is always driven by emotion, and that purely rational arguments over cost or deterrence will never carry the day.

What research there is on the characteristics of capital punishment supporters shows, unsurprisingly, that they are likely to have more conservative or authoritarian attitudes than the rest of the population (Tyler and Weber 1982:26, citing previous studies). They are also drawn disproportionately from the less-educated portions of society. American survey research shows that support for capital punishment declines with increasing education (Greenberg and West 2008:310). Evidence from other countries also shows higher levels of education associated with lower support for capital punishment. A set of two French polls, one conducted in 1983 and the other in 1998, asked respondents whether they would like to see the death penalty reintroduced in France. Overall, the polls revealed a sharp drop in support for capital punishment in France over the 15-year interval. In both polls, respondents who identified themselves as educated office workers or members of the liberal professions were opposed to the reintroduction of the death penalty by a much wider margin than all other social groups, such as general or agricultural workers. For instance, in 1998, only 25% of the liberal/management group wanted to see capital punishment reintroduced in France. The next highest group was non-management employees, 43% of whom were favorable (IFOP/France Soir 1998). According to the director of the Czech opinion research institute CVVK, a 2005 death penalty poll found the greatest support for capital punishment among those who were unaffiliated with a religion and those who had the lowest levels of education. The lowest levels of support for capital punishment were found among students, college graduates, and believing Christians (Schubert 2005). A survey conducted on 24 October 1969 by *The Times* of London broke down support for capital punishment by social class, and found that the working class provided the bulk of support for capital punishment (Times Political Editor 1969). Finally, Karl-Heinz Reuband, in a survey of the German post-war literature on public opinion about capital punishment, noted that opposition to the death penalty always increased dramatically with increasing levels of education, and that this effect seemed to have grown even more pronounced as of the mid-1960s (1980:546–7).

At an individual level, thus, increasing levels of education drive down support for capital punishment. The next chapter will look at some possible explanations for this fact. But to put this insight into context, it is worth remembering that generally about 60–80% of the population of most Western countries does not possess the equivalent of a degree from a four-year college (OECD 2008:28). By itself, this clear educational divide on capital punishment is an intriguing factor. However, as we will see in Chapter 3, it seems that the educational divide may also point to underlying structural differences in the way educated and less-educated people think about capital punishment. That is, higher levels of education actually change the way people gather information and form opinions about social issues like capital punishment. There are supporters and opponents of capital punishment at every socioeconomic level, but the consistent pattern is that widespread opposition to capital punishment takes root and becomes the norm only among social elites.

Support for the Death Penalty in the Developed World: the Stabilization Effect

For all the evidence that increasing education reduces support for capital punishment on the individual level, there is little evidence that a nation's *overall* level of educational attainment has any significant effect on support for capital punishment. Two contemporary cases in point are Japan and the United States, both of which have high levels of overall educational attainment and consistent support for the death penalty. For that matter, most Western European nations, in the post-war period, also had high levels of general educational attainment, and steady majority support for capital punishment. Several explanations for this phenomenon suggest themselves. The most basic is the exclusivity of education: even in the most highly educated societies, only about a quarter of the population has a four-year degree from an institution of higher education. Post-secondary education is generally is associated with the most significant reductions in support for capital punishment.

However, there is a structural factor – which I call the stabilization effect – which also plays a role. In an article reflecting on two decades of Supreme Court regulation of capital punishment, Professors Jordan and Carol Steiker (1995) identified what they called a 'legitimation effect' arising from the intensive constitutional regulation of capital punishment undertaken by the United States Supreme Court since the 1970s. The Court radically overhauled the system for inflicting capital punishment in the U.S., significantly limiting the death penalty's scope and mandating sweeping reforms in the trial and sentencing process used in capital cases. The result was a system that came to be known informally as 'super due process.' These reforms, argue the Steikers, produced two kinds of 'legitimation effects.' One was internal to the legal system: legal actors' sense of responsibility was eroded by the belief that the procedure for inflicting death had been made entirely rational, and by the diffusion of responsibility for death sentencing decisions among dozens of disparate decision makers (from juries to appeals court judges to governors). Steiker and Steiker also identified what they called an external legitimation effect: 'The public develops a strong but false sense that many levels of safeguards protect against unjust or arbitrary executions. They are thus likely to accept any executions that finally make it through the system as being more than fair enough.' (ibid.:436). The public's vague sense that the process leading to execution has been refined to the point of near perfection reduces pressure to abolish capital punishment once and for all.

The Steikers developed their theory of the legitimation effect in the context of modern American death penalty law. However, evidence of a similar process can be found in many different nations. By the mid-20th century (and often earlier), favorable opinion on capital punishment in most developed nations had become stabilized. The stabilization effect takes hold when the following basic conditions are met: first, the nation must be free of considerable political upheaval such as a war or occupation, and must have a smoothly functioning judicial system which affords criminals reasonably fair trials and appeals. Second, the death penalty must have already been legally or practically restricted only to murder or other very serious crimes. Britain and France, for instance, satisfied these conditions by the early 1950s. In Britain, capital punishment had been reserved for murder since the 1860s, and Section 5 of the 1957 Homicide Act further restricted the availability of the death penalty only to particularly aggravated killings, such as killing in the course of theft, or killing a police officer. Capital punishment was available for some non-murder ordinary crimes in France during the 1950s and 1960s, but was as a practical matter limited only to those crimes which resulted in the loss of life. Setting the special case of Algeria aside, from 1958 (the beginning of the Fifth Republic under de Gaulle) to 1981, only 17 criminals were executed in France, while during the same time period, 37 death sentences were commuted (Costa 2001:161).

By the 1950s and 1960s, developed nations had all achieved what can be called a modern state of stabilization. Legal reforms had ensured that the death penalty would be inflicted relatively rarely, only after thorough trials, and only against those who had committed especially heinous crimes. An ordinary citizen of Paris or London, in the 20th century, could expect to read of death sentences being handed down and carried out only against murderers. Some of these persons may have been relatively sympathetic victims of circumstance, but most others were not. Over a longer period of legal equilibrium, it seems safe to assume that the image of the 'typical' death row inmate among ordinary newspaper readers would become more and more closely associated with particular kinds of aggravated murder. The public had long since lost all memory of people being sentenced to death for political crimes or minor property offenses. There were still sympathetic death row inmates and cases of possible innocence, of course, and these cases dominated the headlines. However, to the extent that most ordinary news consumers paid close attention to such cases, they seem to have viewed them as exceptions to the rule, rather than indications of a fundamental flaw in the legal system. The cases of Ruth Ellis, Derek Bentley, and Timothy Evans, for instance, became the focus of intense activism and media controversy in Great Britain in the 1950s, especially after evidence of Evans' likely innocence came to light in 1953. These cases affected elite opinion on the death penalty. However, there is little evidence that these cases significantly affected *overall public support* for capital punishment, which remained strong. Thus, the stabilization effect and the legitimation effect resemble an instance of Zeno's famous dichotomy paradox, in which an arrow can never reach its target because it must first travel half of the way there, and then half of the remaining distance, and so on. Because there will always be a half of some remaining distance yet left to travel, the arrow never reaches its destination. The more the death penalty is reformed and rationalized, the less of a pressing issue it seems to be, and the harder it is to finally eliminate it.

There are considerable caveats to this picture of the stabilization effect, of course. The first is that the U.S., in the mid-1960s, was an exception to the rule. Throughout the 1960s, support for capital punishment among the broader public declined considerably, even in the face of a stable modern death penalty equilibrium. This interesting anomaly will be dealt with later in Chapter 8. However, *modern* death penalty sentiment in the U.S. is stabilized. The U.S. now has restrictive death penalty statutes: capital punishment can only be assessed in cases of intentional homicide, convicted murderers are given a separate sentencing trial during which they are permitted to present mitigating evidence, and the sentence itself will generally only be carried out after the inmate has exhausted an appeals process lasting at least a decade. As we have seen, Japanese sentiment on capital punishment also seems to be stabilized. The legal landscape in Japan is similar.

A recent survey of capital punishment in Japan observed that Japanese law gives prosecutors and judges almost complete discretion over the penalty to be sought in homicide cases. As a practical matter, though, these decision makers reserve capital punishment only for those who have committed multiple murders or who have previous criminal records (Johnson 2005:262–3). Japan executes only 2–3 death row inmates per year maximum.

Thus, in both Japan and the United States today, the average citizen is likely to associate the phrase 'death row inmate' with a person who has committed a heinous murder and whose case has been analyzed at great length and expense by the judicial system. We have noted several studies from France and Germany showing that survey respondents' support for capital punishment increased significantly when they were 'primed' by asking whether they would support capital punishment for *specific heinous crimes*. The stabilization effect may well be a generalized, background instance of this priming effect: years and years of newspaper stories describing highly aggravated murders are likely to cement a frightening image of the 'typical' recipient of capital punishment in the average citizen's consciousness. This impression survives doubts about capital punishment as an institution. This may explain why miscarriages of justice do not seem to actually spur many people to change their view and oppose capital punishment. A recent report by the Death Penalty Information Center revealed that Americans' confidence in the legal process leading to death sentences has been considerably eroded, with only 39% of Americans expressing confidence in death penalty adjudication, almost 90% believing an innocent person has already been executed and 75% calling for a higher standard of proof in death penalty cases (2007:3–5). Nevertheless, even these startling results have not led a majority of U.S. citizens to reject the death penalty. A 2001 study found that requiring college students to read an essay about the high risk of executing an innocent person 'only weakly reduced support for capital punishment' (Lambert and Clarke 2001:227).

These findings harmonize with the conclusion this and the following chapter urge: most people do not support the death penalty because they are rationally convinced that the process for inflicting it is fair. Instead, they support it because – in their view – it metes out fitting justice to people who have committed savage crimes. Just as many opponents of the death penalty *in general* can nevertheless support it for particular heinous criminals, it appears that many supporters of the death penalty can acknowledge flaws in the process and the occurrence of wrongful executions without affecting their judgment on the overall issue. These seeming internal contradictions are best explained by the assumption that most peoples' view of capital punishment is driven primarily by emotion, not by logic.

The stabilization effect is thus based on three elements. *First*, the 'background' impulse toward retribution anchored in human nature, which leads majorities to favor the death penalty for those convicted of murder. *Second*, the effect of legal reform in reducing the scope of capital punishment only to those convicted of aggravated murder, a subset of the population which is unlikely to evoke much sympathy among the public. *Third*, an analogue of the legitimation effect described by Steiker and Steiker: the conviction that the criminal justice system is reliable enough to *generally* select the right people for potential execution, despite occasional highly publicized miscarriages of justice. All of these elements need not be present. As the experience of the contemporary United States and Great Britain in the 1950s shows, the first two elements are strong enough to maintain overall majority support for capital punishment even in the presence of doubts as to element number three.

The stabilization effect likely explains the longevity of capital punishment as an institution. How does a society break the spell of the stabilization effect and take the decisive step toward total abolition? As we will see in Part II of this book, it is a long, difficult process, depending on committed leadership, good luck, and good timing. Great Britain's abolition movement was strong enough among social elites to achieve repeated votes for total abolition in the British House of Commons in the 1940s and 1950s. Nevertheless, public support for capital punishment remained strong, and formed the backdrop to retention of capital punishment until the mid-1960s. In France, opposition to capital punishment remained a distinct minority view, and could only finally be achieved by a seismic leftward political shift in the early 1980s, which permitted a Socialist presidential candidate to adopt total abolition as a plank of his campaign platform without fear of a public backlash. In Germany, the abolition of capital punishment by Article 102 of the postwar German constitution took place in the atmosphere of uncertainty and chaos after World War II, and almost did not happen at all. Even after it was adopted, it had to be defended against repeated Parliamentary attempts to reintroduce capital punishment.

Of course, the most direct way to change public opinion on capital punishment would seem to be through a public-education campaign. Many abolitionist groups have led such campaigns, in all of the countries addressed in this book. Members of these groups distribute flyers, give speeches and debates, write newspaper editorials and pamphlets, and carry the torch of abolition into their circles of family and friends. However, the results are generally disappointing. There is no real evidence of a public relations campaign ever having had a significant, sustained effect on mass public opinion on capital punishment. This is not to say these campaigns are useless: they influence the views of social elites. And, as we will see, this fact is of decisive importance, since only social elites have the practical ability to secure the abolition of capital punishment.

3
The Hollow Hope of Public Education

In a democracy, the most legitimate path to abolition would seem to be a large-scale shift in public opinion away from support for the death penalty. This is one of the declared goals of the American abolition movement. Richard Dieter, Executive Director of the Death Penalty Information Center (DPIC), described the task facing America's abolitionists thus: 'We need to work in all parts of the educational process, in schools, churches, on the Internet, and through the media to reach every segment of the population with the message that the death penalty is seriously flawed.' (2007:7). To this end, the DPIC generates and publicizes data on issues such as the cost of executions, risk of executing an innocent person, and lack of deterrence. Other American scholars question the reliance on policy-based arguments such as cost and deterrence. They urge death penalty abolitionists instead to 'acknowledge emotion as the legitimate battlefield of criminal justice' (Berman and Bibas 2008:356). Only by confronting capital punishment's supporters with 'non-rational' perspectives such as the grisly realities of execution, and passionate arguments about mercy and fallibility, can abolitionists hope to sway opinion.

Susan Bandes (2007), an expert on the role of emotions in the legal system, voiced a similar opinion when addressing the 'strange persistence' of capital punishment in America (to quote from the title of her article). Discourse about the goals of punishment and the rationale for the death penalty downplays emotion to focus on 'philosophical' approaches to the issue. Especially within legal discourse, 'opposition to capital punishment is often denigrated as emotional and moral, and therefore lacking in the rationality and tough-mindedness the law requires' (ibid.:24). Bandes argues that accepting these parameters of discourse is a significant error. The most powerful arguments for *and* against capital punishment are profoundly emotionally resonant. Capital punishment's supporters rarely miss an opportunity to highlight dramatic stories of victimization and the devastating loss suffered by the victims' families. Capital punishment's opponents, Bandes argues, should do the same, emphasizing the unsettling realities of state killing and the loss suffered by the offender's family. Pretending that the issue of capital punishment can be resolved on purely rational grounds, she argues, only plays into the hands of its supporters.

Underlying both sides of the debate are several unanswered questions: first, what is the audience for arguments against capital punishment, elites or ordinary citizens? Second, is there any empirical evidence about which kinds of arguments against capital punishment might actually work? If the American anti-death-penalty movement took the advice of critics such as Susan Bandes and began emphasizing emotionally laden arguments rather than ones based on policy analysis, could we expect to see a significant change in public opinion on capital punishment? This chapter will draw on recent psychological literature to try to shed some light on both questions. The answers, unfortunately, are not encouraging for those who hope to drive large-scale change in public opinion on capital punishment. This is not to say that public education efforts against the death penalty are useless. As we will see in Part II, these efforts influence elites, and that is important. There is no evidence, however, that public education efforts have ever significantly altered mass opinion on capital punishment.

As we have seen, the desire to see criminal wrongdoers suffer retribution for their actions – and to see those who commit aggravated murders executed – seems to be rooted in human nature, and appears in many different cultures. The retributive instinct alone helps explain the resistance to change of opinion on the death penalty. Abolitionists must, in essence, struggle against the 'default' position of a majority of their fellow citizens – against a punishment that strikes the majority as simply 'just', especially as applied to those who commit aggravated murder. However, as this chapter will show, there are further obstacles to changing mass public opinion on capital punishment.

The Landscape of Political Knowledge

The 'Marshall hypothesis', briefly discussed in Chapter 2, suggests that Americans are generally ignorant about capital punishment, but would change their minds if presented with evidence of its injustice and inefficiency. At the outset, it should be noted that an education campaign that aims to have a wholesale impact on public opinion will have to succeed on an unprecedented scale. To use the United States as an example, with an electorate of roughly 139 million voters (Center for the Study of the American Electorate 2006), a change in support large enough to make support for capital punishment a minority proposition (a 20% reduction, from 65% to 45% of the population) would require changing approximately 30 million minds. The Marshall hypothesis would not only have to prove true, it would have to do so on a massive scale. Millions of Americans would have to decide to inform themselves on the issue of capital punishment, mull over the new information, and then change their minds on the death penalty.

This will not happen – at least not in the near future. The first obstacle is the fact that most ordinary citizens who have an opinion about capital punishment know little about the issue and have no particular incentive to learn more. A recent survey of capital punishment in Japan remarked on the fact that there was almost no public discussion of capital punishment in that country, very little reporting about the issue, and little public concern (Johnson 2005). The same cannot be said of the United States, in which capital punishment receives a great deal of press attention. However, average Americans – despite their strong opinions on the issue – tend to know very little about how the death penalty is implemented and carried out. During jury selection in a capital case, large 'venire' panels of prospective jurors are selected at random, called into court and extensively questioned by lawyers for both sides. To ferret out potential bias, prospective jurors are questioned about their knowledge of the criminal justice system and the death penalty. As all capital litigators can confirm, most jurors, when asked to explain their position on the death penalty respond with some variant of: 'Well, you know, I've never really given it much thought.' Almost without exception, jurors turn out to have very little detailed knowledge of questions such as how capital punishment is carried out, what the criteria are for assessing the death penalty, the jury's role in the procedure, and other issues. As the Carlsmith study discussed in Chapter 2 revealed, even Princeton students did not know what retributive or deterrent arguments for punishment entailed.

The Marshall hypothesis, of course, takes this ignorance as its starting point. It then proposes that public opinion will be changed by reasoned debate. The sort of informed debate the Marshall hypothesis envisions, resembles the model of 'deliberative democracy' developed in recent years by American scholars and partly inspired by the work of Jürgen Habermas. One scholar has defined deliberative democracy as follows: 'The notion of a deliberate democracy is rooted in the intuitive ideal of a democratic association in which the justification of the terms and conditions of association proceeds through public argument and reasoning among equal citizens' (Cohen 1989). Law professor Ilya Somin identifies a serious reservation to this theory: to engage in the kind of opinion-forming debate that deliberative democracy calls for, citizens 'must be able to engage in fairly sophisticated deliberation about public policy', since they 'must have sufficient reasoning ability and philosophical knowledge to be able to analyze and debate the issue in the way that the theory demands' (2004:1303, 1304). In other words, a profound change in public opinion about capital punishment would require ordinary citizens to *want* to become much more well-informed about the process.

This is unlikely. Political ignorance in the United States is widespread and persistent. Political scientist John Ferejohn (1990:3) states succinctly, '[n]othing strikes the student of public opinion and democracy more forcefully than the paucity of information most people possess about politics.' Law professor Ilya Somin lists just some of the research findings underpinning this conclusion:

> [T]he majority of American adults do not know the respective functions of the three branches of government, who has the power to declare war, or what institution controls monetary policy. A related problem is that citizens are often ignorant of which political party controls what institutions of government. A survey taken immediately after the November 2002 congressional elections found that only about 32% of respondents knew that the Republicans had held control of the House of Representatives prior to the election. This result is consistent with research showing widespread ignorance of congressional party control in previous elections ... In particular, most ordinary citizens seem not to understand the meaning of the liberal and conservative ideologies that serve as useful organizing principles to categorize issues for political activists and elites. Obviously, failure to understand the basics of the major competing political ideologies is itself a serious informational deficiency. (Somin 2004:1305–6)

Further, most voters do not have much reason to learn more about government. Economist Bryan Caplan (2007), drawing on political science terminology, calls these voters 'rationally ignorant' – since one person's vote has so little influence on policy outcomes, most voters simply have no reason to gather information about public policy, as opposed to other subjects that have a much more direct connection to their lives. As a result, only a small fraction of the best-educated Americans – the 15–20% best-informed – has more than a rudimentary grasp of government structure and public policies. The American political scientist Philip Converse, writing in 1964 (Converse 2006:65), spoke of a 'continental shelf' separating the small elite of the well-informed from the mass of the poorly informed. These numbers have remained stable for decades, despite dramatic improvements in American education and changes in the media landscape, including the advent of the Internet. As Somin (2004:1325) puts it, 'political ignorance is a long-established fact that is unlikely to change in the foreseeable future.' The problem of political ignorance also exists in other countries, but studies suggest that voters in many other countries (especially in Canada and Western Europe) are better informed about their own system and about international affairs than their American counterparts (Delli Carpini and Keeter 1996:89–91).

Here we see one weakness of the Marshall hypothesis – it suggests that voters who obtain more information about capital punishment will change their minds, but does not suggest *why* voters might seek out that information, given that many of them are uninterested in detailed political information. Perhaps an even more fundamental weakness of the Marshall hypothesis is its unsophisticated view of opinion formation. As linguist George Lakoff (2006:10) recently argued, years of study simply do not show 'that hard facts will persuade voters, that voters are "rational," [or that] they vote in their self-interest and on the issues.' Many abolitionists have had the experience of forcing a capital punishment supporter to concede pragmatic arguments against the death penalty (cost, lack of deterrence, inevitability of executing the innocent), only to hear that 'we simply still must' have the death penalty for certain heinous murderers. This is precisely the kind of language psychologists encounter when studying 'social intuitionist' modes of reasoning about moral issues. Haidt, for instance, reports that study subjects could rarely articulate precisely *why* it was wrong to clean a toilet with their nation's flag, but insisted it 'just' was. Haidt labeled such viewpoints moral intuitions, which he defines as 'the sudden appearance in consciousness of a moral judgment, including an affective valence (good–bad, like–dislike), without any conscious awareness of having gone through steps of search, weighing evidence, or inferring a conclusion' (2001:818). For most people, support for capital punishment usually rests on just such a moral intuition.

There are yet more explanations for voters' frequent inability to attach specific reasons to their support for capital punishment. In the terminology of political science, capital punishment is a 'heuristic shortcut.' That is, many voters support the death penalty not necessarily because they have given it careful study, but because it gestures at values with which they identify – commitment to protecting the community, enforcement of social discipline, solidarity with victims of horrific crimes. Their reasoning may be something like the following: 'I may not have studied and compared various proposals to reduce crime, but a candidate who supports capital punishment shows me that she takes crime-fighting seriously, and will enact tough policies that protect me and my family.' Cognitive psychologists have found that most people use heuristic reasoning such as this pervasively: 'Because people have limited cognitive resources, and because heuristic processing is easy and adequate for most tasks, heuristic processing (the intuitive process) is generally used unless there is a special need to engage in systematic processing' (Haidt 2001:820).

Voters are especially apt to use heuristic shortcuts and symbolic thinking when evaluating emotionally fraught public issues. This can lead to distorted policy choices. As Somin (2004:1319) puts it, '[i]nstead of choosing shortcuts for their effectiveness, [voters] may choose them based on the degree to which they conform to preexisting prejudices or create other forms of psychological gratification.' And, of course, few issues are as fraught as capital punishment. Caplan (2007:132–3) observed: '[M]ost people with definite views on the effectiveness of the death penalty never feel the need to examine the extensive empirical literature. Instead, they start with strong emotions about the death penalty, and heatedly "infer" its effect.' Political scientists cite crime policy in general as perhaps the classic example of an area in which voters form their views primarily based on symbolism and emotion. Politicians propose symbolic solutions – such as three-strikes laws, or expansion of the death penalty – which resonate emotionally, regardless of whether they have been proven to improve public safety. Voters who apply heuristic shortcuts are unable accurately to gauge the effectiveness of such policies: 'If voters are applying information shortcuts to determine which side to support on the crime issue, they can easily fall for ... "soft on crime" rhetoric and not give serious consideration to the alternative proposals of those who believe that crime is better reduced by other means' (Somin 2004:1322).

Another factor driving the stubbornness of pro-death-penalty sentiment is what psychologist Jonathan Barron (1998:13) calls 'opinion overkill,' which he defines as 'wishful thinking' which leads people to 'convince themselves that all good arguments are on one side.' Thus, people who strongly favor capital punishment on emotional, just-desert grounds also tend to believe that its costs are justified and that it has a deterrent effect – even though it would be possible to favor capital punishment without believing these things. We saw precisely this effect in the studies discussed in Chapter 2, in which respondents denied that their thinking on punishment was motivated by a desire for retribution, even though that rationale best explained their actual policy choices. Conversely, even if a death penalty supporter can be convinced that the death penalty is costly or unreliable, this is unlikely to sway his or her opinion notably. As we have seen, Americans seem to be able to reconcile doubts about the implementation of capital punishment with continuing support for it in principle.

Finally, majority support for capital punishment may also have a self-reinforcing effect. In daily life, people who disagree with majority opinion on an emotionally laden issue will rarely openly discuss the issue with other people they meet in their everyday lives. This behavior is driven by a desire to avoid conflict with family members or colleagues. As explained by political scientist Michael MacKuen (1990) this tendency to 'clam up,' multiplied across millions of instances, tends to entrench the status quo concerning emotionally laden issues on which a clear majority viewpoint has been formed. The 'clamming-up' effect can go so far as to remove a particular position from the agenda of public debate for a time. During the 1990s, when support for capital punishment in the United States climbed to nearly 80%, debate on capital punishment seemed almost to vanish. The few nationally prominent abolitionist politicians avoided the issue in public. Anti-death-penalty activists had a difficult time broadcasting their views to a national audience. Opinion on the issue seemed so monolithic that Democratic presidential candidate Bill Clinton interrupted his campaign to fly back to Arkansas to preside over the execution of a mentally impaired death row inmate (Frady 1993). Clearly, Clinton was not concerned about offending death penalty abolitionists. If abolitionists 'clam up' in everyday life and have little access to the airwaves, it will be difficult for ordinary citizens even to gain access to arguments against the death penalty.

The final theoretical problem with the Marshall hypothesis is that it ignores the phenomenon of 'motivated reasoning,' the catchall term for the distorted forms of reasoning people use to justify a stance they are already committed to. One form of motivated reasoning is confirmation or 'my-side' bias. When confronted with new information on a subject on which they already have emotional commitments, most people typically ignore or rationalize facts that conflict with their existing views, and focus selectively on items that confirm their beliefs. The effect of this ubiquitous cognitive distortion is that it 'preserves beliefs from challenge, even when the evidence for them is weak and the evidence against them strong' (Barron 1998:83). Opponents of the death penalty, convinced that the evidence favors their position, run into a wall of my-side bias when arguing with death penalty supporters. Of course, those same death penalty opponents fall victim to the same cognitive distortion themselves. There may be a partial biological basis for these effects. A recent study used functional MRI imaging to study the reactions of test subjects with strong political opinions to information that threatened or challenged those opinions. The study's authors concluded that there were visible, qualitative differences in the way subjects reasoned when they were asked to reconsider beliefs in which they were emotionally invested, as opposed to neutral information. The challenging information elicited a primarily emotional response, whereas the neutral information elicited responses from parts of the brain associated with reflection and cogitation (Westen et al. 2006).

The Marshall Hypothesis Scrutinized

Given the above obstacles to changing strongly held opinions, we should not be surprised to find that the Marshall hypothesis, when tested, is generally not confirmed. Perhaps the broadest study of the hypothesis was published in 2001 (Lambert and Clarke). It involved 730 college students who were asked their opinion of capital punishment at the outset of the study. The students were divided into three groups: one was given an essay describing the death penalty's lack of deterrence; another an essay on innocent people who had been sentenced to death; and the third control group was given a general essay on punishment. Only the group which had read the essay about innocence and capital punishment displayed a statistically significant change in their views on capital punishment, and that change was only moderate; supporters of the death penalty became somewhat less convinced, without changing their view on the fundamental issue. The study's authors hypothesized that the effect of information on death penalty views was small either because the students had only been presented with a limited amount of information or because, as many other studies had already shown, 'level of support for the death penalty is an emotional decision that is not easily changed by facts and logic' (ibid.:228).

Motivated reasoning is a key factor in the formation and defense of opinions on capital punishment. A 1979 study (Lord et al.) found that those with fixed views specifically on capital punishment will defend those views with bias and motivated reasoning when challenged with contrary information. In particular, they often engage in 'biased assimilation', ignoring or hypercritically evaluating anti-capital punishment arguments, while accepting even weak arguments in its favor. Another study found that people who cited deterrence to justify their support of capital punishment rarely changed their minds after being provided with evidence that capital punishment did not deter crime (Ellsworth and Ross 1983). Even when arguments against capital punishment do have an effect, researchers have noted a 'rebound effect.' College students who changed their minds to oppose capital punishment after taking a course on the subject generally reverted to their prior opinion with a few months of the course's completion (Bohm and Vogel 2004).

Of course, these psychological studies need to be evaluated carefully, given their small sample sizes and non-random construction. However, there is a strong argument that the effects they measure may be even stronger in the population as a whole. As the authors of one study noted, the subjects chosen for that study were, like most college students, less likely to be motivated by a desire for retribution than the population as a whole (Carlsmith et al. 2002). Further, the college students in these studies were exposed to a great deal of information about capital punishment – sometimes an entire college course on the subject. Very few members of the general public are likely to undertake that much research on their own, and even if they do, they may encounter just as many arguments in favor of capital punishment as against, unlike the college students, who were exposed only to information designed to raise doubt about capital punishment.

Finally, a recent study in an emerging discipline suggests a particularly intriguing reason for the durability of pro-capital punishment. Researchers John R. Alford, Carolyn L. Funk, and John R. Hibbing recently published a study entitled 'Are Political Orientations Genetically Transmitted?' (2005). Previous studies of twins raised in different environments had isolated a hereditary component to personality characteristics such as susceptibility to alcoholism, religiosity, types of hobbies, and risk-taking propensities. The authors decided to broaden the traits studied to include political opinions. The result showed a 'pervasive' genetic influence on study respondents' attitudes to such issues as school prayer, property taxes, pacifism, and unions. Among the strongly correlated views was support for capital punishment, which earned a correlation score of .32 (with the highest score being .41 and the lowest .18). Of course, as the study's authors caution, a genetic influence on political attitudes expresses itself only in a complex interplay with other factors, such as upbringing and environment. Nevertheless, the genetic component is unmistakable. It is also directly relevant to efforts to change opinion, since attitudes higher in heritability are 'manifested more quickly, are more resistant to change, and increase the likelihood that people will be attracted to those who share those particular attitudes' (ibid.:164).

Why Does Education Erode Death Penalty Support?

Many of the above studies also single out the role of education level in determining how people think about issues such as capital punishment. As one would expect, the persons who constitute the top best-informed sector of the populace are also better educated than the rest of the population. They are composed mostly of 'scholars, politicians, political activists, [and] journalists' who constitute 'professional consumers of political information,' as well as people who are simply interested in politics (Somin 2006:260). Higher levels of education are also associated with greater sensitivity to the distorting effects of motivated reasoning. Although almost everyone uses biased reasoning to some extent (as Haidt points out, people who never used motivated reasoning would face constant conflict), higher levels of intelligence are associated with a reduced susceptibility to use motivated reasoning, and a greater ability to objectively weigh competing arguments and evidence. Higher intelligence enables people to postpone instant 'hot' emotional gratification and to follow longer term 'cool' trains of thought that may conflict with their initial emotional reactions (Haidt 2001:823–4). In fact, studies have found that trained philosophers seem to be the only group of people capable of consistently neutralizing their own cognitive biases (Kuhn 1991).

These findings may help to explain the lower levels of support for capital punishment that we see among the better educated. First, those with higher education levels are more likely to follow the news and build up a solid base of political information. They are thus likely to acquire more than superficial knowledge about capital punishment. They are also in a somewhat better position to actually use this knowledge, by situating capital punishment within abstract value systems and political commitments such as those expressed by 'human rights,' 'human dignity,' and the like. As Haidt and others have found, those with higher intelligence seem to be somewhat more likely to permit newly acquired information to challenge their existing beliefs, and more likely to attempt to try to structure their world view according to consistent principles. Thus, they are more likely to actually be persuaded by arguments against capital punishment. This argument does not, of course, exclude the possibility of highly educated people supporting capital punishment, or uneducated people opposing it. Higher intelligence and higher levels of education are closely correlated but not identical, and the effects of higher intelligence in reducing cognitive biases are neither monolithic nor uniform. However, given the observed cross-cultural differences in levels of support for capital punishment associated with education, it seems reasonable to assume that these factors play a role.

As we will see, European abolitionists feel no compunction about associating higher levels of education with opposition to capital punishment. Victor Hugo (as quoted in Smets 2003:7) wrote in 1862: 'It is by a certain mysterious respect for life that one recognizes *the thinking man*' (my translation, emphasis added). Europeans discuss issues of social class and education with a directness Americans often find disconcerting (Fussell 1983:18–19). To most Europeans, the notion that people from different social classes see the world differently is not particularly controversial. A typical member of the European elite would thus find it predictable that the less-educated would disproportionately support capital punishment. Support for capital punishment, in the elite European world view, is based on humankind's natural desire for revenge. Those with little education simply do not possess the cognitive equipment to question this satisfying emotional impulse. Education, however, equips people to think rationally, to weigh policy arguments, and to support principled solutions to social problems. To use a word whose importance to European discourse can hardly be overestimated, education 'enlightens' people. Thus, education should usually lead people to the conclusion that capital punishment is a brutal, inhumane policy inconsistent with civilized values. And even if they remain ambivalent about capital punishment, in many social circles, educated people see the benefit of at least being *perceived* to be on the 'enlightened' side of the issue.

Conclusion

What strikes the observer of the history of capital punishment is that there seems to be no recorded instance of the death penalty being abolished as a result of a popular, grass-roots political movement. The previous two chapters suggest why that might be the case. Almost all humans seem to share a desire to exact retribution for violent crimes, either personally or vicariously through the tribe or state. Those who permit religious or philosophical considerations to blunt this impulse may come to oppose capital punishment for condemned murderers, but they are generally a minority in most countries. Attempts to increase that minority by 'converting' supporters of capital punishment have met with only modest success. People come to support capital punishment because it satisfies a deeply rooted emotional need, not because they have conducted a careful analysis of the alternatives. Thus, attempts to change their view encounter the formidable obstacle of their emotional investment in the practice; their 'moral intuition' that execution is the proper fate of murderers. Perhaps more people can be converted by 'emotional' arguments against the death penalty, as suggested by the authors

I cited at the beginning of this chapter. However, such arguments have yet to be tested.

In any case, for grass-roots-driven abolition to have a chance of success, those arguments would have to achieve the same ambitious goal as the more 'objective' policy-oriented arguments (cost, deterrence) detailed in the Marshall hypothesis studies – they would have to change the minds of millions of people. Stories of individual conversions to the abolitionist cause are, of course, common. Mass shifts in opinion on capital punishment are another matter entirely – especially in societies in which opinion on the death penalty has stabilized and the fundamental legitimacy of executions is no longer a topic of urgent public debate. The only well-documented mass shifts in public opinion against capital punishment we have seen in modern times took place in France and the United States in the mid-1960s and Western Europe today. And in Western Europe, the change in opinion on capital punishment only took place decades after executions had ceased throughout the entire continent.

Chapters 2 and 3 have suggested the many obstacles the public-education model must contend with. For public education to change opinion on the scale needed to bring about fundamental political change, the following conditions must apply:

1. Large numbers of capital punishment supporters must decide that educating themselves about the issue is a worthwhile investment of their time;

2. They must expose themselves primarily to information that tends to undermine support for capital punishment (such as statistics about innocent people sentenced to death), rather than information that reinforces support for it (such as ubiquitous news reporting about violent crimes);

3. They must then counteract forms of motivated reasoning such as biased assimilation and confirmation bias, in order to give the anti-death-penalty arguments a chance to change their previously held opinions;

4. They must then actually *change* their opinion – that is, they must actually find the arguments against capital punishment persuasive;

5. They must then maintain their new stance against capital punishment in the face of possible opposition from co-workers or family members, and in the face of continued new coverage of heinous crimes; and finally

6. They must decide that capital punishment is such an important issue that it will decisively shape their political behavior.

The chance that large numbers of death penalty supporters will arrive at a firm opinion against capital punishment – especially when the death penalty has been stabilized – is thus vanishingly small.

At the beginning of this chapter, I suggested that changing mass public opinion would seem to be the only legitimately 'democratic' way of eliminating capital punishment. Yet if the average voter's 'default' position is support for the death penalty, and public education seems to have no chance of generating large-scale opposition to capital punishment, how did the democracies of Western Europe manage to end executions? As we will see, most European death penalty reformers, at some point, came to the same conclusions as the ones argued in these past two chapters: the general public simply could not be convinced to oppose capital punishment. European abolitionists thus set their sights on convincing members of social elites, and quite openly pursued the abolition of the death penalty against the wishes of a majority of their constituents. Precisely how they succeeded is the subject of Part II.

Part II
Abolition in Germany, Great Britain, and France

'Since Beccaria, Sonnenfels and other worthy and popular authors have declared war on the death penalty and torture, everyone now wants to be an "enlightened thinker", and a horde of writers has formed itself behind them.'
– Christian Gottlieb Gmelin, 1785,
quoted in Schmidt (1948:446)

Preface to Part II

I will now present three detailed case histories of modern abolition movements in Germany, the United Kingdom, and France. The order of the case histories is determined by when capital punishment was ended: Germany abolished the death penalty in 1949, the United Kingdom in 1969, and France in 1981. Throughout the discussion of abolition in each country, I will concentrate primarily on the modern phase of the abolition movement – the decades leading up to the actual elimination of capital punishment for ordinary crimes. However, to frame the discussion, I will present a short historical overview of the emergence of the idea of abolition of capital punishment in Europe in the 18th century, since the ideas developed by Enlightenment criminal-law reformers in this era had a profound impact on the rhetoric and structure of later abolition movements.

Before the Enlightenment, there were some notable proponents of abolition, including the Waldensians, followers of a 13th-century offshoot of Catholicism, and the Quaker thinkers George Fox and John Bellers, who by the late 17th century had evolved to a position of complete rejection of capital punishment on Christian grounds (Megivern 1997:99–107, 205–507). The modern European death-penalty abolition movement was launched by Cesare Beccaria, a minor Italian nobleman, when he was just twenty-six years old. His book, *On Crimes and Punishments*, grew out of discussions within a group of young, philosophically minded Italian noblemen calling itself the 'Academy of Fists,' an ironic reference to the 'pugilistic' debating style favored during the group's discussions (Thomas 2008:xvii). The group debated the criminal law over a period of several months, and Beccaria decided to reduce the group's conclusions to written form. First published anonymously in 1764, *On Crimes and Punishments* is nothing less than a brief Enlightenment manifesto for reform of the entire criminal law, addressing subjects as varied as proportionality of offense and punishment (a key theme), degrees of crimes, dueling, and the punishment of nobles. Beccaria accepted the principle that wrongdoers must be punished, but, drawing upon social contract theory, argued that punishment should inflict only that level of suffering necessary to prevent the crime at issue. Individuals might have conferred upon the state the power to punish, but they could hardly have agreed to assign any more punishing power to the state than the absolute minimum needed to eliminate the mischief at hand. Swift and certain punishment was, in any case, preferable to occasional, tortuous punishment. Richard J. Evans, author of a magisterial English-language history of Germany's death penalty – by far the best work on the subject in any language and the basis for much of the historical discussion in the next chapter – argues that Beccaria's famous treatise 'remained the most influential tract on penal policy well into the second half of the nineteenth century' (Evans 1996:127).

In Section XXVIII of his book, entitled 'On the Death Penalty,' Beccaria (2008:51–7) presents a series of arguments against capital punishment. He first condemns the paradox of the state asserting the right to take its citizens' lives, while forbidding them to take their own. The death penalty is not a right possessed by the state, but rather the 'war of a nation against a citizen, which has deemed the destruction of his being to be necessary or useful.' Executions may be necessary during times of unrest, Beccaria concedes, but when the 'calm rule of law' prevails, their only purpose can be to deter criminals. Yet centuries of experience have taught mankind that executions do not deter men from committing crimes. Further, executions themselves harm public morals: 'the death penalty becomes a spectacle and for some an object of compassion mixed with indignation.'

It is not the intensity of punishment that deters, Beccaria argues, but rather its length. Setting criminals to hard labor provides a lifelong example that will strike fear and awe into citizens' hearts for years to come. It also discourages those who, out of 'fanaticism or vanity,' might actually welcome a public martyrdom at the hands of the state. The death penalty is nothing but an 'example of cruelty,' all the more absurd in that it is a killing committed in the name of laws that 'execrate and punish homicide.' Adopting the voice of a hypothetical citizen to venture some particularly daring observations, Beccaria then suggests that the spectacle of prosperous, untouchable magistrates handing down death sentences on poor wretches may excite the impression that 'these laws are nothing but pretexts for power' and the condemned 'victims offered in sacrifice to the insatiable idol of despotism.' Beccaria concludes with a majestic three-paragraph peroration. Most human societies have indeed practiced capital punishment, but he counters that 'that this objection amounts to nothing in the face of the truth – against which there is no legal remedy – that the history of mankind gives us the impression of a vast sea of errors, in which a few confused truths float about with large and distant gaps between them.' The philosopher's plea for abolition will at first be drowned out by the 'cries of so many people who are guided by blind habit,' but it is Beccaria's sincere wish that 'benevolent monarchs' should take his arguments to heart.

On Crimes and Punishments was originally published anonymously, and the reaction to it was 'swift and widespread' (Thomas 2008:xxiii). The book was banned by the Venetian Inquisition and placed on the Roman Inquisition's Index of Prohibited Books in 1766. A Venetian monk published a ferocious attack on the volume, prompting Beccaria's friends to respond with a pamphlet in which they emphasized that Beccaria questioned only the utility of capital punishment, not the sovereign's right to inflict it. The small volume's fame soon spread far beyond the borders of Italy. The book was translated into French in 1765, prompting Voltaire to publish a favorable commentary on the work in the guise of a 'provincial lawyer.' In the commentary Voltaire echoed Beccaria's argument on the usefulness of hard labor as punishment: 'It is clear that twenty robust thieves, sentenced to labor on some public works all their lives, serve the state through their suffering' (Voltaire 2008). Many murderers who had been transported or exiled transformed themselves into respectable citizens by virtue of being forced to work. If executions are deemed to be necessary, Voltaire argued, they should be exceptionally rare.

Voltaire was, at the time, one of the Western world's most famous men. In 1830, Goethe recalled: 'You ... have no idea of the influence Voltaire and his great contemporaries had in my youth, and how they governed the whole civilized world.' (Goethe 1976:542). Voltaire's positive commentary helped spread the book's fame. Beccaria's treatise was translated into several languages, including English, when it was read and discussed by such American luminaries as John Adams and Thomas Jefferson. Beccaria himself was invited to Paris to meet prominent '*philosophes*' in 1766, but became homesick and quickly returned to Italy. Nevertheless, many of the reforms he proposed in *On Crimes and Punishments* were enacted by Europe's more benevolent monarchs in the late 18th century. Beccaria's thought truly came into its own years after his death in 1794, when several European nations undertook overhauls and codifications of their patchwork criminal codes. Beccaria's thought and arguments set the stage for the gradual abolition of torture and an increasingly selective use of the death penalty.

On Crimes and Punishments is only the most famous example of Enlightenment intellectual ferment on the subject of criminal law. Another example is the 'Prize of Justice and Humanity' sponsored in 1777 by the Economic Society of Berne (Voltaire 1999:17–18), which encouraged submissions from leading thinkers of comprehensive criminal-law schemes which would combine effective punishment with humanity. Voltaire, himself a member of the Society, submitted his own proposed philosophical outline of a criminal code. In the section 'On Murder,' he cited Beccaria to propose punishing murderers by forced labor instead of execution. In fact, he even proposed forcing the murderer to pay the victim's survivors a large sum of money and serve as their slave (Voltaire 1999:17–18).

German-speaking Europe claimed its own Enlightenment criminal-law reformer, Joseph von Sonnenfels. Von Sonnenfels, son of a North German rabbi, assumed a chair in 'policy and cameralism' (the study of high-level administrative affairs in the absolutist state) at the University of Vienna in 1763. There, he advocated proportionality of punishments and lectured against torture and the death penalty. His influence was so great that in 1772, Empress Maria Theresa specifically forbade von Sonnenfels to further address these two subjects, since torture and capital punishment were allowed under Austrian law at the time (Conrad 1967/68). In his massive work *Grundsätze der Polizey* ('Principles of Policy'), published in several volumes in the early 1770s, von Sonnenfels (1769–76:377–87) advocated strict restrictions on capital punishment. The state may exact capital punishment only when other means to defend public security are insufficient. As soon as the offender is in custody, this potential rationale no longer applies, since the danger he poses is neutralized by custody. Generally, therefore, the death penalty could only be imposed in emergency situations, such as someone leading an insurrection or violating plague quarantine. In any case, the death penalty must be subject to the same test for proportionality as other penalties; it may only be used when other penalties would not be sufficient to deter potential wrongdoers. Like Beccaria, von Sonnenfels pointed to the non-deterrability of criminals motivated by fanaticism or revenge (who may be eager to pay the ultimate penalty) and he advocated hard labor as a less glamorous and more practical substitute for the death penalty. As one German historian (Kann 1960:187) notes, von Sonnenfels was careful to avoid explicitly humanitarian arguments against capital punishment, believing these would offend the authorities, bring further restrictions on his teaching, and reduce the chances of realizing other parts of his reform agenda.

For the purposes of this book, the status of Beccaria, Voltaire, and von Sonnenfels is almost as important as the arguments they made. The work of these men stands for the proposition that defining the principles of criminal justice and procedure is properly the domain of intellectual elites, be they philosophers or trained jurists. Indeed, the late 18th and early 19th centuries saw the emergence of a privileged class of Enlightenment thinkers and reformers who traveled from court to court, advising rulers who were eager to rule according to the principles of benevolent despotism. Monarchs and princes interested in projecting an enlightened absolutism even competed to secure the services of the most prominent of these men: 'Leibniz and Christian Wolff, Voltaire and Diderot, Bentham and Herder, all enjoyed imperial patronage; they were translated and consulted, subsidized and often invited to St. Petersburg by a series of emperors and empresses, climaxing in Catherine the Great, who hoped to construct rational and utilitarian facades for their power.' (Berman 1982:178). Beccaria, like other reformers, became the object of a sort of bidding war between Empress Catherine of Russia and the Habsburg Empire, which led Austrian sociologist Dieter Reicher to memorably compare Enlightenment reformers to 'modern professional football players' (Reicher, forthcoming).

The ultimate recognition that could be accorded to one of these philosophers was seeing his ideas enacted into law. Von Sonnenfels responded to Empress Maria Theresa of Austria's 1772 edict forbidding him to publicly discuss torture (used mainly during interrogations) or capital punishment, by submitting to her court chancellery a private defense of his positions, along with a request that the state subject the issue of torture to a comprehensive official investigation. After the investigation began, von Sonnenfels – who held a senior government position in addition to his teaching post – had the right to submit his own brief against torture. His contribution to the report was, predictably, a searing indictment of torture. It was published in Switzerland; ostensibly without his knowledge (though most historians believe he had a hand in its publication). The revelation of the government's secret investigation, as well as von Sonnenfels' arguments, put supporters of torture on the defensive. Eventually, von Sonnenfels' skilled bureaucratic maneuvering – along with a horrifying incident in which a prisoner's hand was ripped from his body under questioning – led Empress Maria Theresa to proclaim the official end of torture in Austria effective from 1 January 1776 (Osterloh 1970:168–9).

Beccaria and like-minded reformers articulated what could be called the first modern, secular arguments against capital punishment, stressing themes such as lack of deterrence, the incoherence of the state denouncing murder by killing in public, the 'brutalization effect' (that is, that executions made spectators more depraved, not more virtuous), and the desirability of permitting offenders a chance to reform and repay their debts to society. None of their arguments was explicitly humanitarian – Enlightenment reformers did not yet press their demands in the modern language of universal human rights, or a 'right to life' – but their thoughts laid the groundwork for the emergence of these ideas in the 19th century. Most fundamentally, these thinkers suggested that it was important for the sovereign to think about what to do with serious offenders on the *level of policy*. The question was not whether individual wrongdoers should be pardoned or executed, but rather how the state's reaction to them could be used to achieve important objectives, such as deterring future wrongdoers and compensating victims. The death-penalty reformers also suggested that there might be limits on the sovereign's authority to execute citizens.

Aside from explicit arguments against capital punishment, the writings of Beccaria, von Sonnenfels, and Voltaire established other tropes that would dominate criminal-law reform debate in the coming centuries. Even when making pragmatic arguments for the abolition of brutal punishments or abstruse crimes, the vocabulary of 'humanity' and 'enlightenment' is pervasive in their discourse. They consciously set up a distinction between the educated, civilized person, who is capable of controlling his animal instincts, and the masses, who take delight in the macabre spectacle of torture and public execution. To take only one of dozens of possible examples, Beccaria, in his attack on capital punishment, contrasts the mild policies favored by 'enlightened citizens' and 'benevolent monarchs' with 'the cries of so many people who are guided by blind habit' (Beccaria 2008:57). As we will see, this rhetoric of civilization, enlightenment, and progress framed the debate on capital punishment for centuries, not only in Europe but also in the United States.

4
Case Study One – Germany

When compared to many other European countries, 18th and 19th-century Germany followed a notably mild approach with regard to capital punishment. Although policy in the various small principalities that formed pre-modern Germany varied widely, use of the death penalty was relatively sparing and merciful, especially compared with contemporary English policy. Under Beccaria's influence – and sometimes at his express urging – Prussian and Austrian rulers often experimented with abolition or moratoriums on capital punishment. Even when capital punishment was retained or reintroduced, the general trend in Central European absolutist monarchies in the late 18th and early 19th centuries was to limit capital punishment to an ever-decreasing number of extremely serious crimes, as part of an overall Enlightenment criminal-law reform agenda (Evans 1996:132–7).

Three times in German history – during the Revolution of 1848, the formation of modern Germany in 1870, and during the 1919 debates on the Weimar Republic's constitution – proposals for the complete abolition of capital punishment were tabled. Amid the social ferment leading up to the Revolution of 1848, the German jurist Carl Joseph Anton Mittermaier led an intellectual crusade against capital punishment which culminated in the adoption of provisions which almost completely abolished it in the so-called *Paulskirche* Constitution. This document was approved by a national assembly which met in St. Paul's Church in Frankfurt am Main (hence the name) in 1848–49. However, the conservative restoration that immediately followed the 1848 revolution in Germany rendered the constitution a dead letter. The 1860s and early 1870s saw a wave of anti-death-penalty sentiment sweep through Europe's smaller states: in Portugal, the Netherlands, and Sweden, the national legislature abolished the death penalty for ordinary crimes, and in Belgium, King Leopold I adopted a policy of sparing all death-sentenced convicts. These moves, which often took place in countries directly neighboring Prussia and the North German States, gave German liberals hope that capital punishment could also be abolished there. Abolitionists won early victories during the complex parliamentary maneuvering leading up to the unification of Germany in 1870–71. However, during the third reading of a bill to prevent the reintroduction of capital punishment in the new legal order, Chancellor Otto von Bismarck intervened with a powerful speech in which he warned that attempting to force through the abolition of capital punishment would endanger plans for German national unity. Bismarck's speech caused a critical mass of abolitionist delegates to change their votes, and capital punishment was kept as a punishment for murder in the new *Strafgesetzbuch* (Penal Code) of 1871, which governed the newly unified German Reich.

Abolitionism as a viable political project revived in the early years of the 20th century. The French National Assembly debated the abolition of capital punishment in 1906–08, and in Germany, the Social Democratic Party, which had established a solid base in the German petty bourgeois and working classes since its founding in 1875, sought with increasing success to convince its clientele to oppose capital punishment. In Germany in the early 1900s, Hans Hyan, a crusading left-wing journalist, 'pioneered the use of emotional appeals based on individual cases as a way of influencing people against the death penalty' (Evans 1996:473). Hyan, for instance, reprinted plaintive letters sent from prison by two Berlin street children who had been condemned as accomplices to a grisly multiple murder. As we will see in Chapter 7, this model of reporting continues to influence the European press to this day.

Despite the abolition movement's growing influence, a 1919 vote in the Weimar National Assembly calling for the abolition of capital punishment was narrowly defeated – owing in large part to the absence of a large bloc of Social Democrats, who would likely have tipped the scales for abolition had they been present and voted. Gustav Radbruch, a liberal jurist and law professor, briefly became Minister of Justice in one of the Weimar Republic's many shifting coalition governments, and proposed a draft criminal code abolishing the death penalty in 1922. The code, however, was never enacted, and Radbruch's two brief terms as Justice Minister were over by the end of 1923. Another near-victory for abolition came in late 1928, when another shift in Weimar power relations brought numerous abolitionists into the legislature. Evans describes the situation:

> A new cabinet committed to abolishing the death penalty; a Reich Minister of Justice who had ordered a nation-wide suspension of executions; a widely felt need to bring German penal practice into line with that of Austria [which had abolished capital punishment]; a major scandal over a wrongful execution; and a probable majority for abolition in the legislature: such were the hopeful circumstances in which the Criminal Law Committee of the Reichstag reconvened on 17 October 1928. (Evans 1996)

Nevertheless, a series of votes held by the Committee on 1 November 1928, which were intended to remove capital punishment from the criminal code, ended in 14–14 deadlock. In 1929, a retentionist Justice Minister replaced the abolitionist Erich Koch-Weser, who had spearheaded the 1928 efforts. Also in that year, Peter Kürten, the 'Düsseldorf Vampire', committed a series of bizarre sex murders in and around Düsseldorf, sparking a massive manhunt. Kürten confessed to the murders, which he said he committed for purposes of sadistic sexual gratification. Court-appointed mental health experts declared him free of serious mental illness. He was eventually convicted of nine murders and seven attempted murders in April 1931, and executed on July 2 1931 in Cologne. Press coverage of the lurid details of his murders, as well as his unsympathetic profile as a confessed and unremorseful serial killer, made clemency out of the question, and brought the abolitionist movement to a standstill. By the time Kürten was executed, the press and mainstream parties, reacting to the growing influence of the National Socialist Party, had moved significantly to the right, further dimming prospects for abolition (Evans 1996:591–610).

During National Socialist rule, the death penalty – carried out by the *Fallbeil*, or guillotine – was used to combat crime and suppress dissent. At least 30,000 'judicial' death sentences were handed down during the Nazi era by German courts, often after summary trials marked by obvious judicial bias. Of course, the number of judicial executions was dwarfed by those killed in programs of mass extermination of 'undesirable' social groups, as 'formal capital punishment was effectively swallowed up in the larger machinery of human destruction' (Evans 1996:875).

After World War II: The Basic Law and the Death Penalty

Germany's post-war constitution, called the 'Basic Law' (*Grundgesetz*) was promulgated on May 23 1949, and is the founding legal document of the Federal Republic of Germany. Article 102 of the German Basic Law is four words long, both in German and in English: 'Capital punishment is abolished' (*Die Todesstrafe ist abgeschafft*). In most nations, abolition of capital punishment was preceded by a decades-long campaign, but Germany accomplished the complete abolition of capital punishment in one ambitious stroke, by enshrining it as constitutional principle at the beginning of its national renewal.

The background to this act of abolition, however, was considerably more complex. In August of 1948, representatives of German political parties, working at the behest of the Minister-Presidents of the German states then under occupation by the Western powers, held a convention on the Bavarian resort island of Herrenchiemsee to develop a framework for a post-war German constitution. The main task of the Herrenchiemsee Convention was to determine the government structure of post-war West

Germany. The delegates decided on a bicameral, federal system with broad powers delegated to the individual West German states. Another point of agreement was the outlawing of popular referenda, which had contributed to the instability of the Weimar Republic. According to the official report of the proceedings (Verfassungsausschuss der Ministerpräsidenten-Konferenz 1948:58), the abolition of the death penalty was discussed 'in the context of the basic rights' which were to be guaranteed by the post-war Constitution, and 'opinions differed.' Because the issue was 'eminently political,' its resolution was committed to the later good graces of the Parliamentary Council.

The Parliamentary Council was composed of representatives from the political parties that had emerged or re-emerged in the early post-war years. The Parliamentary Council, which convened on 1 September 1948, was to use the fundamental framework hammered out during the Herrenchiemsee Convention as the basis for a final, full constitution for West Germany. The Council consisted of 65 voting members and 5 non-voting members, each of whom had been nominated by a state parliament from one of the German states then under occupation by the Western powers. The states were represented by population, with the most populous – Northern Rhine-Westphalia – sending 16 delegates. Each delegate represented, on average, 750,000 Germans. The most important political parties were the mainstream conservative bloc of the Christian Democratic Union (CDU) and the Christian Social Union (CSU), the Social Democratic Party (SPD), and the Liberal party (later known as the Free Democratic Party, or FDP). However, some smaller fractional parties were also represented, such as the Communist Party of Germany (which would be banned by the Federal Constitutional Court in 1956) and the nationalist-conservative German Party (DP or *Deutsche Partei*).

Although the Social Democratic Party had favored abolition of capital punishment for decades, it was a delegate from the *Deutsche Partei*, Hans-Christoph Seebohm, who first proposed a constitutional provision banning capital punishment. During the first session of the Parliamentary Council in December 1948, Seebohm, in Evans' words, 'surprised everybody' (1996:781) by proposing that a clause be added to Article 2 of the draft constitution reading: 'Potential (*keimende*) life shall be protected. Corporal and bodily punishments are forbidden. The death penalty is abolished' (Düsing 1952:279). Seebohm, a wealthy industrialist who had collaborated with the National Socialist regime and whose party represented some of the farthest right tendencies permitted under the new dispensation, urged adoption of the resolution to express the German people's 'revulsion at the large number of death sentences carried out in the last few years' (as quoted in Evans 1996:781). As Evans notes, this language clearly includes not only past sentences handed out under National Socialism, but also post-war executions of war criminals by the Allied occupying powers – which were fiercely opposed by nationalist-right parties such as Seebohm's. As important as this motive may have been, Seebohm also made broader arguments against the death penalty, noting the various European states which had recently abolished capital punishment, and arguing that criminals should be given a chance to transform and purify themselves in prison.

The Social Democratic party, despite its long-standing record of opposition to capital punishment, did not immediately support Seebohm's motion. Only during the third reading of the proposed Basic Law did the remaining political parties, including the Social Democrats, rally to idea of abolishing capital punishment. Carlo Schmid, a leading Social Democratic Party politician, argued that:

> [T]oday one must not approach the death penalty from the standpoint of criminal-justice policy but from fundamental issues, and one must eliminate instrumental considerations. The death penalty is, like torture, simply barbaric; in addition to the possibility of judicial murders, an especially important point is that the state degrades itself with every execution. The sentence 'Que messieurs les assassins commencenent' [a famous phrase coined by French journalist Alphonse Karr, which means 'let the gentlemen who do the murders begin', that is by ceasing to kill] should not apply – rather, the State should cease killing in its name; as it has the greater dignity and the primary obligation to do so. (as paraphrased in Düsing 1952:281)

The Social Democrats eventually lined up solidly behind abolition, and were joined by a substantial number of mainstream conservatives.

After further deliberations, the clause abolishing capital punishment was incorporated into Article 102 of the constitution as a stand-alone provision. During the debate over this provision, a member of the center-right Christian Democratic Union, Paul de Chapeaurouge, argued against giving the death penalty provision constitutional status. The Basic Law, he argued, should contain only the most necessary provisions for setting up a post-war government. Out of consideration for the greater democratic legitimacy of the parliament, Chapeaurouge argued, one should leave the decision on the death penalty to that body. Social Democrat Friedrich Wilhelm Wagner countered that the time had come for a decisive break with the Hitler dictatorship, and that the people 'in their deepest soul' understood the need to anchor the abolition of capital punishment in the post-war constitution itself (Werner 1996:478–9, 480).

All motions to remove Article 102 from the draft constitution were defeated, and the document was approved by a solid majority of the delegates on 8 May 1949. After being ratified by every German state except Bavaria, the law was officially promulgated on 23 May 1949. Because the new legal framework was seen as a provisional measure that would be replaced upon the eventual unification of West and East Germany, it was decided to call it not a 'constitution' but rather the 'Basic Law' (*Grundgesetz*) of the Federal Republic of Germany. As post-war German Chancellor Konrad Adenauer told the delegates (with his typical pragmatism): 'We're not adopting the Ten Commandments here, just a law that will be in force for an interim period' (as quoted in Schulze 1998:297). Nevertheless, the Basic Law set out a complete governmental structure. In particular, Article 79(2) provided that any constitutional provision could be changed only by a two-thirds vote of both houses of the German parliament.

The enshrinement of abolition in the Basic Law of post-war Germany came, in Evans' words, as a 'considerable shock to most observers' (Evans 1996:785). Church groups were generally in favor of capital punishment, and thus opposed the Parliamentary Council's decision. Most right-wing death penalty supporters focused on common criminals: they may have opposed executing 'respectable' officers convicted of war crimes, but saw no particular reason why ordinary rapists or armed robbers should be spared the ultimate punishment. Death penalty opponents were surprised by the decision to abolish capital punishment, and quickly had to rally to defend Article 102.

The fact that abolition had been firmly anchored in the Basic Law turned out to be of decisive importance, as the 1950s saw a series of attempts to bring back capital punishment. These attempts were prompted mainly by capital punishment's popularity in post-war Germany. In 1949, an opinion poll by the Allensbacher Institute showed 77% of Germans to be in favor of capital punishment, and 18% against. According to Evans, '[t]he tide of popular opinion continued to flow in favor of the death penalty throughout the 1950s and showed no sign of ebbing.' (1996:798). The first attempt to bring back the guillotine was not long in coming: in the very first electoral session of the new parliament, in 1949, a representative of the Bavarian Party filed a motion to abolish Article 102 of the Basic Law and bring back the death penalty. Speaking in support of the motion on the floor of the German parliament, Dr. Hermann Etzel delivered a long defense of capital punishment. He argued that the inclusion of Article 102 in the Basic Law might once have been thought necessary to distance the fledgling republic from its Nazi past, but that the wave of criminality in the wake of the Second World War demanded the death penalty's reintroduction. In any event, the adoption of Article 102 constituted a 'weighty and wide-ranging decision taken without consultation of the people' (German Parliament Reporting Service 1950:1893).

The motion was opposed by Dr. Thomas Dehler of the Free Democratic Party, an attorney who was at that time the Justice Minister in the Christian Democrat–Free Democrat coalition government. Dehler argued that, at the very least, more time was necessary to evaluate the consequences of the death penalty ban. In any event, Dehler continued, 'there is a higher measure of legal consciousness than we see in the dumb, instinctual [*dumpfe, triebhafte*] desire for the death penalty' (German Parliament Reporting Service 1950:1896). Members of the right-wing Bavarian Party interrupted his speech with cries that 90% of the population wanted the death penalty, but their motion was nonetheless defeated. Dehler soon emerged as a key figure in the struggle to maintain Germany's abolitionist stance. In the immediate post-war years, the Free Democratic Party enjoyed a mixed reputation, since one wing of the party (until its exclusion from the party in 1953) was associated with right-wing nationalistic tendencies. The more respectable wing of the party, to which Dehler unquestionably belonged, drew upon a decades-long tradition of German liberal thought favoring limited state intervention in the economy and strong protection for individual rights. However, despite their generally libertarian views, most FDP party members, as of the 1950s, favored reintroducing the death penalty.

Dehler himself had been persecuted during the National Socialist regime on the grounds of his 'mixed' marriage to a Jewish woman. He compounded his problems with the Party by continuing to represent Jewish clients, and even members of the resistance. As a result, he was continuously attacked in the Nazi press as a 'comrade of the Jews' and briefly interned in a forced-labor camp. His opposition to capital punishment put him at odds with his party, whose coalition agreement with the center-right Christian Democrats had elevated Dehler to the post of Justice Minister. Konrad Adenauer, the Christian Democrats' Federal Chancellor, also supported capital punishment. Given the discomfort his outspoken abolitionism caused among his political allies, there seems to be no question that Dehler's motives were sincere: he argued on the floor of the German parliament in 1950 that the abolition of the death penalty was a part of his 'liberal and humane view of the world'. In private correspondence quoted by Dehler's biographer Udo Wengst (1997:202), Dehler stressed three main reasons for his opposition to capital punishment. First, the requirement to respect human dignity required the state to show respect for human life in direct proportion to the disrespect shown by the murderer. Second, capital punishment was a 'relic' of bygone times, and had no place in a modern justice system. Third, capital punishment essentially meant treating human beings like 'wild animals,' which resembled the kind of contempt for human life that had defined National Socialism. Definitively rejecting the death penalty would be a symbol of the 'renewal' of Germany.

On 2 October 1952, Dehler took the floor of the Bundestag to deliver a detailed and comprehensive critical analysis of capital punishment. The occasion was a motion by the *Deutsche Partei* to reintroduce capital punishment. The party had evidently changed its position since Hans-Christoph Seebohm had sponsored Article 102 three years before. Dehler thought so highly of his speech that he used it as the basis for a radio address delivered in 1964. The radio address was subsequently published along with several of Dehler's other speeches and essays (Dehler 1969). In the speech, Dehler combines several general arguments against capital punishment (lack of deterrence, the brutalization effect) with repeated references to the need to distance Germany from its murderous recent past. However, almost a third of Dehler's address was devoted to one of his adversaries' most powerful arguments: the popularity of capital punishment. Dehler bluntly rejected the idea that the popular will should control this question. Comparing the death penalty, demanded by the 'dumb feelings' of the masses, to witch-burning, Dehler continued:

> I say in all clarity: I do not care about the 'people's conviction', that is, the opinion of the man on the street, when the question on the table is of the highest political and legal order. In any sort of trade, in any profession, we impose preconditions of apprenticeship, training, experience, ability, and lastly official certification. When the question on the table is crafting the right social order, the correct law, we should insist on the highest measure of insight and strength of character! The delegates Friedrich Kühn and Konrad Adenauer have achieved their goal of exciting primitive impulses by accusing the Parliamentary Council of creating a 'gray [that is, not fully legitimate] democracy' and the Bundestag of living in 'cloud-cuckoo land'...
>
> In 1950 [during an earlier parliamentary speech], I spoke a 'heretical phrase' when I said: 'One fails to recognize the true meaning of democracy when one believes that the parliament is the executor of the people's will. The essence of representative democracy is something else – it is parliamentary aristocracy. The parliamentarians have the opportunity and the duty to act with greater insight, with better understanding, and with weightier responsibility than the citizen can.' The parliament is not the people in 1:100,000 scale, it must be a select few, an elite; the voter must give his trust to the best among the people, but he must give his trust nonetheless. The parliamentarian is bound by a great responsibility, he is – as the Basic Law requires – beholden only to his conscience, and is not required to carry out any other person's orders, not even those of the voters. (Dehler 1969:62–3)

In part of the original 1952 speech which he omitted from later printed versions, Dehler added this intriguing postscript to the discussion of public opinion:

> If one sets to one side contemporary stimuli [*Reizen*] to public opinion, the 'people's opinion' [*Volksüberzeugung*] still contains residues in its bloodstream, remainders left over from earlier stages of development that still have some power. These are moods that cannot be rationally controlled, and simple people are not as effective in controlling them as the

more intellectually differentiated sort of person. Psychoanalysts tell us that there is an impulse toward destruction, toward annihilation in every person, and that people attempt to transfer this impulse toward others, and perhaps even toward the state. In a very interesting report submitted by the jurist Liepmann, written for the Vienna Conference of Jurists [which debated capital punishment in 1912], he says that supporters of the death penalty everywhere are subject to genetically inherited feelings. We might wish to keep this sentence before us as we discuss the problem. (German Parliament Reporting Service 1952:10613)

It cannot be said that Dehler's impassioned attack on capital punishment carried the day, since the motion to abolish Article 102 was doomed to failure in any event. However, the speech itself garnered stormy applause from the left, and was praised as an impressive success by a leading broadsheet (Wengst 1997:201).

The speech also exemplifies one part of the European world view sketched in Chapter 1: the relationship between elected representatives and the people. Germany has a mixed proportional-representation system in which some members of the federal parliament are elected directly by the voters (the so-called *Direktmandat*), whereas others are nominated by their political party to a candidate list. No matter which path is chosen, German parliamentary candidates are always selected after a party-internal vetting process. Before they have a chance of being selected for a federal parliamentary seat, they must prove their talent and dedication through years of work in the party organization. Ideally, this process weeds out the less capable, resulting in a Bundestag assembly in which parties are represented by an 'aristocracy' of their ablest members. The members prove themselves worthy of their responsibility by, in Dehler's words, demonstrating greater insight, understanding, and responsibility than the great mass of citizens. In consequence, they may be called upon occasionally to substitute their will for the will of their constituents. As Dehler notes, Article 38(1) of the Basic Law, in the official English translation, provides: 'The Members of the German Bundestag shall be elected in general, direct, free, equal, and secret elections. They shall be representatives of the whole people; they shall not be bound by any instructions, only by their conscience.'

Dehler's speech endorses the 'Burkean trusteeship' model of political representation, based on the writings of the 18th-century Irish/English parliamentarian and political theorist Edmund Burke. In her classic monograph *The Concept of Representation*, political scientist Hanna Fenichel Pitkin presents a précis of Burke's thought on the role of political representatives:

A well-appointed state … is one which breeds and trains a true natural aristocracy and allows it to rule, recognizing that it can perform this function best. Representatives should be superior men of wisdom and ability, not average or typical or even popular men. What matters is their capacity for practical reasoning, for Burke conceives of their function as essentially ratiocinative. Only, in Burke's view, reasoning is not purely an intellectual matter, but is intimately bound up with morality and what is right. (1967:169)

In Burke's vision, reason, informed by morality, finds its fullest expression during parliamentary deliberation, where the 'natural aristocracy' gathers to debate fully a particular issue. Because an MP's constituents have no expertise and are not present at this discussion, their views have little weight. Because governing is not an act of will, but rather a search for policies which reflect reason tempered by morality, the 'will' of the constituents plays little role. Pitkin describes this idea as the 'first' Burkean concept of representation. Taken to an extreme, it 'seems to preclude democratic responsiveness to the electorate. It makes no sense for wise, superior men to take counsel with stupid, inferior ones ... Representation has nothing to do with obeying popular wishes, but means the enactment of the national good by a select elite.' (170). Pitkin notes that Burke later modified his first concept of representation to include more room for consultation of constituents' interests. However, he continues to maintain that parliamentary delegates should represent broad interests, not the 'will' of their constituents as persons, however that might be measured. 'Burkean trusteeship,' thus suggests that representatives act more as 'trustees' of the public good than as agents of their constituencies.

Dehler's Bundestag speech is framed in language that few German parliamentarians would likely use today. However, the context is important: the constituents represented by the parliamentarians to whom Dehler spoke had recently demonstrated their allegiance to one of the most brutal and sinister dictatorships in human history. So soon after that episode, Dehler asks, should one really permit *their* will to prevail in a life-and-death matter of political morality – which is also a question of the legitimate extent of state power? Dehler's answer is clear. Of course, this power to act as a kind of Platonic guardian does not extend to routine issues, only to those of the 'highest legal and political order.' But when 'primitive' instincts and emotions are especially likely to cloud the average voter's judgment, the Burkean trustee may, in fact must, step in and apply his own superior judgment. Dehler thus makes his case by pointing to the 'residues' of 'inherited' attitudes which prompted the average person to support capital punishment. Like all European abolitionists, Dehler seeks firmly to anchor the abolition of the death penalty among the group of 'pre-emptible' issues suitable for elite decision. As Dehler wrote in the Foreword to a 1952 history of the abolition of capital punishment: 'If this [book] contributes to the replacement of the dumb, instinctual (*dumpfe und triebhafte*) demand of the public for the death penalty with a balanced and well-thought-out judgment, it will have completely achieved its goal.' (Düsing 1952, *Vorwort* (Foreword)).

Passing the Issue to the Criminal Law Commission

Another point made by Dehler at the beginning of his 1964 radio address related to the results of a recent consideration of capital punishment by the *Große Strafrechtskomission* (literally, the 'Large Criminal Law Commission'). Any decision to reintroduce capital punishment, Dehler stressed, would have to be preceded by extensive consultations with 'criminal-law attorneys, psychiatrists, criminologists, judges, prosecutors, and corrections officers.' Writing in 1964, Dehler observed that those who favored reintroduction of capital punishment, 'have simply chosen to ignore that the criminal-justice reform commission which has been tasked with drafting a new Penal Code just conducted exemplary hearings with testimony from these sorts of experts, and voted overwhelmingly against the death penalty!' (Dehler 1969:62).

The *Große Strafrechtskommission*, to which Dehler was referring, was convened in 1954 to draft a comprehensive revision of Germany's criminal laws. Throughout the 1950s, the federal government had promised a fundamental reform of German criminal law, to purge the Penal Code and other criminal laws of outdated provisions and to institutionalize modern correctional practices. Among the questions the Criminal Law Commission would address was whether it recommended the reintroduction of capital punishment in Germany. As we have seen, right-wing parties throughout the 1950s repeatedly tried to overturn Article 102 of the Basic Law. Although these attempts were largely symbolic, they still presented conservative politicians from the Adenauer government with a delicate dilemma, since the public, and Chancellor Adenauer himself, supported the death penalty. Dehler was succeeded as Justice Minister in 1953 by Fritz Neumayer, a Free Democratic Party colleague who was personally pro-death penalty. Unlike Dehler, Neumayer and his successors were wary of direct affronts to public opinion. However, they were equally aware of the need to foster respect for the Basic Law, and were thus loath to overturn one of its provisions so soon after passage. The creation of a criminal-law reform commission presented these ministers with an escape hatch: punting the issue to a blue-ribbon commission.

As described by a leading German-language history of German penal reform (Busch 2005), the Criminal Law Commission met regularly from 1954 to 1959, and was charged with updating Germany's Penal Code, which had remained largely unchanged since its passage in 1871. There were two large plenary sessions in which drafts of the proposed new Penal Code were read, and 237 individual sessions on sub-topics. The Commission finally presented the federal government with its final draft in 1960. As we will see later, the 1960 reformed Penal Code maintained the ban on capital punishment. The proposal, however, was submitted in the middle of a general election, and, amidst the uncertainty caused by such events in Germany, never came to a vote. During the 1960s, a general overhaul of the criminal code was delayed again and again by lack of consensus and a general sense that the proposed new Penal Code drafts that were eventually agreed on were already behind the times in an era of rapidly changing social mores (ibid.:120–5).

Although the Commission's work did not directly result in the passage of a reformed criminal code, its deliberations were crucial to understanding death penalty politics in the late 1950s. The German Federal Cabinet effectively delegated to the Commission the task of weighing the death penalty's reintroduction. Under the German federal scheme, individual lawmakers in the Bundestag (parliament) rarely take the initiative in submitting important legislation. Instead, legislation is normally worked out in relevant government ministries, and then voted on by the Federal Cabinet, which then sends it to the parliament for a discussion and a vote (Dann 2006:26–7). Because of its importance, legislators will often seek to spur the Cabinet to give its imprimatur to issues of particular interest to them.

By the late 1950s, pressure for the return of capital punishment had exceeded the bounds of the right-wing parties, and began to be felt in the center-right bloc. In a meeting held on January 28 1958, for example, the Cabinet of Christian Democratic Chancellor Konrad Adenauer discussed a parliamentary question from Christian Democrat Bundestag representative Friedrich Werber: whether the government planned to submit a bill for the reintroduction of capital punishment 'in especially severe murder cases' (Enders and Schawe 2002:98). The Cabinet – which was divided on the question of capital punishment – decided not to take any particular position on the question, given that the question of capital punishment was currently under review by the Criminal Law Commission. On April 23 1959, the Cabinet was again asked whether it would support the motion of several conservative members of the Bundestag to reintroduce capital punishment. Upon the urging of the Justice Minister, the Cabinet decided that, since the Commission had recently voted against including capital punishment in a revised criminal code, the Federal Cabinet would not, on its own, take any action to reintroduce the death penalty (Henke and Rössel 2003:190 and n.11). The Commission thus played an important role in deferring and defusing the contentious issue of capital punishment. Before its 1958 vote against the reintroduction of the death penalty, politicians could point to its ongoing deliberations as an excuse to defer considering the question themselves. After its vote, they could avoid taking personal responsibility for any position on the death penalty by pointing to the Commission's careful consideration of the issue and the rejection of capital punishment.

The Commission's debates were not only historically important; they provide unparalleled insight into elite opinion on capital punishment in post-war Germany. The personnel gathered to debate the death penalty during the 108th sitting of the Commission, on October 17 1958, included former Justice Minister Neumayer (who had left office in 1956) sitting as President; one representative from each of the Bundestag's three largest parties (by profession, two attorneys and one church official); six professors of criminal law; seven senior judges, a variety of prosecutors from both the state and national level; a 14-member team from the Federal Justice Ministry; a delegate from the Bar Association's Criminal Law division; and an assortment of high-ranking civil servants whose titles have no English equivalents (for example, *Ministerialdirigent*) (Grosse Strafrechtskommission 1959:1–2). The Commission did not include, nor did it hear testimony from, any 'average citizens' or victims of crime. The very idea of doing so would have struck this illustrious assembly – almost all of whom possessed doctoral degrees from German universities – as bizarre. As the excerpts from the speeches and arguments reprinted below demonstrate, many of the Commission's members viewed the 'peoples' opinion' with quite as much distrust as Dehler.

At the outset, the chairman of the Commission, Justice Minister Fritz Neumayer, Dehler's successor, announced the ground rules: the Commission would hear one main presentation for the reintroduction of the death penalty, and then one of roughly equal length against. After the two main speeches, each member would be permitted brief remarks before the final vote. One Dr. Skott, retired President of the Berlin Court of Appeal, presented the arguments in favor of capital punishment (Grosse Strafrechtskommission 1959:7–14). First, he argued that the decision to abolish the death penalty by adopting Article 102 of the Basic Law was something of a fluke, and could in no way be seen as the logical culmination of a process of historical development. The theme of the death penalty was indeed 'fraught with emotion,' but it was wrong to dismiss it as a mere historical relic, as Dr. Dehler was wont to do. Although opinion on capital punishment was subject to swings, in the ten years since the penalty's abolition, public opinion had registered a 'strong and constant' majority for the death penalty. 'The legislator can hardly be expected to ignore this fact,' Skott warned. Turning to more legalistic arguments, Skott conceded that there was little direct evidence that the death penalty deterred crime, although the possibility could not be discounted, given the anecdotal evidence that criminals respected and feared the death penalty. The death penalty was surely irreparable once carried out, but the likelihood of a miscarriage of justice was extremely remote, since courts were likely to be 'extremely cautious' in its assessment. In any event, it was wrong, Skott argued, to criticize the retributive impulse as backward or primitive. Even opponents of the death penalty conceded that retribution was the essence of punishment. Properly understood, retribution was not about reforming the offender, but rather 'in an objective sense, restoring the legal order by means of fair retribution.' Even opponents of capital punishment admitted that it may be necessary in times of war or emergency. If this was so, then it was all the better to establish a procedure for administering it rationally in advance of possible need. Given all these reasons, Skott concluded, the death penalty must be retained 'for the most serious cases of criminality.'

Paul Bockelmann, a professor of criminal law, criminal procedure, and criminology at the University of Göttingen, then delivered the principal speech against the reintroduction of capital punishment (Grosse Strafrechtskommission 1959:15–24). First, he emphasized, the Commission should give heed to continuity and stability in the law. Granted, the Basic Law was meant only to be provisional until the reunification of Germany – but to overturn one of its key provisions a mere ten years after passage would send the wrong signal. It was also wrong to speak of the adoption of Article 102 as a fluke. Seen in context, it was clearly enacted in response to the disturbing overuse of capital punishment in recent German history – according to the most conservative count, German courts pronounced an average of at least ten death sentences for every day of the Second World War, not to mention the unprecedented 'bloodletting' (*Blutvergießen*) that occurred in countries occupied by Germany. This historical background, Bockelmann asserted, was by itself sufficient to justify the preservation of Article 102. In any event, the notion that society 'demands' retribution by death was really, at heart, a 'mystical' or 'religious' supposition that had no place in a modern, rational justice system.

Also 'thoroughly irrational' was the argument from the 'will of the people' (*Volksüberzeugung*) of which death penalty supporters 'are so fond.' Of course, a majority of citizens favored capital punishment. However, it was just as certain that the legislator must ignore this opinion, because it was completely 'unfounded.' Setting aside those who favored capital punishment merely out of 'hidden cruelty,' the vast majority of death penalty supporters cited the 'naïve assumption' that the death penalty deterred: 'The will of the people rests solely on this half-baked supposition, which is not supported by the slightest amount of research.' Further, the will of the people was notoriously inconstant. The press and public often developed fixations upon the innocence of those sentenced to death in foreign countries, and it was certain that if executions were allowed in Germany, there would be cases where the press and public suddenly and 'furiously' took the side of the condemned. Besides, if they let the 'voice of the people' drive their policy, then what could they make of the common man's complaint about the cost of imprisoning someone for life? 'Of course,' Bockelmann assured his distinguished audience, 'none of us would ever say something like this, but the voice of the people does.'

The question of deterrence was inconclusive: those who had experience with criminals knew that most of them never reckoned with getting caught, and many were also driven by irrational urges which rendered them insensible to the death penalty's supposed deterrent effect. Thus, those claiming a deterrent effect for capital punishment had the burden of proof, which even Dr. Skott would likely concede they were unable to carry. Individual anecdotes of criminals who said they would have been deterred by capital punishment were easily canceled out by the many stories of those who committed crimes despite having just witnessed sentencing proceedings or even executions for similar offenses. To retain the death penalty for states of emergency or war would weaken the message of total abolition contained in Article 102, and was in any case unnecessary, since in such a drastic situation, the state would likely have much more pressing problems. Finally, permitting the death penalty in emergencies would weaken the Commission's ultimate message, which, Bockelmann predicted, would be the 'repudiation' (*Verwerfung*) of the death penalty by a 'large majority' of the Commission.

After thus refuting Dr. Skott's arguments for the death penalty, Bockelmann came to the 'positive' arguments against capital punishment. The first was the fundamental and insoluble problem of defining the prerequisites for capital punishment. Experience had taught that defining death-eligible crimes with the kind of precision and reliability that the ultimate punishment demanded was simply beyond the capacity of any justice system (I will call this the 'non-justiciability' argument). Bockelmann then turned to what was to him the unanswerable ultimate argument against the death penalty: its irreparability. One could only support the death penalty if one were convinced that the possibility of a miscarriage of justice was essentially non-existent. His own experience had taught him that this was certainly not the case. Bockelmann finally cited the 'corrupting effect' of capital punishment. He recalled 'with horror' the sight of schoolchildren, during the war, practicing their newly acquired skills by reading the 'well-known red posters' listing those who had been executed.

Also disturbing was the enormous public appetite for executions – huge masses of people inevitably 'crowd into' courtrooms to watch murder trials, and a senior official once told Bockelmann that the Reich Justice Ministry received so many applications for the office of executioner that they had to develop a general rejection letter to deal with them all. Bockelmann personally oversaw three executions during the war (not resulting from his own sentences), and could testify that the primary job of the execution team was to recruit a 'small army' of soldiers to keep 'the curious' away from the actual place of execution. Bockelmann recalls being extremely disturbed by the first execution he was required to stage, but by the third, he was treating it as a 'routine job,' which bothered him even more. He concluded with the following peroration:

> My outrage is not directed at someone who is capable of beheading the fifteen-thousandth person. Rather, it is directed at the person who is capable of beheading the first. The habituation to horror takes place with frightful speed even in those people who claim to be somewhat more differentiated in their thinking. It is the fear of this habituation that, for me, delivers the decisive argument against the death penalty.

Bockelmann was then thanked by Neumayer, the chairman of the Commission, for his 'interesting' and 'impressive' speech.

After the two main speeches for and against capital punishment had been delivered, the Commission heard shorter remarks from other Commission members. Dr. Baldus, the presiding judge (*Senatspräsident*) of an appeals court, spoke at some length (Grosse Strafrechtskommission 1959:24–6). He first registered his dismay at theologians, the majority of whom claimed that the death penalty was not only compatible with, but perhaps even required under Christian principles: 'I can understand these arguments only as a sign of the complete exhaustion of any religious impulse.' As a judge, Baldus wished to make the Commission aware of the terrible dilemma the death penalty posed for the judges who must actually hand down such sentences. The Commission should not 'believe itself required to follow the peoples' opinion rather than the conviction of many judges.' When one thought of miscarriages of justice, one should also take into account the many people who had been executed despite doubts as to their mental competency; to do otherwise would be to 'fall back on a unacknowledged barbaric assumption: namely, that it is "not so bad" when a mentally ill lust-murderer is executed.' Apparently referring to a specific case, Baldus noted that the 'peoples' opinion,' would demand the execution of a 16-year-old sex criminal. In any event, Baldus noted, the just application of any death penalty statute would demand a level of consistency that is beyond the capacity of the legal system to deliver.

Professor Dr. Rudolf Sieverts, a professor of criminal law and criminology, then registered his belief (Grosse Strafrechtskommission 1959:26) that the notion that the death penalty deterred was absurd. In the course of teaching a colloquium in forensic psychiatry, Sieverts had thoroughly examined 57 murderers, and could say with certainty that not one would have refrained from committing the killing had it been punishable by the death penalty. Sieverts also argued that the ultimate penalty demanded the ultimate level of proof of the defendant's unmitigated mental culpability, yet the number of cases in which that might be possible was much too small to justify introducing a penalty with so many other deeply problematic aspects. Next came brief remarks from the Federal Attorney General (*Generalbundesanwalt*) Dr. Güde. Although he did not regard the abolition of the death penalty as an 'inevitable' development in 1949, Güde argued that the death penalty should not be reintroduced, since 'this generation' of Germans had grievously abused the state machinery of justice in the recent past. With an oblique reference to public opinion, Güde argued that the death penalty could be reintroduced only when 'not just the individual, but also the entire community (*Gemeinschaft*) possesses a reliable standard which, at a very minimum, guarantees the just implementation of the death penalty.'

In the Appendices to the transcript of the hearing, the written submissions of various Commission members on the question of capital punishment are reprinted. It is striking how many written submissions contain (in addition to more conventional arguments against capital punishment) harsh denunciations of the public's instincts and preferences, especially as they played out in recent German history. Professor Eberhard Schmidt from Heidelberg maintained (Grosse Strafrechtskommission 1959:31–3) that the 'strong cries of support for capital punishment among the general public are nothing more than a scream for vengeance and retribution.' After endorsing the arguments of irreparability and non-justiciability, Schmidt returned to more moralistic themes: the death penalty simply harmed public morals in a way that could not be ignored. Why else, he asked, would the task of execution be consigned to 'a morally inferior individual' who kills other humans to 'earn money' and feel a 'thrill'? If Germans, as a society, genuinely believed in the appropriateness of capital punishment, they would give the task to their most senior corrections officials.

The next comments were submitted by Assistant Attorney General (*Bundesanwalt*) Wolfgang Fränkel, whose position required him to represent the German state in criminal appeals before the highest federal court of general jurisdiction, the *Bundesgerichtshof*. Fränkel, a former Nazi party member with years of experience as a prosecutor, would later be promoted to the higher post of Federal Attorney General (*Generalbundesanwalt*) in 1962. In his testimony (Grosse Strafrechtskommission 1959:33–5), Fränkel first denied that the death penalty could be supported on transcendental or 'immanent' grounds. Fränkel also made several more legal arguments, such as the inevitability of mistake and the non-justiciability of the death penalty. Fränkel devoted considerable space to attacking the German national character. Given that Germans had shown an 'unmistakable tendency to uncritically follow any state authority, it is simply irresponsible, after the experience of the last decades, to entrust the state, even through its courts, to decide over the life or death of human beings.' Permitting executions weakens respect for human life, a particularly dangerous factor in reference to the German people whose labile 'moral self-control' (*sittliche Selbstkontrolle*) was so evident. Fränkel returned to the theme when addressing the disturbing ease with which executioners could be found:

[E]xperience shows that even in recent times, it is apparently very easy to find quite a number of creatures willing to do such 'work' among the German people. But precisely the fact that the desire to kill for a possible payment is still widely found among the population – perhaps owing to 12 years of training by a criminal, authoritarian regime or perhaps even owing to inborn tendencies – we must take it as an unmistakable warning against permitting people to indulge this bloodlust, sanctioned by an official court decision.

Nevertheless, Fränkel endorsed a very limited exception permitting the death penalty in cases of national emergency. Later events show Fränkel's testimony on capital punishment in an ironic light. Shortly after his appointment as Federal Attorney General in 1962, an East German publication revealed that Fränkel, as an assistant in the prosecutorial office of the Reich during the Nazi era, had filed numerous motions requesting harsher penalties – including capital punishment – against persons convicted of theft or ideological 'crimes' such as having an 'anti-German attitude' (*deutschfeind-licher Gesinnung*). The sources cited by the East Germans turned out to be credible, and Fränkel was forced from his post into 'temporary retirement' just months after his appointment (*Bundesminister der Justiz* 1989:373–81).

The remaining written submissions sounded similar themes. Prof. Dr. Hans-Heinrich Jescheck, from Freiburg, considered himself a follower of the 'deeply humane outlook' of Gustav Radbruch, which naturally condemned capital punishment. Jescheck recalled with horror his experience in wartime, in which it was always necessary to turn away volunteers for firing squads. The possibility of error was highlighted by a speech given on February 10 1955 in the House of Commons by former Interior Minister Chuter Ede (Hansard HC 1955), quoted at length by Jescheck, in which Ede registered his anguish at having permitted the execution of Timothy Evans, who was very likely innocent (see Chapter 5 for more on the Evans case). Scientifically, Jescheck continued, the death penalty's deterrent effect could not be proven, and from a Christian perspective, an execution forestalls a criminal's opportunity to experience 'God's mercy.'

Following these extended arguments came a number of shorter submissions from judges, prosecutors, and professors, all opposing the reintroduction of capital punishment. Most of these submissions invoked the non-justiciability and irreparability arguments, as well as the death penalty's lack of deterrence and the abuse of capital punishment under the Third Reich. However, many also invoked anti-populist themes. Federal Judge Else Koffka, the only woman to submit an opinion to the Commission, rejected the death penalty on the grounds that it 'awakens dangerous instincts among the people' and placed unacceptable burdens on judges. A high-ranking state court judge from Bavaria, Dr. Voll, sounded similar themes: no definition of murder sufficiently clear and reliable to permit the ultimate punishment could ever be found; the 'sensational and judgmental reporting' of the press on notorious crimes created a craving for vengeance among the public that may 'infect' judges; the 'dignity' of capital punishment, which once expressed the 'majesty' of the state, had been forever lost by the 'outrageously inflationary use of the death penalty in the Third Reich.' Prof. Dr. Dahs from Bonn noted that the public always despised executioners, which was understandable considering the 'sadistic drives of this mercenary.' The only argument for the death penalty was 'expiation' (*Sühne*), which drove the support of the people for capital punishment. However, the strong 'emotional component' to that argument made it untrustworthy: the arguments against capital punishment were valid independently of our emotional convictions, and thus must be considered stronger. The Chief District Attorney of Frankfurt followed. He argued that the 'satisfaction that the victims and the public apparently feel [when the death penalty is carried out] is, in the final analysis, nothing but the satisfaction of the drive for revenge.'

Prof. Dr. Richard Lange, a criminal-law professor from Cologne, submitted a long statement (Grosse Strafrechtskommission 1959:43–6). Lange's was the longest of only four written statements to expressly favor capital punishment. The question of capital punishment was, Lange argued, more a political question than a fundamental question of criminal-justice policy. One might ask whether the political constellation giving rise to Article 102's abolition of the death penalty still existed today. The answer was no: the post-war situation was today 'so clearly overcome on political, legal and psychological grounds' that it could no longer justify Article 102. Many other advanced countries, such as England, France, and the USA continued to employ capital punishment. Further, 'the question of what the people's will means in a democracy remains unresolved.' One could not deny the fact, confirmed by many polls, that 75–80% of the population supported the reintroduction of capital punishment for murder. Lange then critiqued the assumption, popular among experts, that men are 'basically good,' and that criminals were the products of their environment. Surely, he argued, recent experience had made it no longer possible to ignore the 'existential evil' of mankind.

Lange then returned to the question of public opinion. The simple fact was that, ten years after its abolition, the death penalty remained 'deeply rooted in the legal consciousness of the people' (*Rechtsüberzeugung des Volkes*). Of course, one saw the occasional spike in support for the death penalty caused by particularly outrageous murders, but that could not account for the constant support of 75–80% of the population. Quoting Dehler's 1952 speech without mentioning Dehler by name, Lange warned against describing support for the death penalty as a 'dumb and instinctual drive.' In fact, the public's support for the death penalty could be seen as quite rational. Ordinary people were capable of limiting the application of the death penalty only to appropriate crimes. Survey respondents, for instance, approved the death penalty for murder while rejecting it for political crimes. Referring to the other members' frequent denunciations of the pro-capital punishment majority, Lange noted drily that '[w]e need not discuss here whether only the most worthless and unreasonable three-quarters or four-fifths of the people register support for capital punishment.' He argued that it was unhealthy for policy and public opinion to diverge so widely, since:

> the morality-reinforcing (*sittenbildende*) power of criminal law can only unfold when it is in accordance with the legitimate legal convictions of

the people, thereby rewarding and strengthening trust in the law. The legislator will have to determine whether it can afford, in such an important question as the death penalty, to continue to ignore the unrest and dissatisfaction that continue to be registered among the people concerning this issue.

Lange then noted that even opponents of the death penalty, such as Radbruch, conceded that the death penalty might be necessary in emergencies. Although the deterrent effect of capital punishment could neither be 'proven nor disproven' by statistics, the critical question from a political point of view was whether it might counteract the 'increasing lack of human connection' (*Bindungslosigkeit*) that modern society brought with it. Lange argued that new kinds of particularly brutal and cold-blooded murders brought about by such alienation could only be answered by the death penalty, and therefore concluded that capital punishment should be reinstated for murder.

After hearing a few more brief speeches and taking cognizance of the written submissions, the Commission finally took a vote on the question 'Will it be considered necessary to provide for the death penalty for murder in the draft Penal Code?' The results of the vote were 19 to 4 against recommending the death penalty – a result in line with expectations. Accordingly, the draft Penal Code submitted to the Bundestag in 1960, at the conclusion of the Commission's work, did not include death penalty provisions. Of course, the draft Code would not have been decisive on its own, since a two-thirds vote of both houses of the German parliament would have been necessary to remove Article 102 from the Constitution. Nevertheless, given the strong public support for capital punishment and its support by leading conservative politicians in the 1950s (Evans 1996:798–9), the unexpected and explicit endorsement of capital punishment by a distinguished panel of experts might well have given the death penalty another chance. The Commission's decisive 'no' vote, however, both reflected and reinforced the growing consensus against capital punishment among social elites.

Further Reforms

The early 1960s saw a series of notorious robbery-murders of taxi drivers, prompting renewed calls to abolish Article 102 of the Basic Law. However, public support for capital punishment had begun to slip by this time. Further, the Bundestag's failure to enact the Criminal Law Commission's proposed Penal Code reform in 1960 and even later in 1962 (when the 1960 proposal was reintroduced with minor modifications) preserved the viability of the tactic of deferring debate over the death penalty for the (long-overdue) Penal Code overhaul. Complicating matters, a large group of progressive German and Swiss criminal-law professors met in 1965 to generate an 'alternative draft' of a revised Penal Code, which not only maintained the ban on capital punishment but also abolished the *Zuchthausstrafe* (imprisonment with hard labor), decriminalized homosexuality, and proposed a much more finely tuned and rehabilitation-oriented system of criminal penalties which treated prison as a last resort (Busch 2005:42–5). The alterative draft injected new vigor into the debate on criminal-justice reform in Germany. Further, the intellectual ferment had consequences outside Germany's borders. Across the world, many legal orders are deeply influenced by concepts of criminal law developed by German scholars, both because of the high reputation of German legal scholarship and because many countries, at one point or another, adopted a version of the German Penal Code into their own legal order. In particular, the 'alternative draft', which represented the latest thinking on penal reform in the civil-law legal family, had profound repercussions in Scandinavia, Austria, Switzerland, Brazil, and Argentina, among other nations (Lüttger 1979).

Ironically, Germany was not the first to adopt many of the legal reforms its scholars proposed. In the mid-1960s, Germany was governed by an unwieldy Grand Coalition of Social Democrats and Christian Democrats, a circumstance which choked off any initiative to undertake controversial and ambitious reforms, no matter how long overdue. Only after the election of Social Democratic Chancellor Willy Brandt in 1969 – under the slogan 'Dare more democracy' – was the way finally open for the first comprehensive reform of the German Penal Code since the late 19th century. By the late 1960s, support for the death penalty had dropped to a plurality of the West German population, and supporters began routinely to be outnumbered by opponents.

By 1969, when the new 'social–liberal' coalition took power, paving the way for the long-delayed reform of the criminal code, the death penalty was no longer an active issue. With the advent of the baby boom generation – the first generation of post-war Germans to be educated in a 'de-nazified' system, public opinion turned decisively against the reintroduction of capital punishment. Reform, not retribution, was the watchword. Between 1969 and 1974, five major reform bills were passed, modeled largely on the 'alternative' reform plan proposed in 1965 by the Swiss and German professors. Together, these new laws revamped the German penal landscape (Busch 2005). Among the innovations was the *Strafvollzugsgesetz*, or 'Law on the Implementation of Punishments', passed in 1972. Section 2 of the law specifies the exclusive goals of punishment: 'While serving his penal sentence, the prisoner should become capable of leading a socially responsible life without further criminal acts. The imposition of a prison sentence also serves to protect the public from further crimes.' All attempts to add a component of punishment or retribution to this provision were defeated during negotiations in the German Bundestag. According to commentaries written by German professors, every section of the *Strafvollzugsgesetz* is to be interpreted in light of Section 2, which, properly interpreted, specifies the offender's re-socialization as the exclusive goal of punishment (Hammel 2006:110).

The public registered this dramatic loosening of criminal sanctions in Germany without protest. There were two spikes in support for the death penalty: one amid the Red Army Faction terror attacks of the mid-1970s, and one following reunification with East Germany. Although East Germany had abolished capital punishment in 1987, East Germans remained more favorable to capital punishment than their West German counterparts in the years immediately following German reunification. Thus, in 1996, 45% of former East Germans supported capital punishment whereas 31% were against, and in 2000, 42% of the supporters of the PDS political party – the successor to the East German Communist Party whose base of support was made up overwhelmingly of former East Germans – supported capital punishment, a percentage 12 points higher than any other political party (Noelle-Neumann and Köcher 2002:676–7). However, it is likely that East German attitudes toward the death penalty have gradually approached the West German norm in the years since these opinion polls were taken. Aside from the 'primed' questions described in Chapter 2 which elicit high levels of support for the death penalty, German public opinion remains opposed to capital punishment. Extreme-right parties such as the National Democratic Party or the German Peoples' Union endorse the reintroduction of capital punishment for sex crimes against children. Aside from these parties, there is no support for the reintroduction of capital punishment in the German political landscape. In any case, reintroduction would be practically inconceivable, given Germany's status as a signatory to Council of Europe treaties which require Member States to abolish capital punishment.

Abolition in Germany: Themes, Strategies, and Structures

Surveying the general themes that dominated the German death penalty debate, we see some aspects of the debate that are conditioned by Germany's unique historical circumstances, and some that are more universal. The most prominent characteristic of German abolition is its 'cart before the horse' nature. The death penalty ended suddenly, during a time of great political upheaval. Had a right-wing delegate to the Parliamentary Council not unexpectedly filed a motion to abolish capital punishment in 1948, it is very likely that abolition would not have been enshrined in German constitutional law. Had it not been made a part of the constitution, but rather been regulated by ordinary German law, abolition could well have been reintroduced by the German parliament during the 1950s, when public opinion ran strongly in favor of capital punishment and leading politicians, including post-war Chancellor Konrad Adenauer, favored its reintroduction. In essence, Germany abolished the death penalty first, and only then had the 'debate' over its abolition – a debate that ran, with greater or lesser intensity, for 15 more years.

Also unique to Germany was the intensity and frequency of references to Germany's post-war history. Although many European commentators voiced doubts about the judgment of 'the masses' in the wake of the 1930s and 1940s, Germany's recent history was obviously the most catastrophic. Among the strongest arguments of German abolitionists, therefore, were the abuses of death penalty legislation under the National Socialists, what I will call the 'institutional' argument from history. Prosecutors and judges, in particular, referred to the importance of Article 102 in signaling Germany's clean break from the perversions of criminal justice under National Socialism. Germany's recent history also furnished the basis for a 'national character' argument. Especially in the written submissions to the Criminal Law Commission, participants suggested either that the German 'national character' was inherently violent, or that 12 years of corruption under National Socialism had deformed it to the point where it could no longer be trusted, at least until a few generations had passed.

Many other themes of the German debate, however, were not unique to Germany. The national-character argument was only one argument among many other arguments deployed to dismiss public opinion as a guide to policy. Given the death penalty's steady popularity in 1950s Germany, it is perhaps remarkable how few members of the Criminal Law Commission argued that public opinion should guide the decision on capital punishment. Skott, the retired judge assigned the task of delivering the principal speech on reintroduction, merely suggested that the legislature could not 'ignore' the consistent and strong post-war majorities in favor of capital punishment. Only Professor Lange from Cologne argued at length that public opinion should be a principal factor in the Commission's deliberations, lest the public lose confidence in a justice system that seemed to be ignoring one of its primary concerns.

In dismissing public opinion, the other Commission members relied on four main lines of argument, which we will see recurring in other national debates:

- *Expertise.* The general public has no specialized training in criminology, psychology, or law, and thus its opinion on capital punishment can and should be trumped by those who do possess such expertise.
- *Variability.* History shows that public opinion swings back and forth depending on the latest sensational case of innocence or mass murder, thus the latest poll tells us little.
- *Burkean Trusteeship.* The public does not have the right to directly control policy in a parliamentary system of delegated democracy. Voters must rely on their elected representatives to shape policy, and must accept that those representatives will occasionally defy the public will in the name

of an important principle, or in the name of the right, enshrined in the Basic Law, to vote according to their conscience.

- *Irrationality/Backwardness.* The general public supports the death penalty principally based on their emotional reactions to specific crimes. They are either ignorant of, or not interested in, the scientific literature on the subject. It is the role of the elite to enact rational, progressive policies based on evidence and research, even if they contradict the public will.

These themes could also be found outside the precincts of the Criminal Law Commission. The most famous post-war political intervention by the German jurist Gustav Radbruch was undoubtedly his 1946 articulation of the 'Radbruch Formula,' a method of questioning the morality of positive law in order to challenge the kind of apolitical, 'scientific' positivism which had stymied institutional opposition to National Socialist lawmaking among the German legal establishment (Radbruch 2002). In a 1949 editorial, 'The Gallows Overthrown,' Radbruch commented upon the abolition of the death penalty. He counseled fellow jurists that the public would surely mobilize to overrule Article 102 and reintroduce capital punishment, and warned against giving in to the demands of the masses. Opponents of the death penalty, he wrote, 'should maintain their standpoint even against occasional public moods in opposition, should not become weak in the face of the bloodlust (*Blutverlangen*) of the unlettered masses, and even more, should prevent the emergence of these instinct-driven demands by an effective popular education campaign (*Volkspädagogik*)' (as quoted in Düsing 1952:288).

Even supporters of capital punishment occasionally made elitist arguments in its favor. During a 1950 parliamentary debate, Fritz Neumayer, who would go on to be named Justice Minister in 1953 and to lead the Criminal Law Commission, set out his party's position on capital punishment. After admitting that the notion of retribution might not be compatible with 'today's humane attitudes' or even 'the Christian idea,' Neumayer nevertheless defended it on what could be called 'primitive' grounds:

This primitive idea – if I may be allowed to call it that – demands that one who takes another's life must give up his own. We [the Free Democratic Party] are of the opinion that despite all the relaxations in thinking and progress in science and culture, we simply cannot do without a certain amount of primitive thinking ... If we ask primitive people today and want to listen to their answer, we will certainly see that in most cases, that they believe the following: when a murder occurs, it should be punished with the death penalty ... A certain measure of primitive thinking often leads us on the right track (German Parliament Reporting Service 1950:1912)

Neumayer admitted that miscarriages of justice were a concern, but maintained these could be eliminated by rigorous standards of proof.

Here we see members of the elite, speaking of and to themselves, drawing a clear line of demarcation between the kind of arguments that 'should' count among highly educated jurists and civil servants, and those that one encounters on the pages of a tabloid or in a bar-room debate. Neumayer endorses the 'primitive' man's desire for revenge while implicitly denying that he personally shares it. Ordinary people might not be able to understand why it would be wrong to execute a mentally ill lust-murderer, but Commission member Baldus assumed that his fellow members (regardless of their position on capital punishment) would have no such difficulty. Professor Bockelmann, for his part, argued that cost (that is, that it is more expensive to support a convicted murderer during a long prison term than to execute him) is excluded as the kind of argument that the Commission members would ever make in favor of the death penalty.

These members of the elite were, in fact, speaking only among themselves. The debates in the German Bundestag were recorded for posterity and broadcast to the public, but they were largely theater, given that all participants knew that the motion to change the Basic Law would fall short of the necessary two-thirds majority. The debates within the Criminal Law Commission were, of course, held exclusively within the illustrious precincts of the Commission itself. There were vigorous debates about capital punishment in quality broadsheet newspapers but, as in most European nations, these papers were read only by a small minority of the best-educated citizens. The fact that opponents of capital punishment did not feel the need to reach the public or change its opinion is seen from the tone of their remarks, in which the pro-death-penalty opinion held by a majority of citizens was described as 'primitive' or 'barbaric.' This is hardly the language a reformer might choose if he were trying to change the public's mind. Radbruch, in fact, was the only commentator to even broach the idea that public opinion on capital punishment could be changed, but qualified this argument by insisting that (1) the death penalty should be abolished contrary to public opinion anyway; and (2) changing public opinion would require a sustained campaign of public education. The German case is a particularly clear case of top-down abolition. However, we will see similar arguments surfacing in the arguments in Great Britain and, especially, France.

5
Case Study Two – The United Kingdom

The English history of the abolition of capital punishment is shaped by that country's distinctive traditions and structures. Unlike Germany and France, the English legal system derives from the common law, a flexible set of legal principles developed largely by judges over a period of centuries. Thus, English law is indifferent to, perhaps even hostile to, the sort of logically structured, all-encompassing legal 'codes' favored by Continental jurists and rulers. The English Parliament is also an institution unto itself. By the late 19th century, when the modern German nation finally took shape, the United Kingdom had existed as an autonomous nation for centuries, and the basic prerogatives, composition, and competencies of its Parliament had remained relatively stable since the late 17th century. Further, Parliament, as the final arbiter of the British Constitutional order, had the exclusive authority in matters of criminal legislation.

These structural differences ensured that the progress of criminal law reform took a different course in England than on the Continent. In most Continental European countries of the 17th and 18th centuries, it was generally enough for a commission of experts to draw up a draft penal code and submit it to the absolutist monarch. The importance of legislative assemblies in European countries, to the extent they existed at all, paled in comparison to that of high-ranking bureaucrats, renowned professors, and expert commissions. In the UK, by contrast, criminal legislation was dominated by parliamentary lawmaking. It came about in a piecemeal way, in the form of individual bills submitted by parties or governments. Strenuous efforts to produce a synoptic, organized British criminal code on the Continental model were started in the 19th century, but failed. In fact, repeated efforts to enact a unified penal code in Great Britain have yet to meet with success.

As important as these structural differences are, however, they should not blind us to the marked similarities between the German, French, and British abolition efforts. In Britain, as in the other two nations under review, the death penalty was progressively narrowed in very similar stages: in the 19th century, torturous methods of execution were outlawed, the scope of the death penalty was narrowed, capital punishment was moved within prison walls, and the number of annual executions showed a general overall downward trend. Further, the final push toward abolition in the 20th century showed similarities in all three countries. In Britain, it was also the case that abolition was carried out in the teeth of popular support for capital punishment. The final legislative moves against the death penalty required the insight and input of a skilled legislative operator (in this case, Sydney Silverman) willing to make the abolition of capital punishment one of his signature issues.

Capital Punishment in Britain at the Beginning of the 19th Century

Any history of the abolition of the death penalty in the United Kingdom begins with the so-called 'bloody code,' the vast catalog of capital crimes that the British Parliament constructed piecemeal from the mid-17th century until the early 19th century. Writing in the late 1760s, Sir William Blackstone observed: 'It is a melancholy truth, that among the variety of actions which men are daily liable to commit, no less than a hundred and sixty have been declared by act of Parliament to be felonies without benefit of clergy; or, in other words, to be worthy of instant death' (Blackstone 1884:286). By the early 19th century, British law foresaw the death penalty for over 200 crimes, including the theft of anything worth more than five shillings. As Blackstone's quotation shows, the proliferation of death-eligible offenses in the 'bloody code' gradually became a serious embarrassment to the British Crown. For one thing, it complicated what many British commentators wished to claim as a key distinction between the 18th-century criminal procedure of the United Kingdom and the European Continent: the fact that England had abolished torture during criminal investigations, whereas most European jurisdictions still permitted the practice. English legal commentators' disdain for the Continent's torturous interrogations (Langbein 2003:340) was met by a matching dismay on the part of European writers for the vast proliferation of potentially capital offenses in the 'bloody code.'

Reasons for this proliferation of capital offences have been offered by many scholars. Peter Linebaugh argues in *The London Hanged* (2003), that the emergence of the British 'thanatocracy', as he calls it, was in large part driven by the need felt by the aristocracy and bourgeoisie to squelch the social disorder fermenting within the itinerant, dispossessed working-class population created by the Industrial Revolution. Other writers, such as Dieter Reicher, contrast the criminal justice policy-making process in England with the typical Continental model, here represented by Austria:

A look at those who shaped legislation in the 18th and 19th centuries in the two countries shows that these were two fully distinct categories.

In the United Kingdom, power emanated from the Parliament. The King had less influence. In Austria, the extraordinary position of the ruler and his official staff are immediately evident. The regional assemblies played only a minor role. (2003:102)

As Reicher shows, many absolutist monarchs on the Continent were eager to showcase the 'enlightened' cast of their rule, and commissioned leading philosophers and jurists to draft criminal codes embodying progressive ideals. These elite experts were well insulated from public feeling, and could foster innovation without concern about a potential public backlash. Thus, when these codes did not abandon capital punishment outright, they nevertheless sought to channel it carefully. By contrast, criminal justice lawmaking in England was solely the province of Parliament, which was not subject to any higher control or guidance, and which was dominated by the propertied classes. Crimes could be, and were, added to the haphazard catalog of capital-eligible offenses without regard to the overall structure or logic of the criminal code, since there *was* no criminal code.

The 'bloody code' had many unwholesome effects on British justice. It encouraged the practice of 'pious perjury,' in which juries would conspire to convict defendants of non-capital offenses, despite evidence of their guilt of the greater offense in order to avoid sending them to the gallows. According to John Langbein, it also contributed to the lawyer-driven, often truth-defeating nature of the English adversarial system, which took modern form at the same time as the 'bloody code' was being created:

English criminal justice threatened more capital punishment than those who administered it were willing to impose. To avoid a bloodbath, evasions of many sorts were practiced ... If we are to understand why the Anglo-American criminal procedure that emerged in this period is so truth-disserving, we must bear in mind that we settled on our procedures for criminal adjudication at a moment when we did not want all that much truth. (2003:336)

Finally, it built enormous arbitrariness into the system. Given the many informal methods used to reduce the number of death sentences actually carried out – prosecutorial and victim discretion to 'downcharge,' evidentiary loopholes, pious perjury, and executive clemency – the unlucky few who actually ended up being hanged at Tyburn often seemed more luckless than culpable; their fates determined not so much by the gravity of their crimes as by a kind of opaque procedural lottery. The attitude of modern scholarship to this era of British criminal justice history can perhaps be best summed up in one sentence: 'There is nothing we can learn from the [bloody code] except that we are well rid of it' (Hogan 1974:116).

Given history's definitive judgment, it is difficult to imagine what humane purpose the bloody code could ever have been thought to serve. Nevertheless, the system had its defenders. By far the most prominent was the Reverend William Paley, a priest and philosopher best known for his Christian apologetics. Paley took up the issue of capital punishment in his hugely influential 1785 treatise *The Principles of Moral and Political Philosophy*. Paley began his discussion of crimes and punishments (1825:370–5) by arguing that 'the proper end of human punishment is, not the satisfaction of justice, but the prevention of crimes.' Paley then contrasts two methods of administering justice. The first 'assigns capital punishment to few offences, and inflicts it invariably,' while the second (which England has chosen) 'assigns capital punishments to many kinds of offences, but inflicts it only upon a few examples of each kind.' Paley defends the latter approach as maximizing the benefits both of deterrence and humanity. Formulating penal statutes broadly provides a unique deterrent, since 'few actually suffer death, whilst the dread and danger of it hang over the crimes of many. The tenderness of the law cannot be taken advantage of.' At the same time, though, the traditional practice of reserving execution only for a small percentage of cases permits judges to tailor each sentence to the particular circumstances of the individual crime: '[T]he selection of proper objects for capital punishment principally depends on circumstances, which however easy to perceive in each particular case after the crime is committed, it is impossible to enumerate or define beforehand.' Despite the sagacity of judges, who applied capital punishment only to the extent necessary, it had become common knowledge by the late 18th century that England executed more of its citizens than most other European countries. Paley attributed this to three factors: 'much liberty, great cities, and the want of a punishment short of death, possessing a sufficient degree of terror.' Unlike 'arbitrary' governments which ruled through 'inspection, scrutiny, and control,' England allowed its citizens great freedom to act, which some few inevitably abused. Large cities multiplied crime by creating refuges for villainy, and England's lack of prisons meant that the only alternative to execution was transportation to the colonies, which was ineffectual as a deterrent, since transported prisoners vanished from public view and could thus no longer serve as visible tokens of deterrence (ibid.:381–2).

Paley's arguments reflect the mindset of the British landed aristocracy and political elite of the late 18th century: England's capital punishment practices were seen as open to question, but justifiable. It was against this background that the United Kingdom's first prominent opponent of capital punishment took the stage. Sir Samuel Romilly, a lawyer of Huguenot extraction influenced by Beccaria's thinking, began to occupy himself with the glaring weaknesses in British criminal justice. Notably, Romilly was not a complete abolitionist – he sought to limit capital punishment only to the most serious crimes and to rationalize the process of inflicting the death penalty, while disclaiming any intention to abolish it altogether. A leading history of capital punishment in England describes Romilly's first successes:

> His first attempts at reform between 1808 and 1812, were successful in having the death penalty repealed for the offences of picking pockets, theft from the premises of a calico printers, and vagrancy by a soldier or sailor. He also secured an end to the punishment of disemboweling alive. (Block and Hostettler 1997:42)

In a famous speech held in the House of Commons on February 9 1810 (Hansard HC Deb:vol. 15, cc366–74), Romilly challenged Paley's apologia for British capital justice. There was 'no country on the face of the earth' in which so many offenses were punishable by death as in England, yet 'not one out of six or seven' of those convicted of capital crimes was actually executed. To be sure, there were some categories of crimes – such as murder, rape or arson – that fully justified a capital sentence. However, there were other 'acts in our Statute book which one could not hear read without horror,' such as laws making it a crime to associate with gypsies or to steal from a dwelling-house. Romilly did not wish to be 'represented as a person wishing to be thought possessed of more refined feelings and a greater degree of humanity than his neighbours' (an intriguing statement), but as articulating an objective and rational critique of the legal situation. Surely no rational observer could defend a system in which large numbers of laws were viewed as simply too harsh to be applied by normal judges and juries. Romilly then critiqued the enormous discretion given to judges under the law, which resulted in many similar crimes being subject to radically varying punishments. Concluding, Romilly begged leave to introduce a bill to remove the automatic death penalty from the offense of stealing goods worth more than five shillings from various locations, and for substituting measures to 'more effectually prevent' such offenses.

Romilly's suggestions were met generally with hostility by other debaters. His attacks on the revered Dr. Paley aroused the ire of some other MPs, and his criticisms of judicial discretion were met with the straw-man argument that he proposed to end all judicial discretion and make sentences mandatory, which he denied. A recent analysis of English sentencing policy in this era included some revealing quotations from Romilly's opponents, displaying the reactionary attitudes with which Romilly had to contend. Romilly noted in his diary during one debate that a young man, the 'brother of a peer,' came up to him and announced: 'I am against your bill. I am for hanging all … There is no good done by mercy. They only get worse; I would hang them all up at once.' Lord Ellenborough, who had himself sponsored an act under George III adding ten new capital felonies to the criminal code, rose to speak against a proposal to remove the death penalty from the offense of stealing from unoccupied premises. The law, he argued, ensures 'the security of every poor cottager who goes out to his daily labour. He, my lords, can leave no one behind to watch his little dwelling ... My Lords, there are cases where mercy and humanity to the few would be injustice and cruelty to the many' (both as quoted in Reicher, forthcoming). A commentator writing at the end of the 19th century observed that Ellenborough 'was as much shocked by a proposal to repeal the punishment of death for stealing to the value of five shillings in a shop, as if it had been to abrogate the Ten Commandments' (Campbell 1899:227). Ellenborough's approach reflected prevailing sentiment in the House of Lords which – not for the last time in British history – proved itself a bastion of conservatism in debates over modernizing the criminal law.

Although Romilly took his life in 1818, the crusade against capital punishment would continue, not least because of the work of the great utilitarian philosopher Jeremy Bentham, whose writings 'show him as one, perhaps the only leading philosopher, who, throughout his adult life, steadily and soberly opposed "Death Punishment" and expressed that opposition in writings that are still instructive' (Bedau 1983:1037). In 1832, the same year Bentham died, Parliament passed the Punishment of Death, etc. Act, which reduced by approximately two-thirds the number of offenses punishable by execution. In 1833, Lord Chancellor Brougham convinced King William IV to convene a Criminal Law Commission to organize and codify Britain's chaotic criminal statutes on a European model. The Commission was staffed with five prominent, well-respected scholars and advocates who were heavily influenced by Bentham's utilitarian approach to legislation and punishment, which, although still considered radical, was increasing in influence. The Commission existed for 16 years, producing a series of eight reports advocating dozens of important reforms. The Commission's proposal for a codification of the English criminal law was not enacted, but other major reforms were, over the course of the following decades. As one history of the era puts it, the Commission 'formed a coherent radical group pursuing a philosophical position, [and] powerfully enhanced the humanitarian movement of the early 19th century by spearheading the mitigation of the cruel criminal law and the legislative extension of individual liberty.' (Block and Hostettler 1997:51). The Commission's second report, published in 1836, dealt specifically with capital punishment. The report condemned the arbitrariness with which hanging was inflicted in the UK, and recommended that it be abolished except as to a small minority of grave offenses. The reformist Whig Party leader in the House of Commons during the 1830s, Lord John Russell, agreed with the Commission's approach, and powerfully advocated for the restriction of capital punishment. During the 1830s, the conviction that the Bloody Code was a disgrace to British justice gradually established itself even in the House of Lords. With a more compliant majority in the Lords, Russell, in the words of historian V. A. C. Gatrell, 'presided over the virtual obliteration of the bloody penal code in 1837' (1996:295). The 19th century saw further progressive reductions in the scope of Britain's capital-punishment laws, especially in the 1860s. By the middle of the 19th century, the death penalty was, de facto, only imposed in Britain for cases of murder.

The 19th century also saw a development of sensibilities among British elites. As in France, intellectuals and writers often took the clearest abolitionist stance. We see a transition from the coolly analytical or policy-based arguments of a Bentham or a Romilly toward a more personal, subjective frame of opposition. William Makepeace Thackeray's essay 'Going to See a Man Hanged' provides an excellent example of the latter. Thackeray, then a struggling 29-year-old writer, conceived of the idea of witnessing the execution of François Benjamin Courvoisier, the French valet of retired Whig nobleman Lord William Russell (brother of abolitionist reformer Lord John Russell). Courvoisier had slit Russell's throat as he slept, then staged a robbery to cover up an earlier theft of his master's silver. After a brief, heavily publicized trial (based on his confession), Courvoisier was sentenced to death, and executed on July 6 1840.

Thackeray's account of the execution was rejected by several outlets before being published by *Fraser's Magazine* in August 1840. 'Going to See a Man Hanged' (reprinted in Thackeray 1946:vol. I, 451–5) begins in an almost jaunty tone: Thackeray and his companion X (a politician who, he notes, had voted for the abolition of capital punishment) had spent most of the night socializing with renowned London wit 'Dash,' who 'kept the company merry all night with appropriate jokes about the coming event.' On the morning of the execution, Thackeray and X arrive very early at Snow Hill near Newgate Prison, where the execution was to take place. Even at that early hour, thousands of commoners – who did not number among the 'six hundred noblemen and gentlemen' who had been given official permission to watch from inside Newgate – had gathered outside the walls of the prison to see the hanging. The atmosphere was one of merrymaking among the 'extraordinarily gentle and good-humoured' mob: vendors sold food, men clambered up trees and drainpipes to get a better view, and wags entertained nearby bystanders with political harangues and bawdy jokes.

As the awful event approached, however, Thackeray's apprehension grew. The sight of the gallows itself shocked him, and he was unable to witness Courvoisier's actual execution: 'I could look no more, but shut my eyes as the last dreadful act was going on which sent this wretched guilty soul into the presence of God.' Thackeray's ambivalence before the execution disappeared: 'The sight has left on my mind an extraordinary feeling of terror and shame. It seems to me that I have been abetting an act of frightful wickedness and violence, performed by a set of men against their fellows; and I pray God that it may soon be out of the power of any man in England to witness such a hideous and degrading sight.' The ironic moralist of *Vanity Fair* is nowhere to be seen in the heartfelt peroration of Thackeray's essay: 'I feel myself ashamed and degraded at the brutal curiosity which took me to that brutal sight; and I pray to Almighty God to cause this disgraceful sin to pass from among us, and to cleanse our land of blood.'

Like Victor Hugo's 1829 anti-capital punishment novel *The Last Day of a Condemned Man*, Thackeray's essay highlights the condemned prisoner's psychological suffering. Drawing from the pamphlets and newspaper accounts published after the execution, Thackeray reconstructs Courvoisier's last hours. The night before, he writes obsessively, finally giving a relatively honest and complete confession of his guilt. He asks to be awakened at four in the morning, since he still has 'much to put down.' As 'bachelors are reeling home after a jolly night' outside, Courvoisier wakes, eats a meager breakfast, and continues his feverish scribbling. He writes to his mother, and finishes his last will and other last documents, leaving most of his 'little miserable property' to his kind jailers. 'As the day of the convict's death draws nigh,' Thackeray observes with pathos, 'it is painful to see how he fastens upon everybody who approaches him, how pitifully he clings to them and loves them.' As historian V. A. C. Gatrell noted, Thackeray's text heralded that a 'great divide' had been crossed in comparison with previous attitudes of English intellectuals to executions: 'pity for a common murderer and disgust at those who took his life had never been so nakedly expressed in print before' (Gatrell 1996:296). Earlier generations of English writers had expressed squeamishness or revulsion at executions, but only in those cases in which the condemned came from a social background roughly comparable to the writer's. Generally, Gatrell shows, not a word was wasted on convicts from London's teeming slums. Thackeray's essay shows the first steps in the development of a critique of capital punishment based on disgust at the brutality of the practice and generalized compassion for the condemned, regardless of social class.

Nevertheless, Thackeray's budding distaste for capital punishment as an institution had no resonance with those in power. The sensibilities of British officialdom stopped well short of endorsing the complete abolition of capital punishment. As Gatrell shows, English judges clung with particular tenacity to their prerogative to inflict capital punishment, and bristled at any attempt to limit their discretion. In fact, English criminal judges – symbolized by the court at the Old Bailey in central London – were widely caricatured for their obtusely reactionary views and deplorable prejudices. Until the capital code was radically streamlined in the 1830s, English trials continued to generate many more death sentences than the political order was willing to actually inflict. This meant that the Home Secretary was routinely called upon to decide which of a recent batch of condemned murderers would be executed, and which spared. In this task, he was advised by a collection of worthies and nobles called the King's Council. As Gatrell shows (1996:543–65), the deliberations of these bodies were anything but rational. Prisoners, knowing their only chance for reprieve was a convincing petition for clemency, submitted groveling pleas for their lives, accompanied by as many testimonies to their good character or reformability as they could muster. During the long, dull deliberations of the King's Council, King George IV himself often fell asleep, or interjected incoherent pleas based more on squeamishness than principle. Often clemency decisions rested on relevant factors such as age, good character, degree of involvement in the crime, and the seriousness of the offense. Just as often, however, they were the product of internecine bureaucratic squabbles, the chance discovery that a prisoner had a noble or well-respected relation, the perceived need to send a 'message' to squelch an outbreak of certain kinds of crimes, or sheer calculation as to the number of executions that could be performed at once without creating an unseemly spectacle. Beccarian and Benthamite ideas about capital punishment – as well as other critiques of the practice – were well-known by the 1820s, but they played no role in the thinking of British legal actors and officialdom. Instead, the leading concern of the authorities was to maintain the proper balance of 'terror' – enough executions to strike fear into the hearts of potential evildoers, but not so many as to violate vague notions of propriety. Given that the production of terror was a principle goal of British capital punishment practice in the early 19th century, a certain arbitrariness in how clemency was granted hardly impeded – and may even be thought to have advanced – the stated goal of the law.

And even the sentiments of opponents of capital punishment proved conditional. Thackeray's sympathy for the terror suffered by an ordinary servant did not translate into thorough, principled opposition to the death penalty. Many British writers – including Carlyle and Dickens – joined the abolitionist bandwagon in the early 1840s. By the accession of Queen Victoria to the English throne in 1837, however, a combination of factors had already led to a significant reduction in the scope of capital punishment in England. First and foremost were the legal reforms mentioned above. The advent of modern policing and prisons increased the rate of successful prosecutions and introduced suitable lesser penalties for property crimes. Reliable prisons and police, in turn, reduced the need to make gruesome 'examples' of the few offenders who were caught, to deter the many who were not. As soon as capital punishment was de facto limited to murderers, many of its erstwhile critics either fell silent or changed their minds (Gatrell 1996:591–2). Capital punishment was 'stabilized.' The real evil was not the practice itself, but rather the unedifying crowd scenes attending public executions. Reformers therefore turned their attention to lobbying to prevent public executions, a goal which was achieved by the 1868 passage of 'A Bill to Provide for Carrying Out Capital Punishment in Prisons.' This move had also been recommended by a Royal Commission on Capital Punishment convened in the mid-1860s, which also proposed various legal reforms to limit the death penalty's scope (these additional reforms were, however, not implemented until much later).

John Stuart Mill might be said to exemplify the cooling of abolitionist passion in the second half of the 19th century. As a leading liberal, he might have been expected to oppose hanging. Once the practice was 'domesticated,' however, he came to its defense. Speaking on April 21 1868, during the Second Reading of the Capital Punishment within Prisons Bill, Mill (1988:266–72), speaking as an independent Member of Parliament representing Westminster, opposed an amendment which would have banned capital punishment altogether. Seeking to stake out a moderate position, Mill first praised the work of 'philanthropists' of earlier generations. Thanks to them, 'our criminal laws ... have so greatly relaxed their most revolting and most impolitic ferocity, that aggravated murder is now practically the only crime which is punished with death by any of our lawful tribunals; and we are even now deliberating whether the extreme penalty should be retained in that solitary case.' This fundamental fact – that executions were now limited only to cases of aggravated murder – permitted, even required, a new approach to the issue of capital punishment. One can seriously ask whether execution is preferable to the only alternative punishment that would come into play for such a heinous criminal – hard labor for life. Society should not deprive itself of a punishment which, 'in the grave cases to which alone it is suitable, effects its purpose at less cost of human suffering than any other; which, while it inspires more terror, is less cruel in actual fact than any punishment we should think of substituting for it.'

Mill proceeds to other arguments against capital punishment, declaring them much weakened by its late restriction only to aggravated murder. The only argument to which Mill concedes force is the chance of executing the innocent. His comments are revealing:

> [T]he objection to irreparable punishment began ... earlier, and is more intense and more widely diffused, in some parts of the Continent of Europe than it is here. There are on the Continent great and enlightened countries, in which the criminal procedure is not so favourable to innocence, does not afford the same security against erroneous conviction, as it does among us; countries where the Courts of Justice seem to think they fail in their duty unless they find somebody guilty; and in their really laudable desire to hunt guilt from its hiding-places, expose themselves to a serious danger of condemning the innocent. If our own procedure and Courts of Justice afforded ground for similar apprehension, I should be the first in withdrawing the power of inflicting irreparable punishment from such tribunals. But we all know that the defects of our procedure are the very opposite. Our rules of evidence are even too favourable to the prisoner: and juries and Judges carry out the maxim, 'It is better that ten guilty should escape than that one innocent person should suffer.'

Mill's remarks understate the reliability of Continental procedure, and overstate the reliability of its English counterpart. Nevertheless, they reflect a basic faith in the reliability of the English judicial process in capital cases that would reign, with some interruptions, until the 1950s. Having essentially assumed away the risk of mistaken executions, Mill reasons that the current state of English justice – inflicting death only for aggravated murder, insisting on procedurally fair trials, and authorizing executive clemency as the final safeguard against error – ensured that capital punishment would be inflicted only where it would be most useful. Therefore, he opposed the amendment, as did a majority of MPs.

Mill's cautious arguments are representative of the British center-left mainstream throughout the remainder of the 19th century and the early 20th century. Now that the number of executions had been strictly limited and executions themselves moved inside prison walls, the issue of whether to eliminate capital punishment altogether had lost much of its urgency. Further, the numerous voices to the right of Mill fought every attempt to abolish capital punishment altogether. The attitude of the mainstream of the English judiciary and legal establishment can be represented by Sir James Fitzjames Stephen, a lawyer and judge who was perhaps the most prominent theorist of criminal law of Victorian England. Stephen once commented that there is as much 'moral cowardice in shrinking from the execution of a murderer as there is in hesitating to blow out the brains of a foreign invader' (as quoted in Smith 2002:58). Smith summarized Stephen's views thus: '[F]ailure to reflect natural human feelings, including those of vengeance and hatred, in the substance and practice of punishment would undermine the system's necessary popularity while dangerously diminishing hostility towards criminality. The ultimate result of such a weakening of this vital relationship of law and common morality would be a potentially catastrophic loss in the general cohesiveness of society' (ibid.). Although Stephen's language is far more robust than Mill's, their ultimate conclusions were not widely separated. Earlier in his career, Stephen had in fact supported modernizing reforms to English capital sentencing laws, and, like Mill, held that those reforms had appropriately narrowed the scope of the death penalty. To the left of both Mill and Stephen, humanitarian penal-reform groups such as the Howard League (formed in 1866) continued to organize against capital punishment, and certain religious orders continued to agitate against the practice. As in France, however, capital punishment had reached a state of stabilization, and activists did not gain enough momentum to bring the question of complete abolition to a decisive vote in the British Parliament until well into the 20th century.

The Mid-20th Century: Sydney Silverman, Commons and Lords

Capital punishment again became an issue in Britain in the 1920s, which saw the formation of the National Council for the Abolition of the Death Penalty (NCADP) in 1925 and the merger of two formerly separate organizations into the Howard League for Penal Reform in 1921. The 1920s in general were a period of intense public scrutiny of law enforcement in the United Kingdom. Tabloid newspapers chose to focus significant attention on stories of police abuse of power, especially those involving women suspects. Abuses included overbearing 'third-degree' interrogation tactics, the circulation of scandalous accusations without proof, and the denial of adequate legal advice. Parliamentary commissions were set up to evaluate the need for legislation limiting police powers. Amid this general civil-liberties ferment, interest in abolishing capital punishment also dramatically increased. The Labour Party adopted abolition as an explicit plank of its political platform in 1923 (Bailey 2000:313). The ferment surrounding the issue led in 1929 to the creation of a select committee on capital punishment. Historian Clive Emsley describes its activity:

> The select committee received passionate, yet detailed and reasoned, evidence from the NCADP. The point was stressed that several European countries and individual American states had abolished the death penalty without any serious and unfavourable results. But twenty-one of the committee's thirty-one witnesses, many of whom held senior official positions within the penal system, favoured the retention of capital punishment … Not all Conservative MPs were retentionists, but all of those on the committee were. The committee divided on party lines with the Conservative members rejecting the final recommendation that there be an experimental five-year trial period of abolition. The division of the committee, together with the weakness of the Labour government, left the matter unresolved and … governments were to remain resistant to proposals for abolition for another thirty years and more. (Emsley 2005:163–4)

As one historian noted, the select committee refused to hear from British judges because 'their opposition to reform was a foregone conclusion' (Bailey 2000:315). From 1920 to the mid 1940s, the murder rate in Great Britain remained relatively stable, with approximately 120–180 murders per year, yielding a number of death sentences per year ranging from 13 (1937) to 34 (1922), and a number of executions ranging from 5 (1930) to 21 (1922) (Block and Hostettler 1997:105).

The final and successful phase of the struggle to abolish capital punishment in Britain is inextricably intertwined with the career of Sydney Silverman. Silverman was born in 1895 in Liverpool to drapers of modest means. As a committed pacifist and conscientious objector, he was sentenced to a total of two years' jail time for refusing the serve during the First World War – an experience that shaped the rest of his long life in the public eye. He took a law degree from Liverpool University in 1927 and qualified as a solicitor, building a career specializing in workers' compensation claims and landlord–tenant disputes. In the 1930s, Silverman began his rapid ascent in the Labour Party, which culminated in his election to the Lancashire constituency of Nelson and Colne in 1935. He was to represent the constituency until 1968. Silverman's rise in the Party coincided with its increasingly active support for the abolition of capital punishment. Silverman made abolition, as well as the fate of Europe's Jews (he was himself Jewish) a key focus of his public career.

Silverman was one of the more interesting figures in 20th century British politics. In addition to his pacifist beliefs (which he modified during World War II) and his prison stints, Silverman also distinguished himself by his Socialist militancy. One friendly biography of Silverman, published by his parliamentary Labour colleague Emrys Hughes, described Silverman as 'an extreme Socialist, opinionative, dogmatic, assertive and quarrelsome,' and noted that he had frequently clashed with the British Home Office 'on questions relating to the entrance into Britain of Continental refugees' (Hughes 1969:96). Referring to Silverman's attempts to build a cross-party coalition against hanging, an English historian wrote that the main problem for Conservative abolitionists was having to accept the leadership of Sydney Silverman, who had 'gained a singular reputation as a vitriolic and effective Tory-baiter' (Christoph 1962:142). Nevertheless, as the following narrative shows, Silverman was also a resourceful and indefatigable parliamentary operator.

Parliament next voted explicitly on the question of abolition in 1938, on a motion by Conservative MP Vyvyan Adams, who served on the Executive Committee of the National Coalition to Abolish the Death Penalty. Adams moved: 'That this House would welcome legislation by which the death penalty should be abolished in time of peace for an experimental period of five years.' Adams made his abolitionist sympathies clear. The motion was made subject to a free vote and passed by a margin of 114 to 89, even though it was opposed by the Home Office. The vote, however, was non-binding, and had no effect on the policy of Neville Chamberlain's government. World War II brought a temporary halt to further anti-death-penalty activism. After the war ended, however, the death penalty returned, perhaps somewhat surprisingly, to near the top of Parliament's agenda. Given Labour's explicit stand against the death penalty, many observers expected the post-war Labour government of Clement Attlee to make abolition a priority. Chuter Ede, Home Secretary to the post-war Labour government, had previously made statements supporting abolition, and announced the Labour government's intention to bring in a comprehensive criminal justice reform bill at the next legislative session.

Ede in fact introduced a criminal justice reform bill in 1947 that reformed probation, ended penal servitude and flogging as a punishment, and sought to reduce the rate at which those committing relatively minor felonies were imprisoned. The bill, however, remained silent on the subject of capital punishment. The Labour government had gotten cold feet, primarily because support for capital punishment had risen sharply in the post-war years. The government was, as well, loath to encumber its toweringly ambitious legislative agenda with unnecessary controversy. Besides, as Labour Commons Speaker Herbert Morrison related, the prevailing assumption was that 'the bulk of the working-class (or broadly Labour) voters favored hanging and that abolition tended to be a middle-class fad' (Bailey 2000:329). Nevertheless, Labour leaders decided to permit the issue to be raised independently of the criminal justice reform bill. The amendment provoked a lively debate in the House of Commons. Ede announced on behalf of the government that although he had voted for abolition in 1938, he did not think the public was ready for that step ten years later. Silverman delivered a lengthy manifesto in favor of abolition, chiding the government for not having the courage to lead on the issue:

> [T]he Home Secretary said that the Government had not put this matter into the Bill because they thought public opinion was not ripe for it. I concede that if that were correct, they would be justified in leaving it out ... because these matters cannot be judged intrinsically in a vacuum. Penalties are not right or wrong only in themselves. They must be seen against the background of the social morality of the time in which they are being discussed, and must not be either too far ahead or too far behind the level of morality of civilization. (Hughes 1969:104)

However, Silverman continued, this only raised the question of how to judge public opinion. Surely one could not propose doing so by 'going down to a constituency and counting heads or going into a club or a cinema or a theatre, posing the question, and saying that is the public opinion of this country.' Rather, one must gather a cross-section of the country, hold an informed debate, and rely on the 'good sense, good judgment and moral integrity' of that cross-section. And where, Silverman asked:

> can we find a better cross-section of the community than this elected House of Commons? We are not delegates; we are not bound to ascertain exactly what a numerical majority of our constituents would wish and then to act accordingly without using our judgment. Edmund Burke long ago destroyed any such theory. We are not delegates. We are representatives. Our business is to act according to our consciences, honestly looking at the facts and coming to as right a judgment as we may. (Hughes 1969:104)

After this explicit invocation of Burkean trusteeship, the motion passed the Commons by a vote of 254 (215 of which were Labour members) to 222.

Now it came time for the Lords to debate the bill. The Lords debate became, for that sedate body, a focus of unusually intense mobilization. Emrys Hughes, the Welsh Labour MP who witnessed the debate, 'had never seen the House of Lords so full before. The police had some difficulty in recognising peers who had very rarely attended or whom they had never seen before' (Hughes 1969:108). The House of Lords contained numerous former high-ranking officials who spoke in favor of capital punishment, but also committed abolitionists who spoke against. Viscount Templewood, who as Sir Samuel Hoare had served as Home Secretary before the war, announced that he had had a change of heart on capital punishment, and adduced several arguments. First was the experience of foreign countries, which showed not only that capital punishment had a questionable deterrent effect, but also that murderers could be reformed. Templewood then addressed the ever-recurring objection of public opinion. Templewood stated he 'had found ... that public opinion was always against changes in penal methods. Public opinion was almost inevitably ignorant of the kind of details being discussed in the debate. If during the last century [legislators] had waited for public opinion before restricting the death penalty to a few crimes they would have found public opinion almost always against the more expert views of Parliament and Whitehall' (Block and Hostettler 1997:117, paraphrasing Templewood's speech).

The majority of the Lords, however, were in favor of retention of capital punishment. The redoubtable retentionist Lord Goddard, nicknamed 'Lord God-Damn' by Churchill, not only fulminated against abolition but also tried to save at least some forms of corporal punishment from legislative oblivion (Bailey 2000:339). The Lords rejected the abolition measure by a margin of 181 to 28. From a constitutional perspective, the Lords' rejection of a measure passed by the House of Commons was somewhat controversial. The House of Lords 'descends directly from the Great Councils of feudal landowners and notables of the Norman Kings,' but by the 1950s, consisted largely of persons granted peerages by royal letters patent after 1800 (Gordon 1964:139). Historically, the responsibilities of the House of Lords in English constitutional law, while nowhere precisely spelled out, were thought to fall into three main categories. First, the House of Lords contains contingents of distinguished experts (such as the Law Lords, the Lords Spiritual, and various distinguished professors or public servants who have been created peers), who can bring their expertise to bear on Commons legislation in an atmosphere relatively free of party political influence. In this capacity, the Lords can blunt the excesses of unreasonable legislation passed by the Commons in a political fever and, as Bagehot observed in the English Constitution, 'prevent the rule of wealth – the religion of gold' (Bagehot 1872:90). As England does not have a tradition of judicial review, the Lords also play a part in preserving the unwritten customary rules that define the English Constitution. Nevertheless, the role of the House of Lords is also itself constrained by the Constitution: 'It is a fairly settled tenet of the system that the government is entitled to get its business through the House of Commons, and to have it considered in the Lords, and that it is in particular entitled to have measures which were promised in its election manifesto given a fair wind in the House of Lords.' (Jowell and Oliver 2004:263). Thus, the House of Lords' decisive rejection of the abolition amendment – not the type of law that would be subject to the Lords' special prerogatives of scrutiny – was controversial. Nevertheless, in their defense, the retentionist Peers could point out not only that the death penalty did not feature in Labour's 1945 manifesto (which was dominated by economic issues), but that even Labour's own Home Secretary opposed the amendment. The Lords' rejection of an officially sponsored government bill is extremely rare and always controversial (Gordon 1964:118), but the Lords are technically free to reject a bill that is merely tolerated by the government.

The abolitionists pressed their cause, protested against the Lords' obstructionism, and put pressure on the government. As a result, the government proposed a compromise amendment which would have significantly limited the scope of application of capital punishment. The compromise measure passed the House. During the debate Winston Churchill, always a strong supporter of capital punishment, denounced the previous Commons vote in favor of abolition as 'casual and irresponsible' and praised the Lords' previous vote as being in harmony with the feelings of the nation (Hughes 1969:111–12). The Lords rejected even the compromise measure, which raised the prospect of the controversial amendment jeopardizing the entire Criminal Justice Bill. The government finally relented, much to the dismay of the abolitionist majority in Commons.

As a further compromise measure, Prime Minister Attlee, in the autumn of 1948, announced yet another Royal Commission on Capital Punishment. The Commission's terms of reference were limited to whether the death penalty should be 'limited or modified.' When pressed on the issue by an abolitionist MP during prime minister's questions in early 1949, Attlee strongly affirmed that the Commission's mandate did not include recommending the abolition of capital punishment, which Attlee regarded as the sole prerogative of Parliament. Abolitionist MPs were deeply disappointed with Attlee's move. Despite Labour's official stance against capital punishment, a select committee report in favor of abolition, and even a vote of the House of Commons for an abolition bill, the government had not only put the issue on ice by recommending it to a commission, but also denied the commission authority to recommend straightforward abolition (Block and Hostettler 1997:122–3). While the commission met, the English death penalty debate cooled significantly, but, as it turns out, the early 1950s were merely the calm before the storm.

The Commission, sometimes called the Gowers Commission after its chairperson, long-time civil servant Sir Ernest Gowers, was not dominated by lawyers. As one historian described the other members of the Commission, they were half specialists and half laypeople; representatives of fields of activity (corrections, psychology, law, and criminology) rather than points of view; and none had recently taken a clear position on capital punishment (Christoph 1962:79). They heard evidence from prison wardens and guards, psychologists, police officials, the official executioner Albert Pierrepoint, and various advocacy groups (including two presentations by the abolitionist Howard League). All told, the Commission met for four years before releasing its 500-page report in 1953. The report endorsed three main recommendations: First, the death penalty was to be made discretionary with the jury upon conviction of murder, moving the instance of discretion from the Home Secretary's judgment, long after conviction, to the trial itself. Second, the age for eligibility for capital offenses should be increased from 18 to 21. Third, the jury should be given discretion to determine whether an offender was legally insane. The report considered other potential reforms, such as changing the method of execution or dividing homicides into different classes, but eventually decided against them. The report's cautious and somewhat ambivalent tone permitted all parties to claim it as a victory.

The Gowers Commission had been set up by a Labour government, but by the time the report was issued, Churchill had regained Number 10. The new government was not particularly eager to schedule a full parliamentary debate on a report issued under a Labour administration, so opponents of capital punishment continuously had to prod the Home Secretary for a statement and to schedule time for a debate on the report's recommendations. After much maneuvering, the parliamentary debate was finally scheduled for 10 February 1955. First to speak was the Home Secretary, Gwilym Lloyd George (Hansard HC 1955:2064–76). Speaking on behalf of the government, Lloyd George rejected each of the commission's three main recommendations. First, he argued, the age of responsibility for homicide should not be raised to 21, given the disturbing recent uptick of crimes committed by persons between the ages of 18 and 21. Second, vesting sentencing discretion in the jury would violate the long-standing tradition that juries were to be used only to decide questions of guilt and innocence, and would introduce the risk of unreviewable discretion entering the sentencing process. Finally, the proposal to determine insanity by jury discretion was unworkable. Lloyd George stressed that he himself would be in favor of abolishing capital punishment in favor of a suitable alternative penalty, but that the government felt that it was inadvisable to do so, given the strong possibility that the penalty had a deterrent effect, especially against professional criminals. Finally:

> the Government have no doubt that it would be entirely wrong to abolish capital punishment unless there were clearly overwhelming public sentiments in favour of this change. The Government have no reason

to think that public opinion is in favour of abolition, or of suspension. Indeed, they believe that the contrary is true. (Ibid.)

The government's opposition to the Commission's recommendations seemed to doom them, at least for the time being.

Next to speak was Chuter Ede (Hansard HC 1955:2076–84), who, while serving as Home Secretary in 1948, had opposed Silverman's motion for a 5-year moratorium on capital punishment. In the meantime, he announced, he had changed his views, and now would vote in favor of the moratorium. He addressed the issue of public opinion head-on:

I doubt very much whether, at the moment, public opinion is in favour of this change, but I doubt, also, whether, at any time during the last hundred years, a plebiscite would have carried any of the great penal reforms that have been made. The appeal in the time of Romilly was always to the belief that public opinion would not stand it, but there are occasions when this House has to say that a certain thing is right, even if the public may not at that moment be of that opinion.

The growing awareness that Timothy Evans, a slow-witted Welsh miner, had been unjustly hanged also played a role in Ede's conversion:

I was the Home Secretary who wrote on Evans' papers, 'The law must take its course.' … I think Evans' case shows, in spite of all that has been done since, that a mistake was possible, and that … a mistake was made. I hope that no future Home Secretary, while in office or after he has left office, will ever have to feel that although he did his best and no one would wish to accuse him of being either careless or inefficient, he sent a man to the gallows who was not 'Guilty as charged.' (Ibid.)

Ede's confession was so powerful that, as we have seen in Chapter 4, it was quoted by a member of the German Criminal Law Commission during that body's debate on capital punishment. Nevertheless, Silverman's motion to suspend capital punishment for a trial period of five years, introduced during the debate, was finally voted down, 245 to 214 (Block and Hostettler 1997:163).

However, the political calculus surrounding capital punishment in Great Britain had begun to yield different results by the mid-to-late 1950s. Historian James Christoph (1962:76) identifies three main reasons for the shift: 'the activities and Report of the Royal Commission on Capital Punishment, a series of peculiar and much-publicized murder cases taking place in the early 1950s, and the formation and work of a new abolitionist organization, the National Campaign for the Abolition of Capital Punishment.' The murder cases were those of Timothy Evans, Derek Bentley, and Ruth Ellis. Evans was convicted of murdering his wife and infant daughter, and hanged in March of 1950. He had made a variety of contradictory and occasionally incriminating statements, but his cognitive limitations made it unclear how much of his confessions he genuinely understood. Years after his conviction, it was discovered that John Reginald Halliday Christie, Evans' landlord and the chief witness against him at trial, was a serial killer, and had in fact hidden the bodies of many of the women he killed in the very apartment he had rented to the Evans family. Christie was convicted of murdering his own wife in 1953. Before he was hanged, he also admitted to murdering Evans' wife (while maintaining his innocence of the baby daughter's murder). The likelihood that the British criminal justice system had hanged an innocent man quickly became the focus of intense and sustained controversy. Shortly after Christie's conviction, Sydney Silverman co-authored a book with fellow lawyer and abolitionist MP Reginald Paget called *Hanged – and Innocent?* (1953). The book presented three detailed, lawyerly analyses of cases of possible innocence, among them that of Timothy Evans. Prominent attorney Michael Eddowes added to the controversy with a book devoted exclusively to the Evans case, *The Man on Your Conscience* (1955).

The other two famous cases, Derek Bentley and Ruth Ellis, did not involve innocence in the 'classical' sense in which the Evans case presented it, but were nevertheless influential. Bentley, a brain-damaged petty criminal with a turbulent history, was convicted and executed at the age of 19 for the murder of a policeman, even though his partner in crime, Christopher Craig, fired the fatal shot after Bentley had already been detained by the police. Under English law at the time (1953), members of a joint criminal enterprise could, under the doctrine of 'constructive malice,' be held liable for felonies committed by another member of the conspiracy, even if they did not participate in the crime or intend it. The application of this doctrine to a mentally limited 19-year-old sparked intense controversy. Ruth Ellis, the last controversial case, confessed to killing her ex-lover and was executed in 1955, when she was 29 years old. Her youth and attractiveness, coupled with the emotional turbulence in her personal life that drove her to her crime, ensured a media frenzy. She became the last woman executed in Great Britain.

The cases of Bentley and Evans, in particular, had a lasting effect on the British debate on capital punishment, as family members and abolitionists kept the cases in the limelight by requesting government investigations and applying for posthumous pardons. The British journalist Ludovic Kennedy wrote a 1961 book called *10 Rillington Place* about the Evans case which made the case for his innocence even more strongly than before. Kennedy's book was made into a gripping 1971 movie of the same name starring John Hurt as Evans and David Attenborough as Christie. In 1966, an official government inquiry into the Evans case, whose final report was 158 pages long, came to the odd conclusion that Evans had probably not murdered his own child (the crime for which he was hanged), but may well have murdered his own wife – the crime to which Christie had earlier confessed (Block and Hostettler 1997:254). Despite the ambiguous conclusion of the report, the case had attracted enough controversy that the Labour Home Secretary, Roy Jenkins, recommended a posthumous free pardon for Evans, which was granted by the Queen. For almost two decades, thus, the case of Timothy Evans was rarely far from the limelight. Although it seems to have had little effect on British elite public opinion as a whole, there is much evidence that the constant focus on a tragic and embarrassing miscarriage of justice helped crystallize British opinion against capital punishment. As two historians argued: '[T]he execution of this innocent simpleton probably did more than anything to accelerate the cause of abolitionists' (Block and Hostettler 1997:155). For his part, the chairman of the Gowers Commission, Sir Ernest Gowers, wrote a short book in 1956 describing how his duties on the Royal Commission had turned him into a convinced abolitionist.

Given this ferment on the issue, Sydney Silverman and his abolitionist allies in the House of Commons sensed that 1956 might be an opportune time for another vote on a five-year death penalty moratorium. Silverman introduced a private member's bill requesting a five-year moratorium on capital punishment. Private members (or back-benchers) of the House of Commons are those members who are neither ministers nor ex-ministers. If they are granted sufficient time to do so by the current government, they are allowed to introduce legislation addressing their own priorities. Despite their name, private members' bills are not limited to merely local matters; they can also be 'public bills' in the parliamentary sense – that is, bills which propose nationwide changes in general policy. This was the nature of the bill Silverman introduced. In light of the solid support for abolition among Labour ranks, and the steadily growing list of Tory MPs and other worthies who had declared themselves in favor of abolition, the Conservative government of Prime Minister Anthony Eden chose to grant Silverman time to introduce his bill. The bill passed after its second reading (during which the bill's merits are debated) by a vote of 286 to 262, and went into committee. In committee, retentionist MPs sought to amend the bill to exclude certain kinds of murders from the blanket prohibition on capital punishment, but all the amendments were defeated save one, which would have retained capital punishment for those prisoners who kill while serving a life sentence. On the floor of the House, Sydney Silverman used a blizzard of arcane motions to strip all the words from this latter amendment save 'provided that this,' and then moved to eliminate the nonsensical remnant (Block and Hostettler 1997:180–1). His 'sleight of hand' provoked some opposition even from Labour Party ranks, but allowed the bill to go to a vote free of amendments, where it was passed by a vote of 152 to 133.

As in 1948, a private members' bill calling for abolition had been passed in the House of Commons and went to the House of Lords for debate.

Since that time, a 1949 parliamentary reform had stripped the Lords of their ability to reject legislation in most cases, replacing it with the power only to delay consideration of a bill for one year. Nevertheless, the Lords again mobilized an unusual number of members to actually attend the debate, prompting the *Spectator* to jibe that opposition in the Lords came from 'hitherto unknown rustics, who thought, perhaps, that abolition was in some way connected to blood sports' (Block and Hostettler 1997:186, quoting the *Spectator*, July 13 1956, p. 51). Lord Mancroft, speaking for the retentionists, counseled against excessive reliance on opinion polls which seemed to reflect a transitory cooling of the British public toward capital punishment:

> Public opinion on this subject is peculiarly variable, and is liable to be influenced by some recent murder in which particular sympathy is felt for the victim, or by a recent execution in which particular sympathy is felt for the murderer. The fluctuations in Gallup Polls in recent years have illustrated this point quite clearly. For example, a poll in October, 1953 (just after the Christie case), showed 73 per cent in favour of the death penalty; another in July, 1955 (just after the execution of Ruth Ellis), showed only 50 per cent in favour and 37 per cent against. (Hansard HL 1956a:vol. 198, col. 689)

The House of Lords again defeated the Commons by a strong majority. H. L. A. Hart, describing the aftermath of the 1956 abolition vote in the Commons, noted:

> There are ways in our curious Constitution of circumventing the opposition of our Upper Chamber, but in practice these are not available unless the Government of the day is in favour of the measures which the House of Commons passes. In this case the Government was opposed to suspension or abolition of the death penalty and refused to lend its aid. (Hart 1968:56)

Nevertheless, the steady succession of Commons votes for abolition – coupled with the steadily increasing number of Tory MPs joining the abolitionist side – contributed to a growing certainty that the question was no longer whether Great Britain would abolish the death penalty, but when.

Eden's government wanted to avoid another embarrassing confrontation between the House of Commons, which apparently now possessed a steadfast majority in favor of abolishing capital punishment, and the House of Lords, which seemed eager to court controversy by steadily opposing abolition. To stave off another confrontation, the government resolved to introduce compromise legislation. The November 1956 Queen's Speech, in which the government traditionally announces its major legislative initiatives, contained the phrase: 'My Ministers will bring forward proposals to amend the law of homicide and to limit the scope of capital punishment' (Hansard HL 1956b: vol. 560, cols 16–19). Throughout the 1957 Parliament, the government used complex maneuvers to stymie an abolition bill sponsored by Labour member Alice Bacon, and to shepherd its own Homicide Act through committee without too many amendments from Labour MPs. The effort was successful; the bill became law in March. The Homicide Act made a variety of relatively non-controversial changes to the law of homicide, including clarifying the doctrine of provocation and introducing the defense of diminished responsibility. The bill also largely eliminated the doctrine of constructive malice, which had been used to convict Derek Bentley of murder based on the actions of his co-conspirator. The most controversial aspect of the bill, however, was Section 5, which limited eligibility for capital punishment to offenders who had committed murder in the course of theft, murder by explosion or shooting, murder of a police officer or prison guard, or murder in the course of escape. Section 6 made offenders who had committed two or more murders in Great Britain death-eligible.

The intent of the government was to try to limit application of the (mandatory) death penalty to those offenders thought to be most susceptible to deterrence – that is, professional criminals. However, the arbitrariness of the government's list came under immediate attack. A lecturer at University College, London, wrote in a 1957 law journal article: '[I]n seeking to restrict a mandatory death penalty to a small group of offenses in which deterrence might have a particularly significant effect, [Parliament] has introduced a number of extremely artificial distinctions which will cause great unevenness and unfairness and inevitably arouse considerable public concern when they are applied in practice' (Prevezer 1957:649). Prevezer, citing hypothetical cases frequently advanced by the Homicide Act's critics, noted that a person who strangled a young girl to death after raping her, or poisoned a family member to inherit money, would not be subject to capital punishment even though these offenses would seem just as heinous, if not more so, as the ones listed in the Homicide Act.

The critics' point of view would, in the course of the following years, be borne out by events. Although British abolitionists were at first disappointed at their inability to eliminate hanging outright, they soon came to see the Homicide Act as a blessing in disguise. The bishops of the Church of England found the arbitrary results of the act, in the phrase of one British legal historian, 'morally shocking' (Radzinowicz 1999:271). The Lord Chief Justice, in a 1965 Lords debate, reported that 'judges are quite disgusted at the results produced by the Homicide Act' (Hansard HL 1965:vol. 268, cols. 480–513). One obvious solution would have been a return to the old law – but the Homicide Act had been passed precisely because even Conservatives recognized that British capital punishment law required modernization. Further, by passing a law which narrowed application of the death penalty,

Conservatives had implicitly accepted the premise that a reduction in the number of capital sentences was, in and of itself, a worthwhile goal of government policy. The only remaining option for retentionists seemed to be yet another revision of the British law of homicide. But if one thoroughly debated reform attempt had turned out so poorly, abolitionists argued, what guarantee could there be that the next one would hit its mark? Overall, retentionists found themselves in a position in which defending the death penalty meant defending a law whose weaknesses had become apparent to every observer (Newburn, forthcoming).

Criminologist Tim Newburn, in a forthcoming paper, identifies several other factors which were crucial for setting the stage for abolition in England. One was the surprisingly non-rancorous nature of the debate on criminal justice policy in England in the late 1950s and 1960s. Despite growing prosperity, crime rose steadily throughout the late 1950s, and became a pressing issue for the Conservative governments of Anthony Eden (who retired in 1957 in the wake of the Suez Crisis) and Harold MacMillan, who governed until 1964. Responding to concern about crime, both Conservative and Labour governments, in the late 1950s and early 1960s, prepared White Papers proposing a sweeping modernization of English criminal justice. Reflecting the approach to crime control which David Garland (1984) has called 'penal welfarism,' English technocrats and civil servants analyzed penal law as one of a series of state interventions in social life designed to address the needs of socially vulnerable populations and support the reintegration of marginalized groups. This approach necessarily entails a view of crime less as a partisan battlefield and more as a social problem in need of humane and well-researched counter-strategies. Thus, it was a Conservative government that published, in 1959, a landmark White Paper called *Penal Practice in a Changing Society*, which proposed sweeping changes to the British criminal justice system, including the establishment of a center of criminology to study the root causes of crime, expanding and modernizing the prison system with an emphasis on rehabilitation, developing alternative sentencing practices to keep young offenders out of prison, streamlining the criminal adjudication process, modernizing psychiatric and psychological care in prisons, and building up prison after-care programs to ease former prisoners' transition into society (Jarvis 2005:21). Regardless of the tone of the debate in the broader society, the bureaucratic elite of post-war Britain valued a 'modern' approach to crime and punishment. MacMillan's Conservative government continued to issue White Papers along similar lines until its ouster in the 1964 general elections. Broadly similar policies were pursued by MacMillan's Labour successors.

This obscuring of partisan boundaries also affected opinion on capital punishment. One recent estimate suggests that in the decade after 1956, the proportion of abolitionists within Conservative ranks doubled from one-eighth of all MPs to one-quarter (Twitchell 2006:333). The composition of the House of Lords had also begun to change dramatically. In April 1958, the Life Peerages Bill became law. Its object was 'to strengthen the House of Lords by widening the area from which men and women of distinction in all walks of life could be recruited to take an active part in its business, since many such are thought nowadays not to desire hereditary peerages.' (Gordon 1964:150). The bill also permitted women to serve in the House of Lords for the first time. As a result of a bipartisan agreement to bring more political balance to the House of Lords, a large number of Labour peers were created in the aftermath of the Life Peerages Act, including famed penal reformer Baroness Wootton and Gerald Gardiner, an indefatigable abolitionist attorney who had served as joint chairman of the National Campaign for the Abolition of Capital Punishment (and who would later become Lord Chief Justice) (Newburn, forthcoming).

In the meantime, Sydney Silverman had not given up his crusade against capital punishment. Shortly after the 1956 vote, Silverman published an article called 'When a Murderer is Hanged,' in which he stated his credo:

> Civilization is doomed unless we learn to preserve our faith in the value of every human being. When a murderer kills, the crime is not his alone; we all share it.
>
> When a murderer is hanged every citizen of a democratic country is morally responsible for his death. We, each, in some degree become in ourselves a murderer too. What the hangman does with his hands, we each do in our hearts. For he acts in our name and by our leave. The guilt of blood rests upon us all.
>
> Nearly every country in Europe abolished the death penalty years ago. No evil consequences followed. We do not need to kill, we change nothing for the better when we do. (As quoted in Hughes 1969:156)

Nevertheless, despite the sea change taking place in the attitudes of British elites toward capital punishment in the late 1950s and early 1960s, the Tories under MacMillan were unwilling to risk another divisive and high-profile parliamentary vote on capital punishment. It appeared that Labour would have to win an election in order to bring the issue to a head once again.

Labour and the End of the Noose

Abolition's fortunes changed decisively when Labour eked out a four-seat majority in the 1964 general elections. The government formed by Harold Wilson raised the hopes of British abolitionists:

> The Prime Minister, Harold Wilson, detested the institution of hanging, as did the Lord Chancellor, Gerald Gardiner, and most of the Cabinet

were middling to strong abolitionists who had consistently voted for abolition. No member of the new Cabinet, and scarcely any member of the junior ministerial ranks for that matter, had voted for its retention since the late 1940s. (Twitchell 2006:332)

The composition of the Labour rank-and-file had also changed markedly in the decades before 1964. Almost one-third of the Labour MPs elected in 1964 had not been MPs as of the most recent election in 1959, and the new MPs were markedly better educated than their predecessors, more likely to be lawyers or educators, and more interested in broad-gauge social and ethical issues as opposed to bread-and-butter concerns (Dorey 2006). Nevertheless, the Wilson government was still unwilling to endorse abolition as official government policy. Public opinion played a role here – Labour's 1964 electoral victory was small, and public opinion, during the 1960s, had shifted dramatically in favor of capital punishment. Instead of making abolition official government policy, Wilson's government decided to simply make time for a private member's abolition bill. Nevertheless, to raise the issue's profile, the government arranged for this policy to be announced in the Queen's Speech, the only time that the Queen has ever mentioned a private member's bill in her official speech. Emrys Hughes, a Labour MP at the time, called it 'a bold and courageous decision for a Government with such a small majority to take' (Hughes 1969:172). The vote would be, as always, a free vote.

The 1964 parliamentary debate on the Murder (Abolition of Death Penalty) Bill was fierce and prolonged, but, as Silverman himself noted during the debate on the bill's second reading: 'This controversy has gone on for long enough. The arguments both ways are clear, and everyone has made up his mind where the balance between the two sets of arguments lies.' A Conservative former Home Secretary, Henry Brooke, gave a speech in which he revealed that he, too, had come to oppose capital punishment since his time in office. Hughes (1969:176) noted: 'This frank and courageous speech from the ex-Conservative Home Secretary created a deep impression and helped to decide the vote. Five Home Secretaries had now come to the conclusion that the death penalty should be abolished: Lord Templewood, Lord Samuel, Herbert Morrison, Chuter Ede and now Henry Brooke.' As in 1956, retentionists tried to clutter the bill with amendments and exceptions, but they were again deflected by Silverman's expert parliamentary skills. Only one amendment was added, which specified that abolition would be introduced only for a trial period of five years. After that time had expired – in July 1970 – Parliament was to assess the trend in crime statistics during the period of abolition and decide whether to continue the policy. The dramatic shift in the British political landscape was shown by the fact that the abolition bill not only easily passed both houses of Parliament, but gained an even larger majority in the Lords than it had in the Commons.

Shortly after the abolition bill passed, two notorious murder cases sparked widespread public outrage and calls for the reintroduction of capital punishment. In October of 1965, the Moors murders were discovered. For almost two years, Myra Hindley and Ian Brady had conspired to abduct young Britons, murder them (often after sexually assaulting them), and bury their bodies in the moors near Manchester, England. The gruesome details of the case – as well as the bizarre *folie à deux* which possessed the working-class couple to perpetrate them – generated saturation press coverage. Hindley and Brady had buried their victims not far from Sydney Silverman's constituency. An uncle of one of the Moors murders victims, Patrick Downey, decided to run against Silverman in the 1966 general election as a member of the 'hanging' party: 'I will be fighting on the hanging issue alone. I consider the Bill introduced by Mr Silverman as stupid and idiotic. I intend to fight Mr Silverman in his own constituency and beat him' (Hughes 1969:183). The Tory candidate in the race, Peter Davies, quickly changed his opinion to supporting capital punishment to try to steal a march on Downey. Although the unusual three-way race in Nelson and Colne attracted considerable media attention, the outcome was another comfortable victory for Silverman. His years of loyal service to his constituency evidently outweighed his unpopular stand on hanging. Shortly thereafter, in 1966, three policemen were murdered in London by career criminals in an incident that became known as the Shepherd's Bush killings. These killings brought sustained calls for the reintroduction of capital punishment for the murder of police officers in the line of duty. However, the Labour Home Secretary, Roy Jenkins, was a staunch abolitionist who had forthrightly denounced capital punishment in his 1959 book *The Labour Case*. Jenkins resisted calls to restore capital punishment, arguing that policy should not be made on the basis of individual cases.

Tim Newburn, in his analysis of abolition in Great Britain, locates the emerging distaste for capital punishment within the context of the 'penal-welfarist' mentality that prevailed in Britain in the mid-1960s. During the Labour premiership of Harold Wilson, which lasted from 1964 to 1970, the series of groundbreaking White Papers on social problems and problems of law enforcement continued. The era also saw a series of Royal Commissions and advisory panels which proposed sweeping changes in British social-welfare and penal laws, all with the aim of integrating crime prevention and offender rehabilitation into an overall social-welfare strategy to improve social support for excluded and marginal populations. These strategies were essentially elite measures, which were crafted and implemented in response to advances in criminology and psychology, rather than to pressure from public opinion. As Newburn sees it, abolition:

fitted neatly with the Labour government's broader modernizing mission. Moreover, like so many other reforms in the penal field, expert opinion played an important role in the process of policy change. Similarly, only more so than the other penal reforms, the abolition of capital punishment was undertaken in the absence of public support. As an elite measure it was in many respects characteristic of the era. (Newburn, forthcoming)

Newburn nevertheless argues that the abolition of capital punishment does not fit completely into the broader context of penal reform, because it remained a more partisan issue than other criminal justice reforms. Therefore, Newburn argues that it can perhaps best be understood within the context of the sweeping group of permissive reforms that loosened British laws on divorce, homosexuality and other morals offenses throughout the 1960s.

Despite the growing elite consensus in favor of death-penalty abolition, high-profile killings, coupled with a modest increase in yearly homicide statistics, contributed to increased public support for capital punishment as the 1960s progressed. In 1965, an opinion poll showed that 65.5% of Britons were in favor of keeping capital punishment, whereas 21.3% were against and 13.2% were undecided (Block and Hostettler 1997:237). Shortly after the triple police murders in 1966, a Conservative MP, Duncan Sandys, formed the 'Society for the Restoration of Capital Punishment,' which served as a focal point for public calls to reinstate hanging (*The Times* 1967). By October of 1969, a Marplan poll sponsored by *The Times* of London found that 38% of Britons supported the return of capital punishment for all types of murders and 47% supported the return for some types of killings. Only 12% were categorically opposed to capital punishment (*The Times* Political Editor 1969).

Given this trend, the Wilson government was anxious to avoid having the issue of capital punishment crop up as a factor in the next general election, which would have to be held by March 1971, at the latest. Thus, instead of waiting until mid-1970 and studying the crime figures for 1966 to 1970, as the original bill foresaw, the Labour government instead decided to call a vote in 1969 to make the abolition of capital punishment permanent. Conservatives and Labour had already agreed not to make capital punishment a party political issue, but Conservatives regarded Labour's decision to move the vote forward as a breach of this understanding, and strongly criticized it (Block and Hostettler 1997: 262–3). Sydney Silverman died in 1968, so he was not present to sponsor the bill that ultimately enshrined abolition. By this time, however, the Labour government was bold enough to sponsor the bill as an official government measure, in both Houses of Parliament. The abolition bill passed the House of Commons with a comfortable majority. One fact of particular significance was that the leaders of all three major parties in the Commons – including the Conservative Party leader Edward Heath – had voted for abolition.

Gerald Gardiner, who had been created a peer in 1963 and was serving as Lord Chancellor in December of 1969, gave a landmark speech in the Lords (Hansard HL Deb 17 December 1969:vol. 306, cols.1106–21) in support of the bill he had introduced:

> The only countries in Western Europe which still practise [capital punishment] are Spain, France, Eire and Northern Ireland ... In the last 10 years the annual number of executions in Northern Ireland has been: 0, 0, 2, 0, 0, 0, 0, 0, 0, 0. In the last 10 years there have been no executions in Eire. In the last 10 years in France, where the number of murders a year is now substantially higher than it is here, the annual number of executions during the last 10 years has been 4, 3, 2, 1, 1, 0, 0, 4, 1, 1. It is I think well known that President Pompidou is a strong abolitionist. He has so far reprieved all the cases, and it may be that we have seen the last execution in France.
>
> Canada has recently abolished capital punishment except for the murder of prison officers and policemen ... Their total number of executions in each of the last 10 years has been: 3, 3, 3, 2, 1, 2, 0, 0, 0, 0. Last year in the United States – I doubted this figure, but I have had it checked from Washington, and they say it is what their computer says—the number of murders was 13,650. When one remembers that their population is four times ours, this makes our little 170 look rather silly. The number of executions for murder in the whole of the United States in each of the last 10 years has been: 41, 54, 33, 41, 18, 9, 7, 1, 2, and last year, for the first time in the history of the United States, none. My Lords, when practically the whole of the Western Christian world has either formally abolished capital punishment or virtually given it up in practice, would it not be an extraordinary time for us to start using the noose again?

Other abolitionist peers stressed the fact that all party leaders in the House of Commons had voted for abolition, which seemed to confirm its status as a non-political issue. Eventually, the bill prevailed with a surprisingly large majority of 46. Among the majority were 100 Labour peers, 41 Conservative peers, 39 'cross-benchers' (peers who have no official party loyalty), 22 Liberals, the Archbishop of Canterbury, and 18 of the 19 bishops present (Noyes 1969). Aside from a few scattered code provisions which were not considered worth the effort of removing, the death penalty had been legally abolished in Great Britain. Efforts to reinstate it were defeated:

> [Abolition has remained in force] despite periodic attempts – most notably in 1973, 1975, 1979, 1983, 1987 (twice), 1988, 1990 and 1994 – by sundry Conservative backbenchers to restore the rope, usually for specific categories

of murder. All these attempts have been defeated, with a discernible trend towards ever larger abolitionist majorities, largely irrespective of the party in power and the balance of forces in the House (Twitchell 2006:337)

Article 21(5) of the Human Rights Act 1998, which Tony Blair's Labour government passed in 1998 in order to harmonize British law with European human-rights provisions, provided for the complete abolition of the death penalty, abrogating isolated laws that had prescribed capital punishment for certain military offenses. Protocol No. 13 to the European Convention on Human Rights and Fundamental Freedoms, which provides for the complete abolition of capital punishment in all circumstances, was signed and ratified by the United Kingdom shortly following its opening for signature in 2002, and entered into force on 21 February 2004. With these actions, the government of the United Kingdom placed formidable, likely insurmountable, legal obstacles in the way of reintroduction of the death penalty.

As the majorities in both Houses of the British Parliament solidified in favor of abolition, public opinion shifted in the opposite direction. As late as 2003, public opinion polls were registering solid and consistent majorities in favor of reintroducing the death penalty in Great Britain. That support may have dropped somewhat in the early 2000s, though, in line with developments in other Western European countries. The British tabloid press is much more aggressive in its approach to capital punishment than its counterparts in Western Europe, which generally refrain from explicit calls for the return of capital punishment. Two examples illustrate the attitude of many British tabloids. In the summer of 2000, *People* conducted a reader survey after a gruesome child murder. Under the headline 'How can we protect our children if these monsters are allowed to live? There is no cure for them ... they must hang' the paper reported (Klein and Fowler 2000) that a 'massive army' of readers had voted for the return of capital punishment for child-killers, the precise count being 48,762 in favor to 440 against. The *Daily Express*, in an article (Lee and Twomey 2005) entitled 'Police Killers Must Hang' suggested that 'Calls for police killers to face the gallows came from across Britain yesterday as the nation mourned the coldblooded killing of [police officer] Sharon Beshenivsky.'

Despite the support lingering in some quarters, the only politicians arguing for a reintroduction of capital punishment in contemporary Britain are the far-right British National Party and Tory outliers such as Ann Widdecombe (also a *Daily Express* columnist), who argued in 2002: 'If it can be shown that it is a real deterrent and its availability, not its regular use, is enough to deter murderers and save innocent lives, then I think that is a case that can be made' (BBC 2002). Nevertheless, Widdecombe has no support in her own party for this notion, and one commentator described the broader context thus:

> Needless to say, there is no chance of the restoration of capital punishment in Britain in the foreseeable future. Almost all MPs oppose it, and support for it, like being anti-gay, is widely seen as a litmus test for being truly, madly, deeply reactionary. Indeed, even Widdecombe is anxious to distance herself from the retributive urge that often underlies it, arguing instead for the deterrent value of the penalty (Benn 2002).

As in other European countries, the very fact that the death penalty has been permanently, irretrievably placed off-limits has, ironically, made it the ideal issue for right-wing populist parties – they can publicly endorse a policy that has considerable lingering support among the population without ever having to worry about the far-reaching consequences of ever following through on their rhetoric.

6
Case Study Three – France

By the late 18th century, the debate about the death penalty in France had achieved recognizably modern form. Explicitly religious arguments, like invocations of the divine right of kings, were largely absent. Beccaria, in introducing the idea of complete abolition of capital punishment for ordinary crimes, drew on social contract theory, utilitarian thinking, and insights into the psychology of criminal offenders. As we have seen, Beccaria's treatise was translated into French almost immediately, and Voltaire lent his fame and renown to the Italian's arguments. Retentionist thinkers, for their part, were forced to confront modern arguments against capital punishment and to develop equally modern responses. Thus, by the 1770s, French thinkers were debating capital punishment in terms that still resonate today. One scholar compared the debate held in the French Estates-General in 1791 with the debate held in the English House of Commons in 1956: 'The first thing one notices is the remarkable similarity in these comments, 165 years apart. There is hardly a single idea in either one of the debates that cannot be found in the other' (Hornum 1967:71–2).

Even before Beccaria, French thinkers had been advocating limits on the sovereign's right to take life. In Book II, Chapter V of *The Social Contract*, entitled 'The Right of Life and Death,' Rousseau (1762) delivered a qualified endorsement of capital punishment. The social contract includes protection against death at the hands of fellow citizens, therefore 'we consent to die if we ourselves turn assassins.' By attacking 'social rights,' the malefactor becomes 'a rebel and traitor to his country' and in putting such a person to death, 'we slay not so much a citizen as the enemy ... not a moral person but merely a man.' Then, somewhat puzzlingly, Rousseau argues that although the state has the right to kill, it may not 'exercise' that right. Further, a state which punishes frequently shows its weakness, and the death penalty must be executed as sparingly as possible: 'The State has no right to put to death, even for the sake of making an example, any one whom it can leave alive without danger.'

Rousseau's arguments influenced the discussion of capital punishment in the 1776 book *De la Législation, ou principes de lois* by Gabriel Bonnot de

Mably, a *philosophe* who enjoyed considerable influence in the 18th century, but whose star has since waned. *De la Législation* takes the form of a debate between an English 'Milord' and a Swedish philosopher, both of whom are legislators in their respective countries. During a long dialogue held during a walk in a garden, the Swede and the Englishman debate many aspects of modern governance and philosophy. According to one scholar, the Swede's views correspond to Mably's own (Lehmann 1975:162). The two statesmen discuss capital punishment in Book III (Mably 1776:97–121). The Swede prefaces the discussion with a general plea for mildness in punishment, arguing that harsh, torturous punishments debase the morals of the public. Increasing the severity of punishment only habituates citizens to cruelty. The legislature should 'advertise [the laws] several times before punishing, should work to instill in us shame for our wrong actions, and punishment … should strike mainly at the soul, not the body.' Milord professes himself 'delighted' (*ravi*) at these comments from his Swedish colleague. The Englishman recognizes the state's right to regulate citizens' conduct, but confesses to a 'secret indignation' at the prospect of judges pronouncing a sentence of death. Perhaps it is a 'trivial axiom,' but the citizen cannot give to the state a right he does not possess, such as the right to take another citizen's life. Of course, the state has the right to take the life of enemies, but this analogy breaks down once the offender is in secure custody, at which point he is no longer capable of harming society.

Perhaps surprisingly, the Swedish philosopher disagrees. Although he admires the humane sentiments of his colleague, and continues to favor the mildest punishments possible, nevertheless the state must be accorded the right to execute, if only as a last resort. The Swede says that every person does, in fact, have the right to take life in self-defense, and has transferred this right to the sovereign:

> In the state of nature, I have the right to kill those who attempt to take my life, and in entering into society, I have accorded this right to the magistrate; why should he then not use it? Citizens have not accorded the magistrate the right to play arbitrarily with their lives; this concession would be senseless and void: they have, however, required the legislator to pursue their security, and that he counter, with sword in hand, the dangers which menace them, to defend them against a domestic enemy which wishes death upon them.

Echoing Rousseau, the Swede argues that since a person who commits violent acts against his fellow man renders himself an enemy of the state, he essentially has the same status as an enemy in wartime; his life is thus forfeit and can legally be taken by the state. Further, there can be 'no order, no rule of law, and no security' when the fate of the killer is superior to that of the 'virtuous citizen' who has lost his life – 'the first, the greatest, and the most irretrievable of goods.' Finally, can we really trust the humane sentiments of capital punishment's opponents, when they suggest replacing the death penalty with a lifetime of humiliating, exhausting, public forced labor? And is it possible that they will never once escape their chains and pose a continued threat to society?

Milord responds that his confidence has been shaken (*ebranlé*) by the Swede's arguments, but nevertheless holds to his position. Strongly echoing Beccaria, Milord argues that the brief spectacle of an execution has little effect on criminals and spectators, whereas the prospect of a life spent 'seeing nothing but dungeon cells, chains, and continuous labors' creates much deeper anguish and reflection. The Swede then offers a kind of compromise to his English interlocutor. While maintaining that the death penalty must be kept in the state's armamentarium, the Swedish philosopher argues equally forcefully that its imposition should be exceedingly rare, both for humanitarian reasons and to preserve its exceptional character. The Swede would, in fact, limit the death penalty only to treason and aggravated cases of murder. He hastens to add that he would never include among the ranks of traitors a person 'who has the courage not to flatter the nation, and who desires changes to increase its happiness.' Further, the Swede would end the 'sinister work' of torture completely, and work to improve the quality of justice by mandating a presumption of innocence and strong procedural protections for the defendant, since 'it would be better to create the possibility of seeing a hundred or a thousand guilty men escape their merited punishment than to see one innocent punished.'

The efforts of Rousseau, Voltaire and Mably had turned the death penalty into a philosophical novelty – an issue as to which all self-respecting *philosophes* were required to have an opinion. Thus, it should come as no surprise that a debate was held on the abolition of the death penalty in the French Constituent Assembly during the French Revolution. The reporter of the drafting commission, Lepelletier de Saint-Fargeau, introduced the debate with a summary of the latest thinking on criminal justice, stressing the requirement that punishments be humane, proportioned to the offense, and that they not discriminate based on the social status of the defendant. Lepelletier, while remaining agnostic on whether the death penalty should be retained, framed the issue in familiar terms, arguing that the only source of legitimacy for capital punishment would be the citizens' right to self-defense transferred to the state, and that the death penalty could only be justified in those cases in which no other punishment would serve to deter potential offenders. Three speakers, Maximilien de Robespierre, Jerôme Pétion de Villeneuve and Adrien Duport, spoke out for complete abolition. Robespierre's arguments, described by Hornum (1967:57) as typical for the abolitionist side of the debate, were as follows:

> The state's execution of the death penalty is legalized murder. The death penalty ... is the weapon of tyrants against their slaves. It is not

a deterrent to would-be murderers and its use diminishes respect for the authority of the law. Punishment should be meted out in response to the emotions which produced the act and not blindly to all crimes of a particular type. Furthermore, the experience of other countries such as Japan, Greece, Rome, and Russia shows that it is possible to do without it. Finally, the risk of error is very great. Human judgments are not infallible and an innocent man may be condemned to death and executed. Most importantly, however, is the denial to the accused of a chance to repent his acts.

His eloquence cannot be doubted, but given his later role in the Terror, one has to wonder about Robespierre's sincerity. Three other delegates spoke in favor of retention. Nevertheless, the supporters of capital punishment were sensitive to issues of barbarity and arbitrariness, especially as highlighted by torturous methods of execution:

Aside from the uselessness of severe punishments which affront nature and humanity ... there is no point of comparison between a fixed penalty which, in certain cases, the crime deserves, and an arbitrary punishment, because the arbitrary often occasions a very real inequality in the uses that judges make of their power ... I allow therefore only the death penalty, that is to say the simple privation of life, without torture, for all kinds of murder. (Smith 2003:32, quoting speech of M. Mougins de Roquefort to the National Assembly, July 31 1791)

Hornum summarizes (1967:60) the overall impressions generated by the debate:

The skill in public speaking exercised by these men, the mixture of strong emotional appeals and references to social and political theories, and their zeal in defending the rightness of their cause, stand out. Another lasting impression is the intellectual prowess of the orators. Their constant references to Montesquieu, Rousseau, Beccaria, Mably, Filangieri and others, and their knowledge of other countries' experiences with the death penalty showed them to be well-read students of political and social classics.

Of course, the debate resulted in the retention of capital punishment. However, the debate revealed a broad consensus on the need to adopt a more humane method of execution. A famous surgeon offered his expertise:

In December 1789, Dr. Joseph-Ignace Guillotin, deputy of the National Assembly, had proposed a reform of capital punishment in keeping with the equal status accorded to all citizens by the Declaration of the Rights of Man.

Instead of barbaric practices which degraded the spectators as much as the criminal, a method of surgical instantaneity was to be adopted. Not only would decapitation spare the prisoner gratuitous pain, it would offer to common criminals the dignified execution hitherto reserved for the privileged orders. The proposal also removed the stigma of guilt by association from the family of the condemned and, most importantly, protected their property from the confiscation required by traditional practice. (Schama 1989:619)

After some intervening parliamentary maneuvers, the guillotine – originally called the 'louison' or 'louisette' after Dr. Louis, perpetual secretary of the Academy of Surgeons, who took up Guillotin's idea – was adopted as the official method of execution. It was first used in April 1792 against a robber named Nicolas Pelletier. Later, of course, the number of executions increased steadily during the Terror. During the reign of Bonaparte, the use of capital punishment was regularized and consolidated by the great Napoleonic codifications of criminal law and procedure, and the scaffold and guillotine became a fixture of French justice.

19th Century: Hugo and *The Last Day of a Condemned Man*

Although the main focus of this book is on the 20th century, a detailed look at the contribution of Victor Hugo in 19th-century France is in order, since Hugo's approach to the death penalty debate has, I will argue, exercised a lasting influence on the modern approach to the issue. Although he started his public life as a royalist, Hugo also opposed capital punishment. His third novel, *The Last Day of a Condemned Man*, was first published anonymously by Gosselin in 1829, after having been composed in approximately three weeks in December 1828. The novel takes the form of a series of brief first-person diary entries written by a man who has been condemned to die by a French court. He recalls being sentenced to death by a French jury, and his transfer to Bicêtre prison, where he waits as his plea for mercy works its way through the various instances. The condemned man reflects on the fates of the previous prisoners to inhabit his cell, who have all scratched their names in the cell's wall. A priest visits him several times to try to convince him to repent, but the prisoner's attitude toward religion seems ambiguous – he confesses a strong faith in God, but finds the prison chaplain's clichés repugnant. His plea for mercy is eventually denied, and he is then taken to the Conciergerie prison for the final day before his actual execution. By this time, the gallows is being constructed and a large crowd of spectators has already gathered. While there, the condemned prisoner meets with his daughter, who does not recognize him in his long beard and prison rags. He is finally conveyed along the narrow streets of the Faubourg de Marceau to the place of execution, but requests one last brief reprieve to record his final impressions. These form the conclusion of the book.

The Last Day is a curious book. We learn nothing of the anonymous author's identity, except that he can read and write and that he appears to have the standing of a gentleman, given the respect with which he is treated by prison personnel. Several times during *The Last Day*, the author admits his guilt of the crime for which he has been condemned, and concedes that the justice system functioned properly in his case. In the words of an early English translation: 'My pleas will be rejected, because all was legal, the counsel pleaded well, the Judges decided carefully ... The plea [for mercy] is a cord which holds you suspended over an abyss, and which you feel giving way at each instant until it breaks! It is as if the axe of the guillotine took six weeks to fall' (Hugo 1840:59). As the excerpt shows, the focus of *The Last Day* is primarily on the condemned man's psychological state. At trial, he recoils in horror as his lawyer suggests that he might receive a sentence of hard labor for life, protesting that he would prefer death (12). 'Until that sentence of death,' the narrator recounts, 'I had felt myself breathe, palpitate, exist like other beings. Now I felt clearly that a barrier existed between me and the world. Nothing appeared to me under the same aspect as hitherto' (14). As he is led from the courtroom, the youngest of 'two young girls who gazed at me with eager eyes' says '*It will take place in six weeks!*' (15). This is the first of many images of young or innocent people being debased by the grim spectacle of punishment and execution.

After being delivered into the enormous, gloomy Bicêtre prison to await the processing of his plea, the author resolves to record his every psychological state, to impress upon the world the barbarity of the death penalty:

[W]ill there not be in this process of agonizing thought, in this ever-increasing progress of pain, in this intellectual dissection of a condemned man, more than one lesson for those who condemned? Perhaps the perusal may render them less heedless, when throwing a human life into what they call the 'scale of justice?' Perhaps they have never reflected on the slow succession of tortures conveyed in the expeditious formula of a death sentence! Have they ever paused on the important idea, that, in the man whose days they shorten, there is an immortal spirit which had calculated on life, a soul which is not prepared for death?' (24)

At one point, the condemned man witnesses the bizarre spectacle of prisoners at hard labor being marched out of their cells into a courtyard visible from his cell. They are all locked into a long iron chain, and led to a trough from which they are allowed to drink some gruel. They are also permitted a short time to themselves, to dance in a circle, chains clanking, chanting rhythmic prison ditties at the top of their lungs. After that, they are driven onto a large carriage and out of the front gate of the prison, to go to work literally as galley slaves. Soon the condemned man is visited by the prison governor, who informs him respectfully that his appeals have been denied, and the narrator follows the galley slaves out of the prison in his own customized carriage. His departure, like that of the galley slaves, is commented on by a large crowd of curious onlookers. The carriage twists through 'those old and crooked streets of the Faubourg St. Marceau and the city, which twist and cross each other like the many paths of an anthill.' (83). It is here, in the Conciergerie prison, that the prisoner will spend the very last hours before his execution. He is housed with a *friauche*, a newly condemned prisoner. The latter is an old man who has just been condemned for murder during a highway robbery, and is awaiting transfer to the death cell the narrator has just occupied. The old rogue recounts his life, which was marked by poverty, desperation and vice ever since his father, a famous thief, had received the 'hempen cravat' (87–8) when the future killer was six. The narrator is both fascinated and intimidated by the elderly criminal, who prevails upon the younger man to trade his fashionable greatcoat for the old man's dirty linen jacket. After the old man is taken away, the narrator loses his composure as the reality of his death nears, and begins reviewing desperate options for renewing his plea for mercy. After the prison chaplain attempts to minister to him once more, the condemned man feels nothing but disgust for the priest's stale, routine phrases. The condemned man instead wishes that the task of consoling those about to be executed be given instead to the nearest 'young curate':

Let them find him at his devotional studies, and, without warning, say to him: 'There is a man who is going to die, and it is reserved for you to console him. You must be there when they bind his hands; you must take a place in the fatal cart, with your crucifix, and conceal the executioner from him. You must pass with him through that horrible crowd which is thirsting for his execution; you must embrace him at the foot of the scaffold, and you must remain there until his soul has flown! (110)

The prisoner is then visited by his daughter Mary. He learns that she has been told that he is dead, and she does not even recognize him, with his long beard and soiled rags. Finally, the prisoner is transferred to the town hall, witnessing the throng gathered to watch his execution at four p.m., and finishes the last entry of his chronicle, the forty-sixth, in which he begs an official visitor on bended knee for just five minutes more to wait for a last-minute pardon. The executioner interrupts the conversation, noting that it is four o'clock and that he is responsible for carrying out the sentence in a timely manner, according to the law. The last entry ends with the prisoner hearing someone ascending the stairs to his room in the town hall.

Speculation as to the identity of the author of *The Last Day* was intense; many commentators apparently believed the slim book to be a translation of an American or English work. A history of Continental anti-death-penalty activism written by a Belgian researcher (Smets 2003:12–15) records the controversy surrounding the book, which began with Hugo's editor, Charles Gosselin, who criticized Hugo's use of underworld slang and his decision to leave out details of the main character's life and crime. Hugo defended his decision to use coarse underworld slang, calling it the 'language of misery.' The initial reviews were largely negative. Jules Janin called the book 'atrocious' and 'three hundred pages of agony': 'success can never justify, nor talent excuse – no, nothing can pardon this author's stubbornness in dissecting the soul of a man and disturbing the peace of a nation.' An anonymous reviewer praised the novelist's evident horror of capital punishment, but took issue with the 'cold solemnity' of the prose. Charles Nodier expressed respect for the 'dark and energetic' talent of Hugo, but declared he would never read the novel again, nor even 'think of it during the day, for fear of descending again into its dark night.'

In 1832, Hugo wrote a preface to a new edition of *The Last Day* (Hugo 1840:157–92) in which he acknowledged his authorship of the novel and justified its treatment of its dark subject. He confirms that *The Last Day*, which he acknowledges to be a 'slight production,' is a 'pleading, direct or indirect, for the *abolition of punishment by death*.' Hugo's argument is a forceful and brilliant attack on capital punishment in general. In one tour de force, Hugo either invokes or creates almost all the tropes of the modern European critique of capital punishment. Hugo first justifies his approach to the book: he left the biographical details of his narrator vague because the debate on capital punishment must not be considered in the light of a specific case; it is rather 'a great point of Human Right.' His plea is for the abolition of capital punishment for 'all persons, innocent or guilty, before all courts, juries or judges.' Unfortunately, history has shown that 'the scaffold is the only edifice which revolutions do not demolish,' indeed, in revolutionary times, the 'first execution' merely 'excites the sanguinary passions of the mob.' Hugo then refers to a series of recent executions which turned into unseemly spectacles: a faulty guillotine that refused to kill the victim, forcing the executioner to 'slowly cut through the neck with a knife' or a case from Dijon which involved 'a woman (a woman!) This time again, the axe of the guillotine failed of its effect, and the head was not quite detached. Then the executioner's servants pulled the feet of the woman; amidst the yells of the populace, thus finished the law!' Even orderly executions corrupt the public, either directly or through the scandal sheets that are distributed before every execution, in which 'the crime of a hapless fellow-creature, its punishment, his torture, his agony' is exploited for financial gain.

Finally, Hugo addresses the most common arguments in favor of capital punishment. Removing a dangerous person from the community can be achieved by 'perpetual imprisonment.' The need for punishment and vengeance is also insufficient: '*vengeance* is an individual act, and *punishment* belongs to God. Society is between the two: punishment is above its power, retaliation beneath it.' As for the need to make an example of wrongdoers, Hugo denies any edifying effect. It is far more common to see crowds turned brutal or callous by executions. One recent example: 'At St. Pol, immediately after the execution of an incendiary named Louis Camus, *a group of masquer-aders came and danced around the still reeking scaffold!*' Executions can never be just, no matter what the situation of the offender. If 'the man you destroy is without family, relations, or friends, in the world … [Y]ou make him pay the penalty of the isolated position in which you left him! You make a crime of his misfortune!' On the other hand, if you execute someone who has a family, you inflict a terrible blow, both emotional and financial, on the surviving relatives. Finally, Hugo invokes the march of civilization:

> During the past century, punishments have become gradually milder: the rack has disappeared, the wheel has disappeared; and now the guillotine is shaken. This mistaken punishment will leave France; and it may go to some barbarous people – not to Turkey, which is becoming civilized, not to the savages, for they will not have it, but let it descend some steps of the ladder of civilization, and take refuge in Spain, or Russia! (ibid.:190)

'Civilization,' continues Hugo, 'is nothing but a series of transformations.' Eventually, he concludes, 'the gentle laws of Christ will penetrate at last' into the legal system, and '[w]e shall look on crime as a disease, and its physicians shall displace the judges, its hospitals displace the galleys.'

Hugo's 1829 novel and 1832 foreword are vital to understanding modern European anti-death-penalty activism, because they either originate or anticipate tropes that dominate European advocacy against capital punishment to this day. First, the approach is dramatic and subjective, as befits a Romantic author. The condemned prisoner is not presented as a victim of misfortune, target of rehabilitation, or as a variable in a utilitarian calculation of interests. Instead, he is presented as an individual, worthwhile human being whose fate and whose thoughts are worthy of our attention. The internal experience of the condemned man is the only theme of the novel, and we are asked to contemplate the idea that capital punishment must be ended *primarily* because it is psychological torture for condemned persons such as the narrator. Hugo's critique also anticipates other characteristics of abolitionist discourse:

- The critique of capital punishment is apodictic and deontological – it sounds less like a man relaying his opinion than a prophet revealing a great truth. In the foreground is the individual human being who is to be executed, and it is this person's human dignity that requires the categorical abolition of capital punishment. Pragmatic questions of cost, deterrence or miscarriages of justice, if they are mentioned at all, are treated as secondary.

- The innocence or guilt of the inmate is unimportant. Hugo here draws on – and helps develop – the idea of human dignity as an inalienable attribute of each human life. It must be respected by the state, and is not diminished by the offender's guilt of a crime, no matter how severe. This conception of human dignity still drives much European human-rights discourse, and helps explain one of the key cultural differences between Europe and America, where abstract notions of human dignity play a much less prominent role in legal reasoning, and in which it is widely accepted that an offender who has been found guilty of a crime can be stripped of many important rights.
- Waiting for execution is itself a type of keen psychological torture. Indeed, it is mostly the anguish and horror experienced while waiting for execution that insult human dignity in a way incompatible with civilized values.
- The march of progress and civilization, which has gradually eliminated many other torturous forms of punishment, will eliminate this one as well.

As will be discussed further in Chapter 7, all of Hugo's tropes continue, to this day, to flourish in European discourse against the death penalty. For example, the decision of the European Court of Human Rights in *Soering* v. *United Kingdom*, which denied the American state of Virginia's request to extradite a German national to face a potentially capital trial in that state, cited the 'the anguish and mounting tension of living in the ever-present shadow of death' (1989: par. 106) as the kind of 'inhuman and degrading treatment' prohibited by Article 3 of the European Convention on Human Rights.

To Hugo, opposition to capital punishment is a mark of societal and personal civilization. He explicitly ranks countries in terms of their degree of civilization as shown in their attitude toward the death penalty. People can be ranked in a similar way. Hugo's foreword to *The Last Day* is aimed at one class of citizens: educated believers in progress, who can be made to recognize that capital punishment is a 'barbarous' institution that must be abandoned in the name of 'civilization.' The ignorant masses, by contrast, are portrayed as manipulable (their 'sanguinary passions' are easily aroused) and corruptible. It should be kept in mind that when Hugo was writing *The Last Day*, France was a largely illiterate country, still only in the first steps of a process of education reform and urbanization that would fundamentally transform the society. Interpersonal violence in French society dropped steadily throughout France in the 19th century, and the rate of illiteracy, as measured by the number of brides and grooms who could write their names on their marriage registrations, 'declined from almost 50% in the middle of the 19th century to near zero at the beginning of World War I' (Gillis 1994). In *The Last Day*, the crowds which press around the narrator's carriage as he is transferred to the place of execution are portrayed alternately as threatening and gleeful. There is no suggestion that witnessing an execution will be in any way edifying. As Hugo shows in the novel and argues in the foreword, the crowds who gather to witness executions are largely sensation seekers. Deprived of education and consigned to a life of meager scraping, they have no overarching moral framework in which to fit the event. Executions are many things to Hugo, but one of them is clearly an illustration of the chasm in sensibility between persons of refinement and the masses. Members of the former group, such as the narrator and the priest, understand an execution to be a grave and awful event. They may have differing opinions on the issue of capital punishment, but they at least understand that it is a serious business, worthy of the most profound reflection. The masses, on the other hand, treat it as little more than a jolly, gruesome spectacle. Every execution brings us face-to-face not only with the horror of state homicide, but also the depraved callousness of the lower orders.

This dichotomy in sensibilities is also present in the novel itself. To narrow the distance between the narrator and the reader, Hugo uses the first-person voice: '[O]ne belonging moreover to a being not born to crime, poverty or ignorance ... [T]he condemned man's deviant exterior mask[s] a nature quite compatible with the bourgeois norm' (Grossman 1986:126). Hugo excites the sympathies of his educated readers by creating a character with whom they themselves could sympathize. Ordinary criminals, by contrast, are depicted as accepting their sentences fatalistically, even gaily. They use coarse underworld slang such as a 'hempen cravat' or 'marrying the widow' to refer to the execution of death sentences, and circulate macabre stories about former inmates who went to their deaths with particular stoicism or panache. This horrifies the narrator, who also registers shock and humiliation at the fate he shares with the convicts: the crazed dancing of the chain gang in the Bicêtre prison courtyard evokes '[t]he deepest pity,' but the sudden recognition that the prisoners are pointing at him and calling him 'comrade' deeply horrifies him: 'I cannot describe what passed within me. I was indeed their *"comrade"*! The Scaffold is sister to the Galleys. Nay, I was even lower than they were; the Convicts had done me an honour. I shuddered: yes! their *"comrade"'* (Hugo 1840:51). The bizarre sight of the chained prisoners dancing rounds, as well as the prisoners' 'phrases of disgusting cordiality' provoke a nightmarish vision that lands the narrator in the prison infirmary.

Despite the early negative reaction among Parisian critics, *The Last Day* gradually established itself as a classic of abolitionist literature. Hugo used his increasing public fame to attack capital punishment. In 1841 he was named to the French nobility, and became a member of the *Chambre des pairs* (Chamber of Peers), an assembly which had been abolished during the 1789 Revolution but was then reinstated under the July Monarchy of Louis-Philippe. When the *Chambre des pairs* was again abolished during the Revolution of 1848, Hugo ran for a position in the newly created Constituent Assembly and was elected as a Republican delegate from Paris. His political oratory, which had been relatively moderate in 'tone and ideas' in the *Chamber des pairs* (Stein 2007), grew more adventurous amid the political turmoil of France's 1848 revolution, which saw the proclamation of the short-lived Second Republic and finally culminated in the coup by Louis-Napoléon Bonaparte in December of 1851.

On September 15 1848, *le citoyen* Hugo delivered a short but famous oration on the occasion of a bill to abolish capital punishment for political crimes. He promised to speak 'few words,' but to speak from a 'long-standing and profound conviction.' What is the death penalty? he asked rhetorically: 'The death penalty is the eternal and particular sign of barbarism. (Sensation). Everywhere the death penalty flourishes, barbarism dominates; everywhere the death penalty is rare, civilization reigns.' The 18th century saw the abolition of torture, the 19th will see, Hugo predicted, the abolition of capital punishment. Three things belong to God alone: the 'irrevocable, the irreparable, and the indissoluble.' If they are introduced into the laws, they will, sooner or later, compromise (*faire plier*) society as a whole. The assembly had recently voted to bring down the throne – now it only remains to bring down the scaffold as well. Hugo concluded: 'I vote for the pure, simple, and definitive abolition of the death penalty.'

Hugo's many political engagements turned him into one of the most outstanding examples of the public intellectual in French history. He even secured a place in the *Dictionary of Accepted Ideas*, a compendium of platitudes assembled by Gustave Flaubert in the 1870s: 'Hugo, Victor: "Made a sad mistake, really, when he entered politics"' (Flaubert 1954:49). Hugo continued his activism even after being forced into exile – first on the isle of Jersey, and then on Guernsey – in the mid-1850s. While living on Guernsey, he intervened with the English Home Secretary, Lord Palmerston, to try to secure a pardon for John Charles Tapner, who, on February 10 1854, became the last person to be executed on that island. In a letter to a Swiss pastor in 1862, Hugo took credit for the fact that one of the addresses he had written to try to save Tapner had induced the government of Canada to spare a condemned prisoner named Julien. His letter, asserted Hugo, 'did not save (if you will permit the expression) its intended beneficiary, Tapner, but Julien, who was unknown to me. Why do I mention this? Because it proves the necessity of persisting.' In 1871, Hugo wrote to the attorney for a condemned Communard:

> When it comes to judging an enemy, we must guard ourselves against the furious urgings of the mob and against praise from our own party; let us

examine the state of rage all around us, which is a form of madness, let us not be pushed, even to severities which we ourselves wish, but rather fear the accession to public rage. (Prévost 2002:57)

Hugo monitored developments in the worldwide abolitionist struggle and kept up a vigorous correspondence with foreign journalists and lawmakers on the death penalty until his death in 1885.

Hugo is an important innovator in the modern European anti-death-penalty movement for several reasons. First, he framed the issue of the death penalty as a stand-alone topic. Beccaria and other thinkers had embedded their opposition to capital punishment within an ambitious framework of overall penal reform. Hugo, while not ignoring other aspects of criminal justice reform (especially prison conditions), did not propose a comprehensive reform of criminal justice, for two reasons. First, he lacked the legal training to credibly address a criminal justice system that had become much more technically complex since the days of Voltaire and Beccaria. More importantly, though, Hugo valued his position as an outsider to the legal system, using it to critique the legal system's collective cowardice in refusing to unflinchingly face the punishments it sanctioned: 'Hugo, the authentic man of letters, revolts against their double abuse by those who confound justice with the letter of the law. Behind lovely legalistic eloquence lies the ugly reality of man's inhumanity to man.' (Grossman 1986:123). Hugo senses the need to extract the debate over capital punishment from the complex, many-layered discussions on penal reform – where law professors and practitioners can obscure moral imperatives in a numbing fog of legalese – and proclaim it to be an issue that transcends legal categories. Abolishing capital punishment is not a legal reform, but a critical phase in the evolution of civilization.

Closely related to the isolation of capital punishment as an independent issue is the primacy of the condemned's personal, subjective experience, as he waits for his execution. We see here the late-18th-century revolution in subjectivity identified by Charles Taylor. As Taylor puts it, before the late 18th century, 'the background that explained what people recognized as important to themselves was to a great extent determined by their place in society, and whatever roles or activities attached to this position.' Gradually, under the influence of Enlightenment thinkers such as Rousseau and Herder, a new form of inwardness develops, in which people come to think of themselves having inner depths. The 'new idea' that the late 18th century brought with it, argues Taylor, is that there is 'a certain way of being human that is *my* way,' and that one of the purposes of life is to live out that way of life as authentically as possible (Taylor 1994:30, 31). It is precisely this innovation which Hugo uses to build a universalistic case against the death penalty: this practice must be opposed primarily because it subjects a unique individual with human dignity to stretches of intense fear and anguish, before finally ending his existence. It is wrong because it reduces a man to an object, and mocks the sanctity of human life.

This critique of capital punishment, couched in the language of subjective human experience and universal human rights, conferred several strategic advantages on abolitionists. First, it renders the normal frameworks of legal and political debate obsolete, and thus cannot be refuted in any meaningful sense. For the same reason, the argument firmly grounds a claim for 'pure, simple and definitive' abolition regardless of the nature of the crime or evidence of guilt. It also applies with undiminished force in all cultural or legal contexts. The argument meshes with Christian and natural-law conceptions of human dignity, allowing death penalty opponents to urge Christian groups to embrace abolitionism from within a shared discourse. Finally, it provides a compelling justification for ignoring the will of the majority. If all executions are inherently and intrinsically evil, then opposition to capital punishment is a non-negotiable moral imperative that cannot be made dependent on the whims of public opinion. Of course, Hugo did not invent this critique of capital punishment. But his forceful advocacy of the issue, sustained during a long and storied life, planted it deeply in European discourse about capital punishment:

> Before him, Beccaria, Condorcet, Le Pelletier Saint-Fargeau, Robespierre, during the Revolution; and Lucas, under the Restauration, denounced the death penalty as useless. But they appealed more to reason than to emotion. Victor Hugo aimed at the heart. He was the first to place the condemned man at the center of the debate. He brought to life the agony of waiting that precedes the agony of execution. The writer employs these descriptions to trump the philosophers and jurists. One cannot topple the scaffold with arguments but with words which give birth to images and emotions. Hugo, the novelist and poet, puts the reader in the place of the condemned man. (Robert Badinter, in Prévost 2002:58)

Radicals and Retrenchment: The Second Half of the Nineteenth Century

Of course, Hugo was not the only abolitionist in 19th-century France. By the mid-19th century, abolition of capital punishment had emerged as an important political theme among the educated bourgeoisie. The Belleville Manifesto of 1869, drafted by Republican radical politicians and social reformers, envisaged a broad series of reforms of French society to realize the values of 1789, and to propagate the model of French civilization abroad. Among other reforms, the program's 17 articles advocated secular, free, and compulsory primary education; universal suffrage; an expansion of civil liberties; and full separation of church and state (Simpson and Jones

2000:282). The Republicans also endorsed a host of reforms to the legal system, including the election of magistrates to temporary terms, the expansion of the institution of the jury, the revision of legal codes in a more egalitarian and democratic direction, and the abolition of the death penalty. Julie le Quang Sang, the leading authority on the historical debate over the death penalty in France, summarizes the support base and outlook of the French Radicals:

> [T]he party was preferred by the petty and middle-class bourgeoisie, the liberal professions, and, in particular, lawyers, who again carried the torch of abolition in 1906. In the 1870s, the proclamation of the [Third] Republic was associated with a considerable movement of legal professionals into the political sphere. The influence of lawyers was considerable throughout the regime, but became predominant during the Radical Republic. On the strength of a specific professional ideology, they left their mark on the great foundational laws of the 1880s. As a vector of progress and social development, the law, more than ever, constituted an instrument of social regulation, in the service of those in power. Political leadership in social and economic conflicts operated increasingly on the basis of legal dogma, practices, and techniques. (Le Quang Sang 2001:37)

After decades of complex maneuvering and internecine strife, the Radical political tendency in France took its modern shape with the party's official founding as a national political party in 1901, as the 'Radical, Republican and Radical-Socialist Party.' The Radicals emerged as the most powerful force in the legislative elections of 1902. The leading role of the Radical Party in successive French governments leads many historians to call the era of Radical Party dominance during the early 20th century the 'Radical Republic.' In January of 1906, Armand Fallières, a Radical lawyer and statesman and member of the Radical Party, was elected President of France. A committed opponent of capital punishment, Fallières proceeded to commute all of the death sentences handed down by French courts during the first years of his presidency. In the meantime, the Radical Party built the groundwork for legislative proposals to abolish capital punishment.

The abolition proposal, however, met resistance from several quarters. Retentionists organized a protest campaign from the *jurys* – citizen consultative bodies which assisted French judges in deciding guilt and punishment. The institution of the jury had been introduced into French criminal law in 1791, and was preserved in the *Code pénal* of 1810 and *Code d'instruction criminelle* of 1808, both of which were developed under Napoleonic influence. Criminal acts were separated into three categories in order of increasing severity: *contravention, délit,* and *crime*. Defendants charged with a *crime* would be tried by a panel of three professional judges and a larger number of *jurés* (from the French word for swearing an oath, *jurer*) generally twelve in number. Throughout the 19th century, the French jury was a hotly contested political terrain (Donovan 1999). Forces on the Left sought to increase the chance for less-educated and non-property-owning classes to serve on juries. The Right, while generally stopping short of calling for the abolition of *jurys*, sought revisions to ensure that respectable bourgeois property owners – the *notables* – would dominate juries. Thus, during the 19th century, the composition of French juries and the rules governing them (such as how many votes were needed to convict) changed with the political winds. The propertied classes' concerns were not misplaced – one recent study showed that French juries, during the more liberal periods, acquitted surprisingly large numbers of defendants (ibid.: 383–5).

In the early 20th century, the pendulum had swung back into the favor of the upper bourgeoisie, who again formed the majority of the standing *jurys* and who opposed many of the Radicals' legislative initiatives, including the strict 1905 law mandating *laïcisme*, the complete separation of church and state. Together, the magistracy and the *jurys* launched a campaign of public protest against President Fallières' policy of granting amnesty to death-sentenced prisoners (including Albert Soleilland, whose condemnation to death for sexually assaulting and murdering the young daughter of one of his neighbors in 1907 became a massive media sensation), and more generally against the Radicals' plan to abolish capital punishment. To the *jurés*, the President's pardon policy amounted to an unauthorized usurpation of their privileges by a public figure remote from the daily realities of life in the districts where they rendered justice. They submitted petitions to the Ministry of Justice protesting the perceived *laxisme* of Radical criminal justice policies. One petition, submitted by the *jury* of the Seine and published in the French newspaper *le Matin*, read as follows:

The undersigned members of the jury
Convinced that the interests of society require the energetic and continuous repression of serious crimes;
Further convinced that the penalty of death – among all penalties provided for in the Penal Code – is the only one which can sufficiently intimidate hardened criminals, and, by its exemplary character, effectively combat the increase in the number of murders;
Hereby solemnly request:
1st: That the penalty of death be allowed to remain in force;
2nd: That it continue to be executed. (Le Quang Sang 2002:para. 12, quoting *Le Matin*, May 16 1907)

Throughout 1907 and 1908, petitions from juries across France continued to trickle in to the Justice Ministry, generating a continuous stream of news reports.

Another retentionist tactic used in the run-up to the 1908 debates on the Radicals' plans to abolish capital punishment was the 'artistic contest' organized by the *Petit Parisien*, a right-wing tabloid which had loudly declaimed President Fallières' pardon of the child-murderer Soleilland as a sign of the feeble state response to the increasingly depraved nature of modern criminality. The *Parisien* organized a popular 'referendum' on capital punishment which it styled as an 'artistic contest.' Readers from France and beyond were to send postcards to the *Parisien's* editorial offices with *oui* or *non* written on them (in response to the question whether the death penalty should be abolished). The most attractive postcards would win the contest – provided that their answer conformed to the overall majority. Given the rules of the contest and the nature of the *Parisien's* readership, the results were a foregone conclusion: retentionists prevailed 3 to 1. One commentator referred to the referendum as a 'naked promotional stunt' hatched by a 'mass press second to none in sensationalism and sheer cynical pandering to fears, particularly those of urban life' (Nye 2003:214, 216).

The debate on abolition took place over the course of five parliamentary sessions in 1908. Prime Minister Georges Clemenceau declared the issue a vote of conscience. The arguments ran along traditional lines, the only new aspect being occasional references to the then-young disciplines of criminal physiognomy and eugenics. Another novel aspect of the French debates was the background influence of public sentiment. None would argue that the *Petit Parisien's* 'artistic contest' was a reliable gauge of public opinion by modern standards. However, for the first time, it attached a set of numbers to the general impression that the majority of ordinary citizens favored the retention of capital punishment. The survey's results were not directly mentioned in official debates on the floor of the assembly, which were elevated in tone and focused on classic death penalty arguments such as deterrence. However, it seems likely that the *Petit Parisien's* contest bolstered retentionists' confidence that, no matter what their other motives for voting to preserve capital punishment, they were also likely to be respecting the public's will by doing so:

> The debates culminated in a December 1908 vote which brought resounding defeat for abolition. The mass press reacted with huge satisfaction. Even 'Father Pardon' Fallières got the message, refusing clemency in two gruesome cases at the end of the year, and heads fell for the first time since 1905. No serious effort to end the death penalty reappeared until the Fifth Republic. (Nye 2003:221)

As Nye notes, the death penalty subsided as a prominent issue after the abolitionists' resounding 1908 defeat. Executions continued to be carried out in public in France until the late date of 1939, when the behavior of the crowd at the execution of Eugen Weidmann was so boisterous that it caused a national scandal. The execution was secretly filmed from a nearby apartment. We see the guillotine from the rear. Weidmann, wearing a white shirt, is quickly tied down, the blade falls, and his headless body flops from the tilted table into the open basket placed to the right of the machine. President Albert Lebrun immediately issued an order banning public executions, which continued in private until the last execution in 1977. Judicial executions for non-military crimes were (perhaps surprisingly) infrequent under the Vichy regime, although Pétain rejected clemency for all of the 50 or so persons condemned to death by the civil justice system, many for violations of strict rationing and anti-black-market laws. Of course, the deportations of French Jews and the executions of real or suspected members of the Resistance greatly increased the human toll of the war. After World War II, there was a general legislative housecleaning intended to rid the French statute books of laws passed under the influence of the occupation and division of France. Law Number 46-2141 of October 4 1946, retained the death penalty as part of France's post-war legal order. After World War II, executions gradually became more and more infrequent, but a serious push to end capital punishment once and for all would have to wait until the 1970s.

The Final Push To Abolition

The last, successful phase of the abolition movement in France was prefigured by Albert Camus' 'Reflections on the Guillotine,' first published in 1957 (Camus 1960). While editor of the influential Resistance journal *Le Combat*, Camus had supported the execution of high-ranking collaborators, editorializing against calls for mercy from the Left-Catholic novelist and journalist François Mauriac (who would win the Nobel Prize in 1952). Shortly after the liberation of France, however, Camus signed clemency petitions for collaborationist writers such as Robert Brasillach, although Camus maintained that his support for clemency stemmed solely from principle, and should not be interpreted as any form of forgiveness. Finally, in 1948, Camus held a speech at a Dominican convent in Latour-Maubourg in which he told the audience that he had changed his mind and come to recognize that Mauriac had been right all along (Bloch-Michel 2002:247–8). From that point on, Camus became a convinced abolitionist, and, as Hugo had before him, publicly intervened to request clemency on behalf of death-sentenced prisoners in France and elsewhere.

Camus' abolitionist activity culminated in *Reflections* (1960) which gained even greater influence given the fact that it was originally published in 1957, the same year Camus won the Nobel Prize. Camus begins with a personal story: his father once witnessed the execution of an Algerian who had murdered several members of a family. Although Camus' father, a 'simple, straightforward man' had abstractly supported capital punishment until that time, the actual sight of an execution made him literally sick – he returned home and vomited. Camus rehearses familiar arguments for abolition: its failure to deter crime; the physical horror of executions by the guillotine; the fact that executions devalue human life; and society's guilty conscience about the practice, demonstrated by the secrecy with which it is carried out. Camus disclaims sentimental humanitarianism, and leaves religious arguments to one side. While avoiding any attempts to whitewash the guilt of those who have committed savage crimes, echoing Hugo (and citing Dostoevsky) Camus notes that the state, through its legal processes, inflicts a punishment worse than execution, by inflicting an agonizing delay between pronouncement and execution of sentence:

> As the weeks pass, hope and despair increase and become equally unbearable. According to all accounts, the color of the skin changes, fear acting like an acid ... Long in advance the condemned man knows that he is going to be killed and that the only thing that can save him is a reprieve, rather similar, for him, to the decrees of heaven. In any case, he cannot intervene, make a plea himself, or convince. He is no longer a man but a thing waiting to be handled by the executioners. He is kept as if he were inert matter, but he still has a consciousness which is his chief enemy. (ibid.:200–1)

Camus also invokes France's sordid recent history. If any society has the requisite moral purity to carry out an irrevocable, 'perfect' punishment, Camus intones, it is surely not France. The past 20 years, Camus observes, have shown that it is governments themselves, rather than individuals, who present the greatest threat to human life.

Arthur Koestler, another European public intellectual joined Camus in making abolition one of his signature issues. Koestler, a former Communist whose novel *Darkness at Noon* had propelled him to world fame, had lived in Britain since the late 1940s. In 1955 he had started a national campaign to abolish capital punishment in England, and began a series of essays for the *Observer* that were later collected into the anti-death-penalty polemic *Reflections on Hanging*. In *Reflections*, Koestler (1957) denounced the British institution of hanging with the rhetorical eagerness associated with Continental – but not necessarily English – political discourse. In France, Camus' essay was published alongside a French translation of Koestler's. Jean Bloch-Michel also added a preface and a historical study on capital punishment in France. As we will see later in Chapter 7, Camus' and Koestler's anti-death-penalty polemics both indicated and fostered a growing anti-death-penalty consensus among center-left intellectuals in developed Western countries.

As influential as Camus' essay was, Camus was, unlike Hugo, unwilling to seek office, and his life was cut short by an automobile accident in 1960.

Nevertheless, the French population, like its German and American counterparts, gradually turned against capital punishment as the 1960s progressed, dropping to 33% support in 1969, after the exit of Charles de Gaulle from the French political stage (Costa 2001:160). As in the United States, though, dwindling public support for capital punishment in the 1960s did not end in its final renunciation, only in its increasingly sparing use. As noted above, throughout the 1960s and 1970s, executions were rare events in France (averaging less than one per year), and were outnumbered by pardons. When the system was moved to condemn a criminal (at least on the French mainland) the crime was usually against a child victim and often had sexual overtones. The defendant was unsympathetic, and his guilt (all executions from 1958 to the end of capital punishment in 1981 were of males) not in doubt. The death penalty was stabilized; no sympathetic defendant or case of innocence emerged to provide a focus for anti-death-penalty forces. Abolition of the death penalty was not going to be propelled to the center stage of French political discourse on its own; it would have to be pushed there by someone.

That someone was Robert Badinter. Badinter, born in 1928, received his legal training at the University of Paris and was called to the Bar in 1951. He obtained a doctorate with a dissertation on American conflict-of-laws principles in 1952, and in 1965, obtained the *agrégation en droit*, a qualification permitting the holder to occupy chairs at French law faculties. As is often the case within the French legal academy, his professorship left him a great deal of time for ordinary legal practice. After initially establishing his career in complex civil litigation, Badinter was persuaded, in the early 1970s, to take over the defense in the case of Roger Bontems. During an attempt to escape from Clairvaux prison, Bontems assisted another prisoner, Claude Buffet, in taking two prisoners, a nurse and a guard, as hostages. During the siege, Buffet killed both of the hostages. Buffet and Bontems were each charged with murder, even though Buffet, the acknowledged mastermind, himself took exclusive credit for the killings in letters sent from prison. Both men were convicted. Bontems' appeals were rejected, and he and Buffet were both executed on November 29, 1972. Badinter accompanied his client until the last moment, when Bontems was led into the prison courtyard, and described the last moments in *L'exécution*, an absorbing account of his involvement in the case (Badinter 1973:218–19). Badinter was outraged that someone could be executed even though it was clear he had never killed anyone. From that moment on, he resolved to work for the abolition of capital punishment. In Badinter, the French anti-death-penalty movement found an ideal exponent. By the mid-1970s, his eloquence and rhetorical skill were already legendary. Throughout the 1970s, Badinter increased his profile by winning life sentences in several French cases in which the prosecutor had sought the death penalty.

In actively crusading against the death penalty, Badinter was swimming against an ever-stronger tide. In the mid-1970s, France's press highlighted a series of brutal crimes against children and the elderly, dramatically increasing the public's fear of crime. In France, a criminal case that attracts considerable press coverage becomes known as an *affaire*, and mid-1970s France saw one *affaire* after another: *l'affaire* Ranucci, *l'affaire* Carrein, and so forth. The most notorious of these cases, however, was *l'affaire* Patrick Henry. Henry, a married computer programmer who had gotten into financial difficulty, abducted 8-year-old Philippe Bertrand in Troyes on February 4 1976 and demanded a ransom from Bertrand's well-to-do parents. Henry, whose precarious financial situation was well-known and who had social contacts with the Bertrands, immediately fell under the suspicion of the police and was questioned several times. Each time he denied his guilt and, in interviews with curious journalists, deplored the crime. A few days into the abduction, for instance, Henry told journalists from the Europe 1 radio station: 'It's really despicable to target children. I hope they can find the child alive and certainly that they arrest his kidnapers ... I myself would be for the death penalty in this case. No one has the right to endanger the life of a child' (Badinter 2000:40, quoting an interview printed in *L'Aurore* on February 18 1976). For weeks, French television broadcast the Bertrands' desperate pleas. Sensing that his chances of receiving any ransom had become vanishingly small in light of the press and police attention on the case, Henry strangled Philippe Bertrand to death in a small studio which he had rented to confine the little boy. Shortly thereafter, the police found out about the studio from a local bar owner, and accosted Henry as he tried to enter it. Henry calmly informed the officers that Bertrand's body was hidden under the bed.

The Henry case inspired an avalanche of press coverage that made it the French equivalent of the Manson Family murders or the Moors murders. The callousness of Henry's crime, coupled with his lack of remorse or apparent mental illness, transformed him into a symbol of what the French tabloid and right-wing press saw as the continuing collapse of French morals in the permissive 1970s. *Le Monde* thundered in 1976:

For ten years, the people in this country whose task it is to educate, to command, and to punish have failed in their mission. The result is Patrick Henry and all the others, from the 'punks' of the suburbs to the murderers, not to mention the sexual obsessives. The guilty ones are you, you parents who are too busy to pay attention to your children, or who have renounced the exercise of your authority for fear of traumatizing the dear little ones. And you, terrified teachers, who have quit teaching in order to organize 'free discussions' with illiterate youngsters ... One thing is sure: periods of rot and decay are always terminated by the advent of iron-fisted rule. (Le Quang Sang 2001:124, quoting from *Le Monde* February 23 1976)

Henry's trial was one of the largest media sensations France had ever seen, and Badinter was drawn into it. By the mid-1970s, Badinter was so closely identified with the abolitionist cause that he had earned the informal nickname *Monsieur Abolition*. He received a call from M. Boucquillon, Henry's principal lawyer, asking him to assist in Henry's defense. Although wary of the strong passions the case had already unleashed, Badinter accepted, reasoning that if he could save Henry from the death penalty, he would demonstrate that the law could spare even the most odious criminal. To prepare for the defense, Badinter met Henry in prison:

> With Henry, the most atrocious crime was clothed in the most ordinary traits. The criminal could have been our neighbor, our colleague from work or sport, a man like us. This seems to have driven the public opinion to even greater excesses of hate. In reading certain newspapers, I was reminded of the fury of anathemas and death which drove the witch-hunts of former days. The witches had also been features of the ordinary life of the villages back then. Nevertheless, [as normal as his exterior was,] it was impossible to exclude the possibility of a gravely altered personality, a profound psychosis, or a dangerous neuropathy hidden under the peaceful exterior of an ordinary man. (Badinter 2000:59)

Badinter elicited somewhat ambiguous testimony from psychiatric experts, but delivered a mesmerizing plea for the defense. The *jury*, composed of three magistrates and nine lay judges, sentenced Henry to life in prison.

The jury's decision to spare Henry provoked widespread outrage. One tabloid declared it a 'license to kill' (Costa 2001:161), and Badinter was inundated with death threats. France experienced a rise in criminality of all kinds throughout the 1970s – a development that (along with broader social transformations) drove public sentiment strongly in favor of capital punishment. Badinter attempted throughout the 1970s to counteract this trend with tireless speaking engagements and editorial interventions against capital punishment. However, he soon determined that chances of changing public opinion on capital punishment were minimal. He describes the lessons he learned from speaking to civic groups about the death penalty:

> The settings were modest, classrooms or meeting halls with metal chairs lined up in front of a conference table, the attendance most often sparse. The sessions would unfold with little variation. The same arguments provoked the same questions that called for the same answers. Often, supporters of the death penalty questioned me with an air of indignation, sometimes bordering on insults. From their perspective, abolitionists were taking the side of the murderers over their victims. In the fervor that drove these advocates of the death penalty, they wanted quick and

summary justice, a kind of permanent Reign of Terror where the guillotine operated without appeal and without delay. To hear them, I realized that it was there, in that obsession with the ritual of death, that lay the core of the irrationality that made abolition so difficult.

In vain, I tried to establish, with the support of various international studies, that wherever the death penalty was abolished there was no rise in violent crime, that it continued along at the same pace, indifferent to the presence or the absence of capital punishment in the criminal code. Yet in the eyes of its most ferocious supporters, it was of little importance that the cruelest types of crime didn't proliferate with the abolition of the death penalty. What they wanted was for murderers to pay for their crimes with their lives. To rally people to their cause, they lent to the death penalty a dissuasive virtue it did not actually have. To all the arguments that a person could reform, that there was the risk of judicial error, that the lottery of criminal court meant a man's life depended on a thousand imponderable factors, to all the moral, historical, scientific, and political considerations, the supporters of the death penalty had one constant response: the criminals must die because death is the only suitable punishment for such crimes. (Badinter 2008:14)

Badinter, unsurprisingly, sensed efforts to build a grass-roots movement against capital punishment had little prospect of success.

The growing cynicism and anger of the French debate over capital punishment at this time was captured in a number of books, including *La Peine de Mort en Question* (The Question of the Death Penalty) by journalist Jean Toulat (1977). Toulat dedicated the book to Patrick Henry's victim: 'To little Philippe Bertrand, who now sees all things in the light of God.' In the first chapter, Toulat interviewed prominent French supporters of capital punishment, including Yves Taron, who formed the Association for the Defense of Children and the Application of the Death Penalty in 1965, shortly after his young son Luc had been murdered. The name of the association was later changed to National League against Crime and for the Application of the Death Penalty. According to Taron, his league had 25,000 members in 1976, and received over 3,000 letters of support after a December 1976 television broadcast which profiled the association. The letters included such sentiments as 'Stop the delusions (*élucubrations*) of all the cretins who think the death penalty doesn't stop crime,' and 'We've had enough of these whining monsters who oppose capital punishment.' Taron's own views reflected an intense distrust of the French criminal justice system:

People talk about life sentences (*réclusion perpetuelle*) but that's nothing but folklore. There's no longer any such thing as punishment or, for that matter, life sentences. There's nothing but prisons, where someone who has killed enjoys the same regime as someone who stole a loaf of bread. And after 12 or 15 years, all the criminals are on the streets again; the death-sentenced prisoner who is granted clemency automatically sees his penalty reduced to 20 years. And then you have further reductions in prison time for good conduct, or good grades ... In brief, you cannot show me a single prisoner condemned to life who has actually died in prison. (Toulat 1977:13)

Toulat also interviewed writers, journalists, professors, a former Justice Minister, and several generals, all of whom declared themselves in favor of capital punishment. Many decried the *laxisme* of the justice system; nearly all invoked the Patrick Henry case as a prototypical example of a crime that should have been punished by death.

At the end of the chapter, Toulat noted a recent song by Michel Sardou, one of France's most popular singers: 'The popular indignation expresses itself in a song, *Je suis pour* (I am in favor), which thousands of Parisians came to applaud at the Olympia [Theatre] in Paris in October 1976.' The song, the lyrics of which Toulat reprints in their entirety, is a hymn of vengeance sung by a father whose son has been murdered. Above a funky start–stop beat, and accompanied by strings and backup singers, Sardou announces to the killer that nobody – not the obedient jury members, not the Christians, not the 'idiotic' philosophers, not the 'humane' and 'informed' people who 'have the time to exist' – will be able to save him from the father's vengeance. At the end of each stanza, the father threatens the murderer 'I'll have your hide' and once even 'I'll put your head on a pole' (Toulat 1977:24).

The death penalty's growing popularity raised a number of strategic problems for abolitionists. One was a legal reform that seemed likely to produce more death sentences: previously, the lists from which lay jurors were selected were composed by municipal authorities, who tended to select better educated members of the population to sit on the *cours d'assises*, the French courts which have jurisdiction over the most serious crimes. According to Article 18 of *Loi No.* 78-888, passed unanimously by the Assembly on July 28 1978, Article 266 of the French Code of Criminal Procedure was altered so that jury lists would henceforth be composed by random drawings of names from a master list containing the names of all registered voters. The law concerned Badinter. Although he disclaimed (2000:215–16) any notion that he wanted to return to 19th century juries of *notables*, who were disposed to defend 'order and property at any price,' he observed, however, that under the previous law, a 'discreet selection' took place with regard to the 'session lists' which, resulted in juries containing 'a large proportion of members of the liberal professions, civil servants, and managers.' In these circles, Badinter reasoned, 'the cultural level is superior to that of the average population,' and therefore 'the number of abolition supporters, and supporters of moderate penal sanctions, is higher.' Badinter acknowledged that the reform, which formed juries by simple random selection from voting lists, was 'more respectful of democratic principles,' but feared that participation of more average people in the sentencing process would lead to more death penalties.

Among French legal elites, however, the momentum in favor of abolition was steadily gaining ground. One left-wing judges' union, the *Syndicat de la magistrature*, voted during its ninth general congress in 1976 that the death penalty 'must disappear from the French penal system' by a margin of 228 to 9, with 10 abstentions (Le Quang Sang 2001:167). The mid-1970s in France also saw the creation of several influential law-reform committees. The Commission for the Study of Violence, Criminality, and Delinquency, composed of civil servants and experts in law, psychology, sociology and urban design, was chartered on April 20 1976 and put under the leadership of Alain Peyrefitte, a center-right lawyer and politician who would be named Justice Minister in March 1977. Recommendation 103 of the Commission's report called for the abolition of the death penalty and its replacement with a long, mandatory prison sentence for particularly severe cases of murder. The Commission reported that its vote for abolition was by secret ballot, with six members for, three against, and two abstentions (Peyrefitte 1977:217). A commission on the revision of the French penal code, composed of 'professionals, theoreticians, and practitioners of law' (Le Quang Sang 2001:129) issued a preliminary report in 1978 advocating the retention of capital punishment only for extremely serious crimes such as torture or hostage-taking (prompting Badinter to question skeptically: 'But for what other crimes was it ever pronounced, in judicial reality?' (Badinter 2000:146)). Peyrefitte, despite being personally in favor of abolition and despite his leadership of a commission that recommended it, refused to pursue the goal once he had been named Justice Minister. He explained his reasons in a candid 1978 speech in Amiens:

> One must permit ideas to evolve, seeing that the public is hostile to abolition of the death penalty. First, one must undertake a careful revision of the laws (*toilette des textes*) to limit the death penalty only to very precise cases, and at the same time give thought to a substitute penalty. (As quoted in Badinter 2000:179)

Peyrefitte continued to temporize on the issue until his departure from office in 1981. Meanwhile, a series of debates on abolition in the French parliament led to the politicization of the debate over the death penalty, and forced the leaders of the four main political parties (The Socialist and Communist parties, the Gaullist RPR, and the center-right UDF) to take positions on the issue. By 1980, the lay of the land was clear: the French left was solidly against capital punishment, and the right was divided. Most favored capital punishment, but some leaders of the center-right, such as

Bernard Stasi of the UDF, actively campaigned for abolition, whereas others, such as Jacques Chirac of the RPR, contented themselves with merely pronouncing their personal opposition to capital punishment (Le Quang Sang 2001:155–6).

Thus, even as French public opinion was coalescing in favor of the death penalty (and French juries were handing down an increased number of death sentences), the French political elite was moving slowly in the opposite direction. Activists such as Badinter and human-rights organizations like the League for the Rights of Man had gradually established opposition to capital punishment as a key element of the left's political profile. The presence of high-profile abolitionists in the center-right parties also legitimized opposition to capital punishment within that camp. From a party-political standpoint, therefore, the prospects for abolition were improving. Badinter sensed an opening. Throughout the 1970s and early 1980s, he had steadily increased his public profile within the French Socialist party. His remarkable legislative and oratorical skills quickly won him a reputation as a rising star, even if his close identification with the unpopular side of the abolition debate represented a slight liability.

In the late 1970s, it became increasingly clear that the tide was turning toward the left in France, as the center-right government of Valéry Giscard D'Estaing appeared ineffectual in dealing with OPEC's *choc pétrolier* and the resulting economic stagnation and rising unemployment. Further, as historian Tony Judt (2007:548–9) notes, the late 1960s and 1970s had witnessed seismic shifts in French society, as the French countryside depopulated and the electorate became more urban, more secular, and less bound to traditional institutions and parties. Amid this upheaval, opinion polls showed increasingly rosy prospects for left parties. François Mitterrand, who had earned a respectable showing running for President in 1965 and 1974, lent his personal popularity to the resurgent Socialist party in the late 1970s, and the French left displayed a rare unity in the run-up to the presidential election of 1981. Badinter, in turn, had gained Mitterrand's trust by supporting his 1974 presidential bid. Badinter approached Mitterrand before the 1981 elections and asked him to publicly announce his intention to abolish capital punishment if elected. Only by so doing, Badinter reasoned, would it be possible to achieve legitimacy for a policy that was consistently rejected by a two-thirds majority of French voters during the late 1970s and early 1980s. During an interview on the French television show *Cartes sur table*, Mitterrand announced his intention to abolish capital punishment if elected: 'In my innermost conscience, like the churches, the Catholic church, the Reformed churches, Judaism, and all the important national and international humanitarian associations, in my heart of hearts, I am opposed to the death penalty' (as quoted in Bae 2007:105). Badinter called Mitterrand 'the least repressive politician I have ever known' (Badinter 2008:189).

Mitterrand's 1981 victory was followed by a sweeping victory for parties of the left in the following 1981 legislative elections. In recognition of the role of the Communist Party in the left coalition, Mitterrand named four Communist cabinet ministers, the first time members of that party had served in the French cabinet in 30 years. The Socialist government quickly undertook an ambitious program of industrial nationalization and expansion of social services. The left coalition also had ambitious plans for introducing reforms to the justice system. Mitterrand first appointed Maurice Faure as Justice Minister (who is technically called *Garde de Sceaux*, or Keeper of the Seals), but Faure quickly determined that the job was not to his taste, and Mitterrand appointed Badinter as a replacement. With Mitterrand's explicit approval, Badinter immediately set about implementing various reforms to the justice system, including Mitterrand's campaign promise to abolish capital punishment. With Mitterrand's express backing and a solid parliamentary majority behind him, Badinter had enormous power over the French justice system. He chose to present abolition as a single issue to the French parliament. To focus the debate yet further, Badinter's proposed bill did not provide for alternative punishments; it would simply strip the death penalty from the French penal code, leaving other provisions intact: 'It was essential that the bill be adopted in its concise form, as it was written. At this stage, any addition would reduce its symbolic force and open the door to a debate in the Senate that I wanted to avoid,' (Badinter 2008:194).

Speed was of the essence, for several reasons. First, just as in the early 19th century, there were signs that French juries were mounting a campaign of resistance to abolition: during 1980 they had handed down an unusually large number of death sentences. Retentionist politicians were eagerly anticipating a series of mini-scandals as Mitterrand would be forced to commute these death sentences – drawing attention, repeatedly, to the most unpopular part of his political platform. Socialist politicians also made it known to Badinter that party discipline on the issue could be maintained only for a few months. Drawing upon the legislative expertise of his staff and his wide network of political acquaintances, Badinter invoked special provisions of parliamentary procedure to procure expedited review of the abolition bill in the legislative committees and the Commission of Laws, a standing commission of the French National Assembly responsible for reviewing legislative proposals. As a result of Badinter's maneuvering, the law passed through all the stages of preliminary review in less than three weeks in August of 1981, and a floor debate was scheduled for September 17. (Le Quang Sang 2001:163–8). The vote on capital punishment would be a *vote de conscience*.

Badinter had no illusions about how the public would receive the abolition of capital punishment: 'I was sure the abolition of the death penalty, an absolute priority in my eyes, would be seen as an outrage by the general public' (Badinter 2008:188). To be sure, French voters had just delivered a sweeping electoral victory to the Left. But their views were hardly monolithic: rising crime, terrorism, and economic uncertainty fostered a mood in which crime control was more important to the public than human rights or civil liberties. Badinter saw no option but to expressly defy the public's mood. His September 17 speech in the French Senate (*Assemblée Nationale de France* 1981) was a model of French parliamentary eloquence. Badinter framed the abolition of the death penalty as the next urgent step in the march of human progress, in which the 'great' nation of France had so often been the leader. In this particular arena, however, France had delayed shamefully. Responding to a rhetorical question about whether it would not be better to wait, Badinter objected: 'Wait, after two centuries! Wait, as if the death penalty or the guillotine were a fruit which one must let ripen before harvesting! Wait? We know in truth that the cause [for the delay in abolition] was fear of public opinion.' Badinter's response to those who charged him with undermining democracy was simple: the Socialist Party, in its platform and the comments of its leading officials, had clearly informed the voters that abolishing capital punishment would be one of their top priorities once entering office. If there was a democratic objection to duly elected legislators carrying out their promises to the voters, Badinter could not see it. Some had proposed submitting the question to a popular referendum yet, as Badinter reminded them: 'But you know as well as I that this path … is precluded by the Constitution.' Badinter concluded:

> by invoking the language of honor and shame, a feature of the French political lexicon: 'Tomorrow, thanks to you, we will no longer have in French prisons, to our common shame, furtive executions at dawn on a dark scaffold. Tomorrow the bloody pages of our history will be turned. At this moment more than any other I have the sentiment of having assumed my ministry in the ancient and noble sense of "service".' (Nye 2003:226)

Badinter's eloquence may have swayed some delegates, but most observers had reckoned with an overwhelming rejection of capital punishment in any event. That indeed took place on September 18 1981, in a vote of 333 for abolition, 117 against, and 6 abstentions in the *Assemblée Nationale*. Shortly thereafter the Senate voted 160 to 126 for abolition, with one abstention.

The vote was not greeted with surprise, since the governing political arrangements had made the outcome a foregone conclusion. As historian Robert A. Nye (2003:226) puts it, somewhat dramatically: 'The abolition of capital punishment in France was accomplished as a *coup d'etat* by a political and intellectual elite against the clearly established sentiments of the vast majority of the public.' Mitterrand and Badinter also pushed ahead with other moves to liberalize the justice system, building on a first wave of prison reforms in the 1970s by adopting further enactments to improve conditions in French prisons and modernize the system of punishments (Whitman 2003:129–31). The general public was not warm to any of these proposals. According to a November 28 1984 survey sponsored by *Le Figaro*, for instance, 63% of the respondents felt that their security had deteriorated in the past few years, 60% felt the police had too few weapons to combat crime, 54% wanted more severe punishments, and 61% believed the death penalty was effective (as cited in Le Quang Sang 2001:199). While public sentiment still favored capital punishment, active support for reintroducing the punishment dwindled steadily among French political elites. By the mid-1980s, reintroduction of the guillotine had the support only of a minority of the center-right deputies. They were, nevertheless, active – 1984 saw the introduction of largely symbolic bills in the French parliament to reintroduce capital punishment for crimes against minors and for the killing of police officers and security officials (Le Quang Sang 2001:198). And, of course, on the far-right flank of French politics, Jean-Marie le Pen advocated tirelessly for the return of the death penalty.

To fully foreclose the prospects for the re-establishment of capital punishment in France, abolitionists turned to the European level. With France's vote for abolition, all of the large nations of Western Europe were now either de facto or *de jure* abolitionist, at least as far as ordinary crimes were concerned. Additional Protocol 6 to the European Convention on Human Rights was opened for signature in 1983, and signed by France in April of that year. It commits signatory states to abolish the death penalty, but permits them, in Article 2, to maintain the supreme penalty 'in respect of acts committed in time of war or of imminent threat of war.' The *Conseil Constitutionnel*, a supreme tribunal for constitutional questions created by the Constitution of the Fifth Republic, was then called upon to judge whether France's signing of the treaty was acceptable under French constitutional law. In a typically brief decision handed down on May 22 1985, the Council held: 'Considering that this international instrument is not incompatible with the duty of the State to assure respect for the institutions of the Republic, the continuity of the life of the nation and the guarantee of the rights and liberties of the citizens ... [the Court holds that] Additional Protocol 6 to the European Convention on Human Rights concerning the abolition of capital punishment does not contain any clause contrary to the [French] Constitution' (*Conseil Constitutionnel*).

With Protocol 6 signed and ratified, the question of whether to bring back capital punishment was effectively taken off the table. Le Quang Sang's analysis is insightful:

Once again, the law was invoked and used for political ends. The legal barring of the death penalty, once it reached its goal, also had the oblique goal of barring the death penalty politically. If the provisions of the European Convention on Human Rights placed constraints on the legal system, these were relative. However, as a matter of political logic, the possibility of re-establishing the death penalty could no longer be envisaged, because of the discrediting effect such a precedent would set. (Le Quang Sang 2001:199)

French lawmakers could no longer pass a law reintroducing capital punishment, since Article 55 of the Constitution of the French Republic provides that: 'Treaties or agreements duly ratified or approved shall, upon publication, prevail over Acts of Parliament, subject, with respect to each agreement or treaty, to its application by the other party' (*Assemblée Nationale de France* 2008). Thus, France's only option would be to 'denounce,' or officially terminate its recognition of Protocol 6. However, Additional Protocol 6 specifies, in its Article 6, that its provisions abolishing capital punishment 'shall be regarded as additional articles to the Convention and all the provisions of the Convention shall apply accordingly.' Thus, any denunciation of Additional Protocol 6 on the death penalty would have to satisfy the preconditions for denouncing the treaty as a whole: the denunciation could take place – at the earliest – 5 years after ratification, and would be subject to a waiting period of six months (Schabas 2002:292–3). These delays would, of course, subject any state which chose to denounce Additional Protocol 6 to a sustained barrage of external criticism. Thus, as of the time France signed the Protocol, the return of capital punishment to France was, for all practical purposes, permanently banned.

Part III
The European Model in a Global Context

'Stepan Arkadyevitch had not chosen his political opinions or his views; these political opinions and views had come to him of themselves, just as he did not choose the shapes of his hat and coat, but simply took those that were being worn. And for him, living in a certain society – owing to the need, ordinarily developed at years of discretion, for some degree of mental activity – to have views was just as indispensable as to have a hat. If there was a reason for his preferring liberal to conservative views, which were held also by many of his circle, it arose not from his considering liberalism more rational, but from its being in closer accordance with his manner of life.'

– Leo Tolstoy, *Anna Karenina* (translation by
Constance Garnett)

7
Elaborating the European Model

Having completed an overview of the abolition movements in three separate European countries, we can abstract from the particulars of each nation's experience. The previous chapters suggest that despite radically differing historical contexts, certain broad historical patterns were common to abolition in all three countries. In this chapter, I will elaborate on some of these broad patterns in an attempt to show how that abolition of capital punishment fits well within the elite-driven European model of criminal justice policy formation.

Phase I: Taking Distance from Vengeance

Before the Enlightenment, organized opposition to the idea of the state's power and prerogative to take life was limited to religious activists (such as the Quaker George Fox) who, for all their zeal, had little influence on public policy. The various forms of intellectual and social ferment that went into what we now call the Enlightenment are too complex to be addressed in detail here. However, one strain of Enlightenment thinking was, of course, the impulse radically to question existing social institutions and practices. Once this process was set in motion, it was only a matter of time before a philosopher would turn his attention to the question of crime and punishment. As we have seen, several philosophers and civil servants converged on the issue almost simultaneously, but Cesare Beccaria enjoyed the distinction of being the first to articulate a thorough and radical critique of inherited punishment practices.

The approach of Beccaria and Hugo was fostered by changes in the notion of personal development aptly described by Charles Taylor. During the Renaissance, Taylor observes, the idea took hold that the enlightened and civilized person is expected to transcend mankind's baser instincts by 'constructing [his] own representation of the world' and 'tak[ing] charge of the processes by which associations form and shape our character and outlook.' This change in the structure of the civilized person's attitude became even more pronounced during the Enlightenment. The purposeful construction of a 'civilized' self requires discipline and a certain amount of self-alienation, 'the ability to take an instrumental stance to one's given properties, desires, inclinations, tendencies, habits of thought and feeling, so that they can be worked on, doing away with some and strengthening others, until one meets the desired specifications' (Taylor 1989:174–5, 159–60). The common man might react to descriptions of heinous crimes with an atavistic cry for vengeance (one of his 'given properties'), but the thinking man showed self-control by distancing himself from his initial emotional reaction and subjecting it to critical analysis. Further, the enlightened thinker was no longer willing to cede the fate of lawbreakers to rulers' unfettered discretion. Although directly challenging the sovereign's right to take the life of his or her subjects was still a delicate matter (as shown by the experiences of Beccaria and von Sonnenfels), Enlightenment philosophers could still urge that the fate of criminals be regarded as an important social problem requiring reasoned discussion and new approaches.

This first phase of the modern critique of capital punishment thus involves the creation of emotional distance. The problem of the death penalty is assessed in the abstract; individual offenders are rarely mentioned by name; and the emphasis is on crafting an effective repressive policy, not advocating humane treatment of offenders for its own sake. This approach is emblematic of the overall Enlightenment approach to criminal law reform, which was to replace an archaic jumble of inherited attitudes and provisions with a coherent system of proportional punishments derived from the application of reason. When Enlightenment critics attacked excessive brutality in punishment, the primary focus was not so much on the suffering of the offender but on the damage such cruelty inflicts on the reputation of the sovereign, and on the morality of the crowds who witness public executions.

Joseph von Sonnenfels, for example, favored replacing capital punishment with hard labor for life, which he argued was a much harsher punishment. Nor was his opposition to torture absolute; he was willing to sanction it in order to accomplish concrete investigative ends, such as forcing conspirators to name their accomplices. As one historian put it, Sonnenfels, to keep the ear of the absolutist rulers he served, was 'eager to prove that he was not motivated by free-thinking, radical-humanitarian motives, but rather by concern for the welfare of the state.' However, where he could, Sonnenfels advocated more humane policies by 'smuggling them through the back door of utilitarianism' (Kann 1960:187–8). Beccaria came closer to a truly 'humanistic' opposition to capital punishment, especially in a section of *On Crimes and Punishments* in which he imagines the thoughts of a typical thief:

> What are these laws that I am supposed to respect, which leave such a great gap between me and the rich man? He denies me the penny I ask of

him and justifies himself by ordering me to work, something with which he himself is unfamiliar. Who made these laws? Rich and powerful men who have never deigned to visit the squalid hovels of the poor, who have never broken mouldy bread amid the innocent cries of hungry children and a wife's tears. Let us break these ties, which are harmful to the majority and useful only to a few and to indolent tyrants; let us attack injustice at its source. (Beccaria 2008:55)

Although these lines certainly offer a sympathetic glimpse into the humanity of the offender, as one sociologist recently observed (Reicher, forthcoming), they are an attack on injustice, not on the death penalty in particular.

This emotional distance from the issue of vengeance and killing was just as evident in supporters of capital punishment as in opponents. Enlightenment jurists and thinkers who supported the death penalty – among others, Montesquieu, Rousseau, Mably, Tommaso Natale and Karl Ferdinand Hommel – took pains to justify their decisions on secular, rationalistic grounds. They also favored limiting capital punishment to a small number of the most serious crimes (Schmidt 1948:444–5). Kant's famous defense of capital punishment, probably the most robust of any Enlightenment thinker, rested on a scrupulous application of the principle of equality, which he derived from the Biblical *ius talionis*, as adapted and modified in Kant's *Metaphysics of Morals* (Ataner 2006). Yet Kant intended his defense of the death penalty to be seen as resting on first principles, not on an emotional reaction either to heinous crimes or to the execution of offenders. For his part, Kant attributed Beccaria's theories to 'the participatory and enthusiastic sentimentality of an affected humanitarianism' (as quoted in Evans 1996:197).

In this early critique of capital punishment, we can already see the seeds of an argument which would become increasingly important in the following centuries – what I will call opposition to capital punishment as a *mark of social distinction*. Whatever else motivated Enlightenment analysts of capital punishment, one purpose was a desire to distinguish oneself from the masses, who were seen as beholden to raw emotion, be it the tribal lust for vengeance or a willful upsurge of sympathy for the trembling wretch on the gallows. Critics of public executions pointed to instances of crowds turning *against* the execution of a sympathetic criminal, and staging volatile impromptu protests as the fatal hour approached. Writing in 1828, the German penal reformer Paul Anselm von Feuerbach argued against 'cruel forms of the death penalty' by contending that these 'barbaric blood-spectacles ... contribute to blunt people's feelings, feed their coarseness, and drive their spirits wild' (Evans 1996:247). Those who have the education and temperament to master their own emotions and consider the issue rationally are a tiny, and self-consciously elect, minority. To quote Beccaria: 'The voice of one philosopher is ... weak against the clamour and the cries of so many people who are guided by blind habit, but the few sages scattered across the face of the earth will echo me in their innermost hearts' (Beccaria 2008:57). As early as 1785, in fact, the German jurist Christian Gottlieb Gmelin remarked: 'Since Beccaria, Sonnenfels and other worthy and popular authors have declared war on the death penalty and torture, everyone now wants to be an "enlightened thinker", and a horde of writers has formed itself behind them' (as quoted in Schmidt 1948:446).

Phase 2: Identification with the Offender; and the Baleful Political Symbolism of the Gallows

If abolitionism in the late 18th century was marked primarily by self-conscious rationalism, the 19th century introduced several new strains in anti-death-penalty rhetoric that would deeply mark abolitionist discourse until the present day and which lent the movement decisive new impulses. The first was extensive exploration of the subjective experience of the condemned person. Until the 19th century, the identity and personal suffering endured by those facing execution were largely irrelevant to the debate over capital punishment. The occasional execution of a high-profile criminal would prompt concern about the life story of that particular condemned person. However, as many commentators such as Linebaugh and Gatrell have pointed out, these occasional episodes of interest and concern were conditioned exclusively by the fact that that rarest of events had occurred – the sentencing of a high-status individual to death. The typical execution was of an anonymous, often illiterate, offender drawn from the slums of London or Paris, and generated little concern.

This is not to say these executions were ignored. Indeed, they were attended by thousands of spectators. Especially in England and the United States, they were staged as spectacles of redemption and repentance: pamphleteers would compose broadsheets reciting the sordid details of the offender's upbringing and crime, and attach a brief moralizing message, often composed in doggerel. In the early American colonies, executions were often preceded by sermons, capped by statements of remorse by the condemned, followed by the awful payment of the wages of sin (Masur 1989:25–49). However, the condemned remained an object, a surface onto which moralizing messages could be projected. Many abolitionist polemics also treated the condemned as faceless tokens of broader social forces. Rather than focus on their individual characteristics, abolitionists painted the condemned as relatively interchangeable end-products of societal neglect. This anonymity allowed arguments both for and against capital punishment to be conducted on the level of abstract principle or religious injunction.

The 19th century saw a new argument against capital punishment being added to this standard repertoire – the argument about the needless personal suffering of the offender. In narratives like Hugo's *Last Days of a Condemned Man* or Thackeray's *Going to See a Man Hanged*, the authors attempt to convey a sense of the intense suffering endured by the condemned person. In 19th-century abolitionist discourse, the condemned person becomes a *subject*. The intensity of their suffering in the final days and hours is portrayed as a unique ordeal, varying in its character but never in its intensity. And that suffering, in and of itself, becomes an argument against capital punishment. This theme plays an important role in Dostoevsky's 1868 novel *The Idiot*. Dostoevsky portrays the moral refinement of the Christ-like hero of the book, the 'positively good' Prince Myshkin, by his reaction to capital punishment. Near the beginning of the novel (2004:21–2), Myshkin describes his recent experience of an execution in France to a footman:

> The criminal was an intelligent, middle-aged man, strong and courageous, called Legros. But I assure you, though you may not believe me, when he mounted the scaffold, he was weeping and was as white as paper. Isn't it incredible? Isn't it awful? Who cries for fear? I'd no idea that a grown man, not a child, a man who never cried, a man of forty-five, could cry for fear! What must be passing in the soul at such a moment; to what anguish must it be brought? It's an outrage on the soul, that's what it is!

The servant meekly responds with the observation that death by guillotine is, at least, painless, which prompts Myshkin to even greater depths of identification:

> 'Do you know,' Myshkin answered warmly, 'you've just made that observation and everyone says the same, and the guillotine was invented with that objective. But the idea occurred to me at the time that perhaps it made it worse. That will seem to you an absurd and wild idea, but if one has some imagination, one may suppose even that. Think! If there were torture, for instance, there would be suffering and wounds, bodily agony, and so all that would distract the mind from spiritual suffering, so that one would only be tortured by wounds till one died. But the chief and worst pain may not be in the bodily suffering but in one's knowing for certain that in an hour, and then in ten minutes, and then in half a minute, and then now, at the very moment, the soul will leave the body and that one will cease to be a man and that that's bound to happen; the worst part of it is that it's *certain*. When you lay your head down under the knife and hear the knife slide over your head, that quarter of a second is the most terrible of all. You know this is not only my imagination, many people have said the same. I believe that so thoroughly that I'll tell you what I think. To kill for murder is a punishment incomparably worse than the crime itself.'

Myshkin returns to the theme several times in the book, always in social situations in which such gloomy subjects are universally avoided.

In addition to the suffering of the victim (which Myshkin obliquely compares to that of Christ), of course, there is the growing disgust with the actual act of execution. Nineteenth-century abolitionist writers are eager to strip away the trappings of justice to focus all attention on the nature of the deed itself – as Thackeray put it, 'an act of frightful wickedness and violence, performed by a set of men against one of their fellows.' Hugo horrifies his bourgeois readers with the image of men pulling at a woman's body to finalize a botched execution. Hugo, Thackeray, and Dostoevsky invoke the supposedly 'natural' revulsion of the enlightened soul against intentional killing as an argument against capital punishment at least as powerful as any philosophical treatise.

These two innovations – identification with the condemned and revulsion toward killing – clearly point toward a civilizing process. The work of the German sociologist Norbert Elias – whose reception in the English-speaking world is now underway – provides a powerful framework for analyzing the issue. In his 1939 classic *The Civilizing Process* (Elias 2000) and in later works, Elias argued, on the basis of research into the evolution of manners in Western Europe, that the social practices we associate with 'civilization' – such as codes of dress and courtliness, table manners and use of utensils, respect for the dignity and autonomy of others, a decrease in the level of general interpersonal violence in society, and the tendency to remove bodily functions, illness and death behind a curtain of privacy – originated among the social elites in the 14th and 15th centuries in Europe, then gradually spread throughout society, as those lower in the social hierarchy adopted 'refined' manners. (As the quotation marks around the word 'civilization' indicate, Elias disclaimed any normative evaluations, and intended only to describe and analyze behavior which is called 'civilized.') Elias' review of the historical record showed a steady decline in the level of interpersonal violence in Western societies since the medieval era, driven by the increasing interdependence and complexity of modern societies, as well as the formation of strong, centralized government. In addition to growing interdependence, however, the civilizing process also involves the gradual spread of patterns of discretion, courtesy and respect for life from social elites to groups lower in the social hierarchy. Thus, 'civilizing' reforms in manners and laws – including constraints on violent impulses – generally originate among elites, and then slowly propagate among lower echelons of society, who wish to improve their perceived social standing by imitating their social betters.

Elias' theoretical framework has proven fruitful to criminologists studying the evolution of violence and norms of punishment. Based on a review of the historical evidence available in 1939, Elias suggested that the level of 'background' interpersonal violence in peacetime in Western Europe had declined gradually, but significantly, since the Middle Ages. Later research confirmed Elias' hypothesis. Several recent studies have found, for instance, that the murder rate in Western Europe and England decreased by something like 90% between the 14th century and the present, despite the development of much deadlier weapons (Gurr 1981; Eisner 2001). After assessing other potential causes, both Ted Gurr and Manuel Eisner come to the conclusion that the decrease in the levels of interpersonal violence was largely a product of evolving social sensibilities toward violence. The decline in violence was particularly steep in the 19th century, a development which coincided with the spread of mass literacy and urbanization in many Continental European countries (Gillis 1994:394).

David Garland (1990) and Ted Gurr, among others, have both noted the explanatory power of Elias' model, which helps make sense not only of the decreasing level of general interpersonal violence in Western societies but also the decreasing harshness of punishment. Garland concludes that 'it seems perfectly clear that Elias' analysis of the development and characteristics of modern sensibilities has a profound importance for the study of punishment, which, as I have argued, is a sphere of social life deeply affected by conceptions of what is and is not "civilized."' (Garland 1990:216). Civilization fosters the elite's ability to empathize with people of different social backgrounds. This empathy leads to internalized restraints that reject violence against others to satisfy cruel desires or gain personal advantage. This enhanced empathy and aversion to violence, in turn, reduces the level of condemnation and sheer hatred felt for criminals, and fosters a legal and moral order which accords even dangerous criminals basic respect and a chance at rehabilitation. Garland, drawing on work by Pieter Spierenburg (1984), traces the development of elite sensibilities:

From the early seventeenth century onwards, in a process that would last for several centuries, the sensibilities and social relations tolerating violence began slowly to change. A fundamental change of attitudes seems to have occurred in The Netherlands and elsewhere by about the middle of the eighteenth century, and after 1800 the shift accelerated to form what is recognizably our own sensibility towards violence, suffering, and the fate of others. Spierenburg traces these changes and the growing appearance of 'verifiable expressions of repugnance and anxiety' in regard to violent public punishments, using the evidence of eyewitness reports, literary accounts, and documents relating to executions. This developing sensitivity, growing from a mild ambivalence in the seventeenth century to the self-declared humanitarianism and sentimentalism of the eighteenth and nineteenth, was first and foremost a characteristic of elites. 'Conscience formation' and the refinement of manners were features of 'polite society', of the upper and middle classes who came to pride themselves on their delicacy and to despise those beneath them for their lack of culture and civilization. It was considered a mark of their uncivilized character that the lower-class crowds 'continued to be attracted to the event until the end' long after the rulers had withdrawn from such scenes, having ceased to take pleasure in the brutal execution of justice. (Garland 1990:227)

In the first half of the 19th century, the rhetorical shift among elite abolitionists was driven by a two-step dynamic that corresponds closely with Elias' framework. Elites first began to see condemned criminals as autonomous subjects whose suffering was – in its own right – worthy of concern. In a related process, they began to see executions as inherently shocking and distasteful. State killing is wrenched out of its legal and procedural framework and presented as the conscious infliction of extreme suffering on a fellow human. Gatrell, in his comprehensive study of capital punishment in Great Britain, broadly endorses the argument from changing sensibilities, but hedges his endorsement by noting that the humanity elites display is rarely unalloyed:

> [H]umane feelings prevail when their costs in terms of security or comfort are bearable; when they can be productively acted upon; and when they bring emotional and status returns to the 'humane'. Culturally dominant groups most deplore brutality when the state's authority or their own is strong enough to obviate the need for its outward display. (1996:12)

Gatrell's emphasis on the social dimension of abolitionism, the 'returns to the "humane",' is also telling. The abolitionist earns these returns when he shifts his gaze to the eager throngs attending the execution. Their boisterous and unpredictable reactions to executions elicit as much disgust as the execution itself, because the crowd, in the eyes of the elite observer, appears to show a deplorable level of voyeuristic callousness.

Nevertheless, as Garland persuasively urges, the genuine humanitarian component in the reformers' disgust at executions should not be ignored. The movement to humanize punishment was comprised of many separate strands of thought. Moderate reformers wished only to see executions made private. But others had already come to the conclusion that all executions were inherently wrong *merely* because they caused needless suffering. The 'needless suffering' argument transcends the frame of criminological or legal dispute, disarming utilitarian or legalistic justifications for capital punishment. Further, this argument can be grasped intuitively, by everybody. It signals that the debate about capital punishment is no longer the province of titled jurists or philosophers; it is an ordinary issue of public morality about which everyone may have an opinion. Further, the objection to executions as needless suffering overlaps closely with religious conceptions of human dignity. Of course, the majority of mainstream churches and believers continued to favor capital punishment well into the 20th century, but the normative, compassion-based argument enabled closer ties with religious groups (such as Quakers) who were unusually effective and persistent advocates of social change. Finally, the execution as needless suffering argument automatically justified – in fact, demanded – the immediate abolition of capital punishment for all crimes, without exception. Essentially, the argument proceeds by assigning such weight to human dignity – regardless of the nature of the crime or the status of the offender – that no possible state interest can outweigh it. It is an analogue of the Kantian argument. According to Kant, the categorical imperative of punishment is so overwhelming that it need not be justified by any merely societal interest. According to the 'needless suffering' argument, the peremptory importance of human dignity is so overwhelming that it cannot be trumped by any societal interest.

The sensibility-based needless suffering argument also added another marker of social distinction to the status of being opposed to capital punishment. The first marker of distinction, we have seen, is the enlightened thinker's ability to gain distance from the raw passions provoked by violent crime. The second marker, emphasized especially by writers, is the superior ability to empathize shown by cultivated members of the elite. What some might call sentimentality is actually a product of their superior moral sensitivity, a faculty which permits them to fully register the suffering felt by the condemned. As Dr. Johnson once observed: 'Pity is not natural to man ... Pity is acquired and improved by the cultivation of reason.' (Boswell 1881:451). Gatrell shows how the imperative to thus cultivate reason spreads: 'Recommended by a culture's prophets and teachers and internalized by dominant groups, shifts in affective patterns develop their own momentum as rules are elaborated. Although some reactions operate automatically, the feelings associated with them are intellectually meditated and highly socialized' (Gatrell 1996:13, citing Elias and others). As soon as the trope was established, persons of refinement could identify one another by their attitude toward capital punishment. This is the recognition Victor Hugo referred to when he stated that one can identify the 'thinking man' by his 'mysterious reverence' for life (see Chapter 6). Of course, this 'mysterious reverence' extends to all of the condemned, not just the unjustly accused. Again, the absolute character of the 'needless suffering' argument comes to the fore: it applies to all condemned persons, regardless of their level of moral guilt. It may be especially terrible to execute an innocent person, but this is only an extreme case of a practice that is always immoral and unjust, because it always extinguishes a unique human life in a manner that inflicts needless terror and suffering. No amount of tinkering with the penal code can remedy the fundamental iniquity of state killing.

A last innovation of the 19th century is worth mention in this context: the idea of capital punishment as the tool of tyrants. This argument gained force during the political unrest across Europe in the 1840s. In 1848, after lengthy deliberations in the *Paulskirche* in Frankfurt-am-Main, Germany, the reformist national parliament adopted the so-called *Paulskirche* Constitution, which was intended to bind all the countries of the German Confederation under a single, unified, progressive legal order. The *Paulskirche* Constitution protected the sanctity of the home and mail against searches, radically expanded suffrage, and guaranteed absolute freedom of religion. Section 139 of the Constitution abolished capital punishment, except in cases of military law and mutinies at sea. It also abolished the pillory, branding, and flogging. During the debates leading up to the adoption of the Constitution, one historian notes, the delegates acknowledged that there was 'widespread popular support for capital punishment,' but 'paid very little attention to the opinions of the mass of the people' (Evans 1996:270).

The debates in the Frankfurt parliament rehearsed all the familiar arguments about capital punishment, but also laid new stress upon its political implications. During the debate on the bill, one speaker urged the parliament not to 'bring the death penalty from the times of the police state into the times of the state ruling by law,' and another suggested that capital punishment perpetuates 'submissiveness and serfdom' by turning an individual into the 'bodily property of state and society.' Of particular importance for a parliament composed largely of political activists, the death penalty was susceptible to abuse by rulers who sought to stifle dissent by abusing laws prohibiting treason (summaries and quotations of arguments in Evans 1996:271–3). Similar arguments could be heard in the French debate about capital punishment in the 1840s. Of course, the revolutions of 1848 in Germany and France ultimately did not bring an end to capital punishment; the *Paulskirche* Constitution was in force only for a few months before it was rendered moot by a military coup staged by a confederation of German princes in 1849. The French National Assembly rejected Victor Hugo's motion to abolish the death penalty completely, but did abolish it for political crimes. Nevertheless, the advent of the Second Empire after Louis Napoleon's 1851 coup put an end to the Second Republic's reforms.

The perception of the death penalty as a tool of tyrants which fosters a 'submissive' attitude among the people could be called the 'liberal' political argument against capital punishment. However, the 1850s also saw the emergence of a radical critique of the practice. To be sure, the leading French radical thinker of the 1840s, Pierre-Joseph Proudhon, was critical of Beccaria and accepted the death penalty (Haubtmann 1982:569–71). Karl Marx, however, was more skeptical. He directly addressed the issue only once (1853), in a column written for the *New York Tribune*. Writing in English as the *Tribune*'s London correspondent, Marx opined that it would be 'very difficult, if not altogether impossible, to establish any principle upon which the justice or expediency of capital punishment could be founded, in a society glorying in its civilization.' Marx then took Kant and Hegel to task for suggesting that eternal principles of justice demanded the execution of murderers. Their glorification of 'free will' ignored the 'real motives' and 'multifarious social circumstances pressing' on criminals, and constituted nothing more than giving 'a transcendental sanction to the rules of existing society.' Relying on recent work by a French criminologist, Marx argued that the number of crimes in a given society was scientifically predictable, and should thus be dealt with in a more scientific way than the 'brutality' of the hangman.

Although Marx never focused again on capital punishment, many of his followers did. Marxist penal theories take two broad approaches. The first attributes serious violent crimes not to the personal characteristics of the offender, but rather to the 'social arrangements of production' (Taylor et al. 1974:225). Violent crime is largely an economic phenomenon, the product of distortions in the human personality created by alienation and exploitation. As one criminologist recently wrote: 'Marx explains that alienated labor alienates nature from human beings; alienates human beings from themselves, from their own active functions, their life activities, and, in so doing, alienates human beings from each other ... Under such conditions, serious violent crime is not surprising' (Bohm 2008:288, 289). This analysis of the origins of violent crime does not directly indict the death penalty, but clearly posits a situational explanation for violent crime which diminishes the offender's personal culpability. The second Marxist approach to crime and punishment suggests that the maintenance of an urban underclass (with the attendant crime it foments) is, in fact, a goal of capitalist policies. The 'criminal underclass' is only a part of a greater group of alienated and dispossessed persons, the 'reserve army' of labor which serves to exert constant downward pressure on wages at the lowest end of the 'legitimate' wage-spectrum. The two Frankfurt School theorists Rusche and Kirchheimer (1939) provided perhaps the most detailed elaboration of this thesis in the 20th century, although the death penalty itself was not the primary focus of their work.

In any event, the influence of Marxist approaches on the death penalty abolition movement has always been marginal. The movement to end capital punishment was dominated by the educated middle classes and liberal professions, who had little time for radical social critique. Further, once Communist governments were created, they did not follow a consistent abolitionist line. Many Communist regimes maintained capital punishment in their repertoire of formal judicial punishments. Their critique of capital punishment was primarily that, under capitalism, it was used by the bourgeoisie to maintain class privilege by state terror. As soon as these illegitimate motives were suppressed by revolution and the dictatorship of the proletariat, the death penalty – now imposed according to pure revolutionary motives – could be retained. The government of East Germany, for instance, justified the preservation of capital punishment:

In so far as the death penalty serves the security and the reliable protection of our sovereign socialist state, the maintenance of peace and the life of its citizens, it possesses a humanitarian character. To apply it to those offenders who threaten the life of our people and the stability of our nation by committing the most serious crimes is an unconditional requirement of socialist legality. (As quoted in Evans 1996:857)

The death penalty was also enforced in most other countries of the former Eastern Bloc, as well as in the Soviet Union.

Of course, our focus on these newer strains of thought should not obscure the fact that traditional anti-death-penalty arguments (such as lack of deterrence) continued to play a prominent role in the thinking of European abolitionists in the 19th century. One of the most prominent of the 'traditional' abolitionists was Carl Joseph Anton Mittermaier, a German criminal and comparative law jurist. In a seminal 1840 article, Mittermaier criticized religious arguments for the death penalty as irrational, took issue with Kantian and Hegelian justifications for the death penalty and, most importantly, assembled statistics from various different nations to demonstrate that the abolition or retention of capital punishment in those countries had no discernible effect on the crime rate. Mittermaier continued to occupy himself with the issue in the ensuing decades. He played an active role in arguing for the abolition of capital punishment during the Frankfurt parliament, and finally collected all of his writings in a seminal book, called *The Death Penalty, According to the Results of Scientific Research, Progress in Legislation, and Experiences* (1862). By the 1860s, Mittermaier's fame was such that the volume was translated into English (in slightly adapted form) in 1865 by a London barrister named John Macrae Moir (1865).

Mittermaier's treatise was based on an ambitious comparative assessment of capital punishment in dozens of different countries, based on surveys of recent legislation, as well as homicide and reprieve statistics. Its logical structure, wealth of specific evidence, and broad-minded curiosity about the customs and practices of other nations make Mittermaier's treatise a minor classic of German legal scholarship. After the statistical analysis, which shows no discernible effect of the death penalty on crime rates, Mittermaier sets out all of the arguments in favor of capital punishment (he counts 11). Before addressing those arguments in detail, however, Mittermaier frames the debate in terms of the increasing civilization of punishment norms:

In analyzing the argument stated in the previous chapter, the inquirer is involuntarily reminded of the time when the struggle was carried on for the abolition of the rack, of bodily chastisement, and of aggravated Death Punishments. At that time also, the adversaries of abolition had a great deal to say of the dangers likely to threaten the safety of society if the State in the administration of law, were deprived of the means hitherto considered indispensable ... [Yet the] rack and bodily chastisement [were] abolished, and the evil consequences so much dreaded never followed. (Moir 1865:172, 173)

Mittermaier then proceeds to refute every one of the 11 arguments in favor of the death penalty. Not content to merely respond to pro-death penalty arguments, Mittermaier then sets out the affirmative case against capital punishment. The arguments here – lack of deterrent effect, distorting effect on the criminal justice system, brutalizing effect on onlookers, irreparability, the ever-present possibility of executing an innocent person, and incompatibility with Christian mildness – are not particularly original, but are set out in a logical and dispassionate fashion, as befits German *Rechtswissenschaft* ('legal science'). Mittermaier's approach was, for its time, by far the most advanced statistical assessment of capital punishment available. Where other authors relied on introspection or speculation to assess claims of deterrence, or cited examples from one or two nations or regions, Mittermaier attempted to construct a much larger matrix of reliable statistical information. In this respect, his work served as a template for later attempts to assess capital punishment on scientific grounds, such as Thorsten Sellin's influential treatise (1959) comparing crime rates in American jurisdictions which had abolished the death penalty with neighboring, demographically similar jurisdictions which had not done so, and finding no evidence of deterrence.

Abolition and the Liberal Professions

As detailed and influential as Mittermaiers's treatise was, most of the arguments in favor of and against capital punishment it rehearsed were all well-known and had already been subject to much discussion. The really new arguments (or new emphases) added by 19th-century thinkers were (1) the focus on the 'needless suffering' of the condemned, prompted by growing disgust at the inhumanity of execution and growing interest in the subjective experience of the condemned; (2) the 'liberal' political critique of capital punishment as a trapping of absolutist rule no longer suited to Europe's increasingly democratic political landscape; and (3) the 'radical' political critique of capital punishment as a tool of oppression used by the bourgeois to keep the dispossessed in check and enforce unjust property relations by state terror. Some combination of these tropes, added to the more traditional arguments (deterrence, irreparability, and so on), formed the basic components of every elite critique of capital punishment until its abolition. They were not, however, equally influential; I would argue that the first two themes were much more prominent and effective than the last, openly Marxist, critique. Further, the arguments were received quite differently depending on the country in which they were used. In 19th-century England, for instance, there was no recent memory of an absolutist sovereign threatening or inflicting capital prominent for political offenses, so the death penalty was much less likely to be critiqued as an instrument of tyranny than on the Continent, where shifting political constellations could (and did) bring rulers to power who might seek to use the threat of the death penalty to punish dissent.

Despite intellectual ferment on the issue, the last half of the 18th century saw very little progress toward complete abolition of capital punishment in the United Kingdom, Germany, and France. Abolition came up for votes before national parliaments only sporadically, and did not come close to prevailing. Of course, reforms continued, including the progressive narrowing of the scope of death penalty statutes, and (in Germany and the UK) the abolition of public executions. These reforms, however, may well have impeded progress toward total abolition, since they domesticated the death penalty into stability, thereby reducing the political salience of capital punishment as an issue. Mill's 1868 speech to Parliament, in which he pronounced himself satisfied with the humane reforms thus far made to capital punishment, is an example of this stabilization effect. As long as executions were infrequent, carried out in private, and limited largely to criminals who seemed unquestionably guilty, the mass public seemed, on the whole, to support them. Indeed, even *after* the introduction of relatively reliable public-opinion polling in the 1930s and 1940s, there emerged very little evidence of lasting changes in public opinion. From the 1940s to the late 1960s, poll numbers fluctuated after notorious crimes or exonerations, but then, in all three countries, returned to a state of equilibrium in which approximately two-thirds of the public voiced support for capital punishment.

The story of abolition in the countries under review here is the story of how abolitionist arguments and attitudes very gradually spread among elites. The emphasis is on the word 'gradually'. It is, of course, impossible to track precisely the growth in abolitionist sentiment among European elites. The manner of transmission, however, is clear. A prominent intellectual, academic or writer (Hugo, Thackeray, Mittermaier, and many lesser lights) penned a compelling presentation of the abolitionist program, inspiring discussion of the subject in educated circles. A solid minority of elite members committed to the cause of complete abolition would gradually build. These abolitionists formed organizations devoted to advancing the cause, thus creating a more or less permanent focus for the abolitionist viewpoint and ensuring the continuous production of abolitionist polemics and analyses. One consistent theme of abolitionist discourse, as we have seen, is claiming the high ground of 'progressive,' 'civilized,' and 'humane' values. Opposition to the death penalty thus gradually established itself as one of the signature issues by which social progressives recognized one another.

Nowhere was this trend more firmly established than among the liberal professions, and among those, the lawyers. The death penalty is regulated within the legal system, and many of the arguments against capital punishment are well tailored to the logical, rationalistic style of analysis taught in all law schools. The second half of the 19th century saw the importance of lawyers grow in Western European societies. In France, Great Britain, and Germany, the state apparatus grew in size, and brought with it a corresponding professionalization and differentiation of the civil service bureaucracy. Great Britain introduced uniform civil service testing, Bismarck established the core of the modern German social welfare state (accident and health insurance, as well as old-age pensions), and France, in the 1990s, passed the 'foundational laws' creating the infrastructure of the modern French administrative state. From the 1880s until its coming into force in 1900, the German *Bürgerliches Gesetzbuch* – the comprehensive codification of all elements of German private law – occupied a committee of illustrious scholars. The resulting law is still in force today. In France, a similar growth and differentiation took place, for instance in the establishment of comprehensive public education and a nationwide curriculum. Lawyers were needed to coordinate these ambitious modernization projects, and a subset of the legal profession began to be associated with progressive social reform and the rationalization and centralization of rule by an enlightened elite of well-trained jurists of 'advanced' views. Lawyers not considered politically reliable enough for government service entered private practice, where they often combined paid legal work with journalism and with the advocacy of causes important to them. This phenomenon was especially pronounced in Wilhelmine Germany (Wehler 2006:862). In other countries, progressive lawyers had direct access to the political system. As Julie le Quang Sang points out, it was the Radical party which took the lead in the organized French abolition movement in the late 19th century. The parliamentary campaign for abolition which took place between 1906 and 1908, for instance, was organized almost exclusively by members of the Socialist and Radical Parties who were also lawyers.

So far, we have assessed a few reasons why lawyers played such an increasingly prominent role in 19th-century abolition movements, among them the suitability of the issue to lawyerly strategies of proof and debate, and the association of abolition with a broader humanitarian legal agenda of modernization and social provision. However, it was abolition's growing popularity among social elites that also spurred greater involvement by lawyers. Simply put, once abolition became thinkable as a *political* possibility; lawyers were needed to make it a *legal* possibility. In the 18th century, an absolutist sovereign could, on the advice of a Beccaria or a Voltaire, abolish capital punishment with the stroke of a pen. After the momentous democratizing reforms and bureaucratic growth of the 19th century, however, even the simplest law abolishing capital punishment inevitably triggered complex debates: What would be the substitute penalty? How would the abolition of the penalty at the top of the sanctioning pyramid affect the distribution of punishments below it? What about the status of scattered provisions in various code books which still mentioned execution? Only those with an understanding of legislative processes and the structure of existing laws would be able to answer these questions. Further, as it became clearer that public opinion in favor of the death penalty was unlikely to change, it became necessary to devise a means by which legislators could insulate themselves from political backlash. As the fierce and ultimately successful resistance to the French attempt to abolish capital punishment in 1908 shows, decades of agitation against capital punishment seemed to have had almost no discernible effect on the opinions of the broad mass of people. The increasing prominence of lawyers in the abolition movements of the 20th century can perhaps be seen as an implicit recognition that abolition 'from below' – from a groundswell of popular opposition – was not on the cards. Abolition would therefore have to come 'from above' – from bureaucratic and policy-making elites.

Law, Politics, and the Final Victory of Abolition

If the need for lawyers in the abolition movement increased the nearer abolition came to realization, then we would expect the final, successful phase of abolition to be overseen primarily by lawyers and politicians. In Great Britain, Sydney Silverman was the undisputed leader of the abolition movement from the 1940s onward, and at his side were prominent and successful barristers such as Gerald Gardiner and Reginald Paget. In Germany, Thomas Dehler was the person most directly responsible for the maintenance of 1949's precarious constitutional ban on capital punishment, but renowned law professors such as Gustav Radbruch lent their support to the struggle. Also prominent were social-democratic jurists such as Carlo Schmid, (a lawyer with a doctoral title) who split his energies between serving as a regional chairman of the Social Democratic Party and as a professor of public law at the University of Tübingen; and Friedrich Wilhelm Wagner, who moved from legal practice into political opposition and ended his legal career as the Vice President of the Federal Constitutional Court. In France, Robert Badinter coordinated the final push for abolition with François Mitterrand, and worked closely with other prominent advocates and politicians of a progressive cast. Badinter was in turn deeply influenced by Marc Ancel, a renowned French professor of comparative law. Ancel, commissioned by the Council of Europe, wrote an influential report on the death penalty in Europe in 1962, and elaborated the 'social defence' theory of criminal law, in which the protection of human rights took precedence over the 'defence of society' (Ancel 1965).

These jurists received support from intellectuals, including most prominently Arthur Koestler and Albert Camus, each of whom penned influential broadsides against capital punishment in 1957. Both Camus and Koestler were prominent public intellectuals of the non-Communist left, and there is no reason to doubt the sincerity of their conviction against capital punishment – especially in the case of Koestler, who had been imprisoned and threatened with execution by Fascist forces during the Spanish Civil War. However, capital punishment was also an ideal issue with which to sharpen their profiles in the complex European political landscape at the beginning of the Cold War. On the one hand, their critique of capital punishment burnished their progressive credentials by associating their names with attacks on a particularly barbaric aspect of the justice system. One need only think of Camus' biting dismissal of the 'empty phrases' with which the legal system sought to obscure the realities of execution, or Koestler's furious denunciations of English judges as 'Abominable Snowmen' and 'wigged fossils,' and mainstream English clergy as feckless servants of the status quo (Koestler 1957:40–1).

A critique of capital punishment was, necessarily, also a critique of an aspect of American society. In the years following World War II, establishing distance from the United States was useful to center-left European intellectuals, who faced accusations from the radical left of maintaining links to the CIA and/or truckling to American interests. These accusations were not always without foundation. Koestler himself was one of the founding members of the Congress for Cultural Freedom, a high-profile organization of progressive European writers and intellectuals founded in 1950 to counter growing Communist influence on the European Continent. It was revealed in 1967 that the Congress had received large amounts of covert funding from the Central Intelligence Agency from its very inception – a fact Koestler had been aware of since 1951 (Cesarani 1998: 368). Attacking the death penalty was one way of establishing distance from the United States, since the American death penalty was a focus of extraordinary attention and concern in post-war Europe. The executions of Julius and Ethel Rosenberg and of Caryl Chessman, a convicted rapist who spent years on California's death row fighting his death sentence, were followed closely by European journalists. This coverage helped establish the European conception of the United States (which survives to this day) as a country with a peculiarly harsh and remorseless brand of justice, meted out by a system in which race and economic resources play an undeniable role in trial outcomes. The prominent French sociologist Michel Crozier, who spent many years studying and teaching at American institutions in the late 1950s and early 1960s, recalled his reaction to American justice in a book originally written for a French audience:

> Another characteristic of American law that ought to be pointed out is its unpitying harshness. Once the machine is set in motion, nothing stops it. It pursues its victims so obstinately and relentlessly one would think it thirsty for vengeance. I shall not cite the Rosenbergs as an example, since their case was too obviously political. But around the same time another affair made headlines in America and the world: Caryl Chessman was

accused of rape and condemned to death ... The evidence of his guilt was not that strong, a lot of time had passed, and meanwhile Chessman had published a book that turned out to be a best-seller. Now, in France some sort of pardon would certainly have come through, but then Governor Pat Brown, though a liberal Catholic and opposed to the death penalty, did not dare to counter inexorable justice with what would have looked elsewhere [like] nothing more than elementary humanity. (Crozier 1984:101)

Chessman's fame within Europe may be gauged by the fact that the Polish poet Zbigniew Herbert, in his excellent travel memoir *Barbarian in the Garden*, discussed Caryl Chessman in a Polish-language book which would first be translated into English more than two decades after its writing. During a visit to Siena in 1960, Herbert noted a front-page story on Chessman's execution in an Italian newspaper:

I buy *Il Messaggero* with a huge photo of Chessman on the front page. So it finally happened? The photograph eternalizes the historical moment: Chessman finishes his last cigarette. Only the butt smouldering in the corner of the mouth in this ugly, cynical, tormented face. (Herbert 1985:64)

Note that Herbert assumes that the story would have been so familiar to his Polish readership that he does not even use Chessman's first name.

Thus, Camus, Koestler and others in their camp could stake out a position which burnished their profile as enlightened progressives, while distancing them from thinkers on the left who justified the state violence of 'progressive' regimes such as the Soviet Union, or the violence of third-world insurgents in European colonies. As Tony Judt described Camus' thought: 'The moral measure that we bring to bear in condemning the death penalty or the violence of Fascist regimes is indivisible and has the same disqualifying effect upon the actions and regimes of the revolution and its children, however "progressive".' (Judt 1998:95). Nor did opposing capital punishment risk too much controversy: by the end of the 1950s, the death penalty seemed to be a withering institution. Parliamentary efforts to restore it in Germany attracted ever-weaker support, and executions in France and Great Britain had become sporadic. Growing numbers of center-right political figures in Great Britain, France, and Germany were joining the abolitionist cause, as were representatives of mainstream Christianity. Thus, capital punishment was less fraught than other issues such as the status of European colonies, or the role of former fascist officials or collaborators in post-war society. Of course, Camus and Koestler also addressed these much more sensitive issues, but it is not hard to imagine them breathing a sigh of relief at the opportunity to move on from these minefields to the much less dangerous terrain of capital punishment. Taking a public stand against capital punishment placed Camus and Koestler within a grand tradition of European thought, and did so without the risk of deeply alienating ideological allies and potential supporters.

For similar reasons, the cause of abolition was increasingly attractive to lawyers. By publicly espousing abolition, a lawyer could signal his or her identification with the forces of progress and humanity; endorse the increasingly popular idea that all criminals could and should be rehabilitated using modern psychological techniques; and implicitly critique other, more callous nations (including the United States), which 'obstinately and relentlessly' demanded the death of wrongdoers. Nevertheless, advocating abolition was hardly seen as a radical attack on the existing social order – such attacks rarely recommending themselves to lawyers, especially those seeking or holding public office. The difference between abolition and more radical critiques of justice is nicely illustrated in an anecdote related by Robert Badinter of a dinner with Michel Foucault in 1981, shortly after the vote to eliminate capital punishment in France. Foucault reportedly joked: 'Yeah, accomplishing abolition is pretty good but also easy; now the essential thing to do is get rid of prisons.' (Nye 2003:223). Badinter and Mitterrand did pass many far-reaching reforms of French prisons, but abolishing them altogether was never on their agenda.

Finally, abolition appealed to lawyers as a mark of distinction, signaling distance from the unreflective and dangerous 'lust for revenge' of the masses. One of the many political ramifications of World War II was rehabilitation of elite distrust of the masses among Continental European governing elites. As we have seen, arguments in Germany against capital punishment were often framed not only in terms of the disastrous excesses of state violence, but also the tacit acceptance of those excesses by the majority, the 'terrible indifference' (*schreckliche Gleichgültigkeit*), as it came to be known in German. World War II lent fresh meaning to the 'liberal' political critique of capital punishment developed in Europe in the 1840s. The protest of the 1840s, directed at authoritarian rulers, now had an additional target: the millions of citizens who had tolerated, or enthusiastically collaborated with, brutal regimes. The state, in voluntarily relinquishing its power to take the lives of its citizens – over the objection of those citizens themselves – could signal a clean break with brutally repressive policies and herald a new era of respect for human rights. The symbolism of abolition as a clean break with an authoritarian path led Portugal and Spain, more recently, to abolish capital punishment after emerging from dictatorship in the mid-1970s (Hodgkinson 1996:206).

The increasing popularity of abolitionism as a mark of distinction for the educated bourgeoisie set the stage for its acceptance by the establishment, including some center-right politicians. In Germany, the decisive vote against the death penalty by the *Große Strafrechtskommission* in 1959 certified the rejection of the death penalty by a majority of German legal scholars and thinkers. During the following decade, efforts to reinstate the death penalty were rejected by increasing margins, and the number of openly abolitionist members of center-right parties grew steadily. Much the same can be said of the United Kingdom, in which the number of Tories opposed to capital punishment rose dramatically during the 1960s. In particular, Conservative Party leader Ted Heath's openly abolitionist views lent decisive impulses to the abolition movement in the late 1960s by giving hesitant Tories cover to vote against the views of their constituents. France is the only country in which the death penalty survived the 1960s. In France, however, the presence of de Gaulle on the political scene – and of political parties so closely linked to his personality that they are still often called 'Gaullist' – sent French politics along a different path from some of its Continental neighbors. Nevertheless, the 1970s saw many prominent center-right politicians such as Valéry Giscard D'Estaing, Jacques Chirac, and Alain Peyrefitte declare their personal opposition to capital punishment, although they did not wish to take responsibility for its ultimate abolition. And in fact, executions became increasingly sporadic in France, and were limited to those who had been convicted of especially serious murders.

Once abolition became acceptable in center-right circles – that is, once a solid minority of, say, 30–40% of conservative lawmakers became willing to vote for abolition – its success became inevitable. All European social democratic parties had rallied behind abolition by the mid-1960s, if not much earlier, and many of the liberal parties (such as the Liberal Party in England and the Free Democratic Party in Germany) joined the movement during the 1960s, as abolition of capital punishment began to be seen as fitting in with their commitment to civil liberties. With the addition of so many non-left politicians to the abolitionist fold, capital punishment increasingly lost its character as a partisan issue, and began simply to be seen as one component of a 'civilized' approach to law enforcement. To be sure, policy differences with the left persisted, but center-right governments – such as the MacMillan government in Great Britain in the late 1950s and early 1960s, or the D'Estaing government in France in the late 1970s – issued official reports and White Papers that urged modernization of criminal justice and an increase in opportunities for rehabilitation of criminal offenders. The last White Paper of the MacMillan administration, for instance, although titled *The War Against Crime in England and Wales 1959–1964*, did not advocate a brutal crackdown on crime, as its title might have suggested. Rather, it stressed that 'the nation was on course to solving the problems of crime through a combination of diligent police methods and technology, the observation and classification of offenders, better informed sentencing decisions, improved treatment regimes in penal institutions, and social work with young offenders and ex-offenders in the community' (Windlesham 1993:92). It is not hard to see the conflict between this approach to crime control and the finality of capital punishment.

Structural Preconditions of Abolition I: Centralized, Parliamentary Political Systems

The political realignment against capital punishment was an important step toward setting the stage for abolition. However, in France and England, capital punishment had been 'stabilized' in the decades before abolition, and few mainstream political figures saw any advantage in unleashing a passionate and unpredictable debate about capital punishment. Intellectuals and activists did their part, but the cause needed vigorous advocacy within the halls of government, by sophisticated parliamentarians. In England and France, it found its apostles in Sydney Silverman and Robert Badinter. They combined a remarkable level of dedication to the cause with considerable political sophistication. They reduced the partisan profile of death penalty votes by forging cross-party coalitions, ensuring that votes would be votes of conscience without party discipline, and separating the death penalty from other, more controversial political issues with which they or their parties were associated. During parliamentary votes, they fought off attempts to weaken or amend abolition bills. Well aware that they were asking their colleagues to vote against public sentiment, they delivered detailed and passionate speeches framing the question of abolition as a milestone in the civilization of penal policies and emphasizing the delegate's Burkean prerogative of occasionally defying public opinion in the service of greater principle.

In all three countries under review, the structure of the country's political institutions eased the abolitionists' burden: to win the day, they needed to convince only one national legislature. In all three countries addressed here, the laws governing major crimes are made by the national parliament, and apply throughout the national territory: in France, there is the *Code Pénal*, and in Germany the *Strafgesetzbuch*. The United Kingdom still does not have a single codification of its criminal laws, but the Constitution grants Parliament the power to pass criminal legislation valid for the entire nation. Germany abolished capital punishment in its Constitution, so from the beginning, there was no doubt as to its nationwide applicability. However, a change to the *Strafgesetzbuch* would have had the same effect, since it lays out the policies and procedures governing the most serious crimes, and judicial review aims to ensure as uniform an application of the *Strafgesetzbuch* as possible throughout the country. Germany likely has the most federalist system of all the countries under discussion here, but its legal system, like the legal systems in France and the UK, explicitly assigns administration of the penal code to the federal lawmaking instance.

The concentration of the ruling elite in one central city (London or Paris) mitigated the influence of regional variations in opinion. A delegate might hail from a part of France or England not known for its abolitionist fervor, but occupying political office in the national capital and associating with the other members of that elite club can have an effect. A vote for abolition which provoked dismay in a rural constituency might well be greeted with approval by colleagues, newspaper editorialists, writers, and civil libertarians in London or Paris. Further, politicians who had compiled a solid record of service to constituents on the national stage had enough political capital to risk a vote against constituents' preferences from time to time. Sydney Silverman himself, in his own pro-death-penalty working-class constituency, handily fought off the 'Hanging Party' candidacy of a relative of a victim of one of England's most notorious murder cases. One can only imagine what obstacles European abolition movements would have faced if, instead of having to carry only one national legislature, they had instead been required to prevail in every single one of the 26 *régions* of France, or in every county in England.

As for Germany, we already have an inkling of how matters would have fared had the death penalty been a matter for the individual states of Germany. Two populous German states – Hessen and Bavaria – kept the death penalty in their own post-war state constitutions for decades after its abolition by the federal constitution. Bavaria's clause was eliminated in 1998 by public referendum as part of a package of reforms designed to ease Bavaria's integration into the EU, but Hessen's clause survives to this day. Horst Dreier, editor of a leading commentary on German constitutional law, argues that these provisions, adopted in the late 1940s, were intended not so much as express endorsement of capital punishment but rather as attempts to assert local control over executions ordained by the Allied powers occupying Hessen and Bavaria (Dreier 2000:593–4). Further, the German Federal Constitutional Court held, in a case called *Auslieferung I* (Extradition I) (1964), that Art. 102, by abolishing capital punishment, definitively overruled all contrary provisions in German law and forbade any executions taking place on German soil. Nevertheless, the clauses have served as occasional rallying points for federalist, anti-EU, and pro-death penalty sentiment in Germany.

Structural Preconditions of Abolition II: Cohesive Elites

Since abolition of the death penalty in France, the United Kingdom, and Germany, the opinion of bureaucratic and policy-making elites has coalesced behind abolition, and the issue has been exiled from the political mainstream. This is not to say, however, that capital punishment has disappeared from the political landscape. The issue has found its home among Europe's far-right parties, which use it to appeal to the substantial minority of European citizens who favor capital punishment. Jean-Marie le Pen, leader of France's extreme right National Front party, routinely calls for the reintroduction of capital punishment for murderers of children. Bringing back capital punishment is also a main theme of the British National Party, which campaigns to '[r]estore the death penalty for child murderers, multiple murderers and terrorists, where proof is beyond all doubt' (British National Party 2008). German far-right parties, such as the National Democratic Party (NPD) and the *Deutsche Volksunion* (German Peoples' Union), which generally get small fractions of the popular vote depending on region, also support reintroduction of capital punishment. Of course, some of these 'fringe' parties win substantial portions of the vote from time to time – most notably in France in 2002, when Le Pen garnered almost 17% of the first-round vote, enough to propel him into the second round of presidential elections. Nevertheless, it is still accurate to say that these far-right parties have very little direct influence, and it is currently impossible to imagine a scenario in which they would become powerful enough to actually reintroduce capital punishment.

Support for the death penalty also persists in the right fringe of centre-Right parties. As noted above in Chapter 5, Tory MP Ann Widdecombe has made the death penalty one of her signature issues. A bill to re-establish capital punishment in France for those who commit terrorist acts (Dell'Agnola et al. 2004) was tabled by center-right *Union pour Mouvement Populaire* (UMP) delegates in 2004, and obtained 47 co-sponsors – out of 577 total members of the *Assemblée Nationale*. However the bill was little more than a political maneuver, since France's treaty commitments preclude the reintroduction of capital punishment. The French death penalty proposal never came close to being enacted; it was transferred to the Commission of Constitutional Laws, Legislation, and General Administration of the Republic, one of six permanent commissions of the Assembly. It was never voted out of this committee, and thus was never even voted upon by the French parliament. These examples, far from showing elite support for capital punishment, prove rather how thoroughly capital punishment has been exiled to the fringe. Politicians can grandstand on the issue, calling for capital punishment for the latest public menace *du jour*, safe in the knowledge that there is no chance of these proposals being enacted.

In fact, the vocal support of right-wing parties for the return of the executioner helps to marginalize support for the issue overall. Of the millions of voters who say, in the abstract, that they might like to see the executioner return, only a fraction are so committed to this view that they will vote for a right-wing fringe party whose other policies they reject. Eventually, active support for the death penalty begins to be tainted by being primarily associated with right-wing demagogues, further undermining its appeal as a political motivating tool. This identification of capital punishment with the fringe right also spurs the increasing identification of opposition to capital punishment with progressive values. To borrow terminology from Pierre Bourdieu, opposition to capital punishment becomes one of the marks of 'distinction' that persons use to signal their membership in the social elite (Bourdieu 2007). Of course, Bourdieu emphasized the use of distinctions of taste and outlook to reproduce and reinforce social hierarchies based on heredity, which were weakened by the advent of the modern social-welfare state. The emergence of opposition to capital punishment as a mark of enlightenment among European elites seems to be an instance of the social forces Bourdieu analyzed fostering progressive outcomes. Members of the elite gradually cease to identify support for capital punishment in terms of the progressive/conservative schema. It becomes something that no self-respecting member of the elite can publicly support, regardless of general political orientation.

The entrenchment of anti-capital punishment among political elites ensures that populist feints in the direction of restoring capital punishment are meaningless, not just because capital punishment is now regulated at the EU level, but also because the criminal justice apparatus of Continental European countries is largely immune to political influence. The aversion to capital punishment which prevails among mainstream politicians is shared by those who form and implement criminal justice policy, such as judges, prosecutors, prison wardens, and high-ranking civil servants. In part, this tendency is determined by the social milieu from which these groups are drawn: these groups are likely to be college educated or to have extensive professional training. As shown in Chapter 3, there is a cross-cultural tendency for support for capital punishment to decline with increasing levels of education.

Ideological cohesion is particularly strong in the professional ranks of law enforcement. In most Western European countries, actors in the criminal justice apparatus show an ideological uniformity that is crucial to understanding how criminal justice policy works on the ground. Johnson and Heijder (1983) observe about Dutch criminal justice:

> The research of a Dutch sociologist [P. J. A. ter Hoeven] indicates that a small professional elite, with a fringe of complementary groups, dominates practice in the field of criminal justice. Shared training, positions, norms, and values provide an effective boundary maintaining system that shields the operations of criminal justice from public opinion.

David Downes, in his groundbreaking comparative study of the sociology of Dutch and English criminal justice systems, outlined the remarkably consistent ideology of tolerance among Dutch criminal justice professionals. A series of in-depth interviews of Dutch prosecutors and judges revealed:

> that judges and prosecutors in The Netherlands have evolved a distinctive institutional culture, central to which is the strongly negative value placed upon imprisonment, which is viewed as at best a necessary evil, and at least as a process likely to inflict progressive damage on a person's capacity to re-enter the community. It should therefore be minimized as far

as possible. The strength of this negative evaluation is a central feature of legal training, in which lawyers are introduced to criminological teaching and research, including that of abolitionists [i.e. scholars who believe prisons should be abolished], which expose them to the weight of evidence against prison as a penalty. (Downes 1988:81)

Dutch criminal trials are more informal than English criminal trials, and the social distance between the judge and the offender is de-emphasized. Dutch prosecutors (who exercise almost complete discretion over charging decisions) and judges share a belief in the absolute primacy of the mission to rehabilitate offenders, except in the most egregious cases. Further, this institutional culture is generally immune to outside political pressure. Even in the face of increasing crime rates and calls by politicians for harsher penal sanctions, the Dutch criminal justice apparatus continued to de-emphasize imprisonment and develop rehabilitation and resocialization programs (ibid.:5–6). Sybille Bedford, in her classic account *The Faces of Justice: A Traveller's Report*, registered surprise at how collegial and informal trials were in Germany and Switzerland in the late 1950s, and praised the 'enlightened mildness' with which German courts treated offenders (1961:163).

In a thought-provoking recent article, Michael Tonry (2004) asked why German imprisonment rates had not risen significantly in response to increased crime in the period from the 1970s to the 1990s, in contrast to many other nations, in which imprisonment had risen sharply. He identified factors similar to the ones Downes attributed to the Dutch penal system. German prosecutors also exert a great deal of control over prosecution policies, and are members of a close-knit institutional system. They are not subject to election, and their secure civil service career paths insulate them from day-to-day politics. Further, Tonry observes, the German public 'accords considerably higher status to elite opinion than do some other places' (ibid.: 1205) including the USA and the United Kingdom. German criminal justice officials are required to avoid imprisonment wherever possible, and to make rehabilitation the primary goal of criminal justice policy. Germany has a nationally binding codified code of law – the *Strafvollzugsgesetz* – which is devoted solely to regulating the purpose and nature of German criminal sanctioning. Section 2 of the law sets out the purpose of the German prison system: 'While serving his penal sentence, the prisoner should become capable of leading a socially responsible life without further criminal acts. The imposition of a prison sentence also serves to protect the public from future crimes.' During the debate over the adoption of this law, attempts by center-right legislators to add punishment or retribution to the list of acceptable goals of punishment were rejected, and later attempts to do so have also met with failure (Hammel 2006:110).

The French criminal justice system also features extensive expert control and relative insulation from day-to-day political pressures. As in Germany,

French judges and magistrates are civil servants, and are chosen from among the best law students after a rigorous round of competitive meritocratic exams. Once they begin their careers, they are subject to close monitoring and supervision to ensure cross-regional consistency of legal interpretation and verdicts. In a recent comparative analysis of the French and American civil judicial systems, Mitchel Lasser observed that the French legal system displayed a remarkable degree of hierarchical formalization and ideological uniformity:

> [Its] elaborate promotion process permits the French civil judicial system to provide both a rational basis for the development of judicial careers and an effective mechanism for the professional control of all the *magistrats* in the French judicial hierarchy ... The organization of the French legal academic and professional spheres demonstrates the same fundamental attributes of concentration, centralization, hierarchy, and expertise. In each case, the institutions associated with the French civil legal system yield a stunningly small and accordingly prestigious elite that plays a particularly influential role in the daily operation of the system (Lasser 2004:185).

Although Lasser was discussing French civil justice, the training and career path of French criminal judges and prosecutors is – from a structural point of view – not significantly different from their civil-law counterparts (Roché 2007:483–4).

The similar backgrounds and close ideological cohesion of the legal elites making criminal justice policy effectively insulate the system from direct political influence. In this sense, what goes for the death penalty also goes for the criminal justice system as a whole: European politicians may denounce individual judicial decisions or promise to 'get tough' on criminals, but they do so in the knowledge that this rhetoric will have little direct impact on the day-to-day workings of the criminal justice bureaucracy. Inside these institutions, a like-minded group of institutional civil servants, working from a clear and explicit set of legal guidelines that rarely changes, pursue the fundamental goals of resocialization and efficiency, not the passing whims of public opinion. James Whitman, in a recent comparative analysis of American and European criminal justice systems, noted how durable the institutional consensus is in these branches:

> [I]ndividualization [in punishment], and its associated value of resocialization, have perdured in Europe, despite all political winds that have blown from the right, and despite a loss of faith in rehabilitation not all that different from the American loss of faith. Like their American counterparts, European penologists make only diffident claims about the success of rehabilitation programs. Nevertheless, European bureaucrats keep

those programs alive. So do European politicians, who remain receptive to professional advice. (Whitman 2003:73)

The insulated nature of these systems is not incidental; it is intended to achieve certain clearly defined substantive goals. Rehabilitation programs continue in France and Germany despite their relatively unimpressive results because preserving the human dignity of offenders is *the overriding goal* of the criminal justice system. Even if resocialization efforts do not reduce crime as much as they might, they cannot but achieve the goal of treating the offender as more than an object, and signaling the system's official belief that offenders can be reclaimed. To dismantle them would be to betray what almost all actors in the criminal justice system accept as one of its fundamental rationales.

The English case is somewhat different. As Downes' comparative study makes clear, the structure and operation of the criminal justice system in England differs substantially from that in the Netherlands and, by extension, most other Continental European countries. Much of this difference can be attributed to the influence of common-law tradition, which – despite increasing European influence – continues to penetrate deep into British legal institutions. This may help account for the fact that British penal outcomes are markedly more punitive than most penal outcomes on the European Continent. Indeed, they look remarkably like American penal trends, albeit on a sharply reduced scale. This fact might have prompted David Garland, in his groundbreaking study the *Culture of Control*, to analyze the United States and Great Britain together for purposes of examining recent trends toward harsher rhetoric, laws, and sentencing. However, despite significant policy and structural differences between the United Kingdom and Continental Europe in overall penal policy, the situation with respect to capital punishment is similar to that on the Continent. That is, the bureaucratic and policy-making elite is firmly opposed, and this fact is enough to ensure it will never return.

In Germany, the elite consensus against capital punishment has now been institutionalized on many levels. On the purely national level, the German Federal Constitutional Court has, as noted above, held that Art. 102 of the German Constitution (the Basic Law) prohibits all executions on German soil. Even if a two-thirds majority of the German parliament could somehow be found for a constitutional amendment reintroducing capital punishment, it is doubtful whether the law would have any effect. German constitutional law has developed a doctrine called the *Wesensgehaltsgarantie*, which can loosely be translated as the guarantee of the integrity of essential rights. According to this interpretation of Article 79(3) of the German Basic Law, there are certain basic values enshrined in the German constitution – such as the essential rules of government organization or the state's duty to protect human dignity – that are so fundamental that they cannot be revoked or altered, even by later constitutional amendment. If the abolition of the death penalty is held subject to this guarantee, then it can never be changed. German legal scholars are divided on this issue, but some believe that the abolition of capital punishment is so protected, which means that any attempt to revoke it would amount to an 'unconstitutional constitutional amendment' (Hohmann 2002:258–9).

Neither in France nor in Great Britain does abolition have the rank of constitutional law. The French judicial system has not addressed the status of the 1981 law abolishing capital punishment in any depth, so it is unclear whether the reintroduction of capital punishment would impinge on any French constitutional guarantees. In the United Kingdom, of course, there is no formal written constitution that could constrain Parliament from reintroducing capital punishment. Thus, in France and Great Britain, from a purely legal standpoint, the status of abolition is somewhat less secure than it is in Germany. However, European legal elites quickly adopted a course to shore up abolition permanently: by making it a core component of the European legal order. Protocol No. 6 to the European Convention for the Protection of Human Rights and Fundamental Freedoms had already required the abolition of capital punishment in times of peace, and Protocol No. 13, which was opened for signature in 2002, required its ultimate abolition in all cases. The exact legal consequences of a country's decision to withdraw from Protocol No. 13 and reintroduce capital punishment are not completely clear. What is clear, though, is that they would likely be at least as far-reaching as withdrawing from Protocol 6, which, as noted above in Chapter 6, would be a time-consuming and controversial procedure.

The European Union elite, which can be seen as a gathering of select members of the bureaucratic and policy-making elites of individual EU states, has taken the issue of capital punishment out of the hands of national lawmakers and permanently relocated it to the level of international treaty, where it is effectively completely out of reach of national majorities. Evi Girling recently argued that opposition to capital punishment has, in the discourse of European elites, changed from a mere policy stance into a constituting element of what it means to be 'European':

> Narratives of European abolitionism unify the fates and sensibilities of people and institutions in Europe and claim a reformist and abolitionist penal identity. The narratives present the European position as a natural consequence of the shared values of a territorially and historically cogent community. Spatial cogency is achieved through the EU's frequent and proud declarations to be a death-penalty-free zone. Historical cogency rests on a recounting of a primitive and uncivilized past which Europeans share (and which culminated in World War II). The European present and its espousal of an abolitionist stance is presented to be a consequence of Europe's triumph over barbarity and a safeguard for

a civilized future in which a death-penalty-free world becomes one of Europe's success stories. (2005:118)

Of course, Girling's analysis, as perceptive as it is, holds true only as long as the focus is on members of the senior officialdom within EU institutions and the political leadership of Western European nations. We see in their rhetoric that the 'needless suffering' argument's signal quality – its power to justify an absolute, universal ban on capital punishment – is now channeled through the modern rhetoric of human rights. As Franklin Zimring observed:

> [The international abolitionist's] appeal to execution-free penal codes as a basic constitutional requirement for a civilized state performs a number of rhetorical functions for the international abolitionist. Seeking out the high ground of limits on government power renders all the traditional death penalty disputes about what terrible crimes and criminals deserve, about deterrence, about risks of error and fairness in administration, literally beside the point. As soon as the human rights/limited government premise is accepted, the policy conclusion is automatic. There are no contingencies, no balancing of costs and benefits, and no reasons to consult public sentiments about crime as soon as the major premise of the human rights/limited government argument is accepted. (Zimring 2003:45–6)

The argument is also universal – if accepted, it transcends all cultural bounds – and furnishes a rationale for immediate abolition everywhere.

This entrenchment of abolition as a fundamental EU value did not proceed without controversy. Former Warsaw Pact nations, informed in no uncertain terms that admission to the Council of Europe (which is a precondition of EU membership) would require the abolition of the death penalty, were markedly unenthusiastic. Not only were their populations strongly in favor of capital punishment (see Chapter 2), so were some members of the political elites. These nations had been largely insulated from the decades-long process of socialization that finally resulted in opposition to capital punishment emerging as a consensus position among Western European elites. In many of these countries, support for the death penalty, far from being relegated to the fringe, was something popular mainstream politicians could voice without fear of scorn. The Kaczynski brothers, for instance, who have occupied various leadership positions in Poland for several years, explicitly support capital punishment, even in the face of Vatican statements condemning the death penalty (Fijalkowski 2005:159).

A recent exchange of letters in an internal European Union newsletter affords a fascinating glimpse into the lingering friction between EU employees from Eastern European and Western European countries in the halls of the EU bureaucracy. *Commission en directe* is an internal newspaper for employees of the European Commission. Responding to a recent article about the dignity of man, a Hungarian member of the General Directorate for Taxation pointed to a recent murder in Hungary and opined: 'I ask myself, by which logic we talk about the human dignity of beings who have obviously none. The esteemed *"goodwill ambassadors"* and abolition-ist activists would surely not be delighted to meet some of the people they are so eager to save.' (Pataki 2007). The first response to Mr. Pataki's letter, under the title 'Chop Their Heads Off?' registered the writer's 'shock' that 'views such as Mr. Pataki's still exist among educated people.' After refer-ring to the fact that Hungary only recently came *'tögether'* with the EU (an apparent mocking reference to the fact that the Hungarian language has no fewer than nine diacritical marks), the author denounces the editors of *Commission en directe* for 'reproducing' Mr. Pataki's 'populist views' (Vopel 2007). The controversy continued into September, when a representative of the EU's directorate for foreign relations wrote reminding readers that 'the EU (all 27 Member States and the Commission), together with the 47 Council of Europe Member States strongly believes that the death penalty is not the answer.' After rehearsing some arguments against the death penalty, the letter noted that '[t]he EU is also the leading institutional actor and lead donor in promoting the abolition of the death penalty around the world' (Lensu 2007). Later, another correspondent acknowledged that most readers would be 'shocked' by Mr. Pataki's views, but defended his right to express them (Andre 2007).

Of course, it would be inappropriate to read too much into this exchange of letters, but it harmonizes with the themes expressed in other recent analyses of European elite opinion on capital punishment. Here, members of the elite are not so much trying to convince an 'errant' insider that his views are *substantively* wrong, but rather that 'educated' people reject capital punishment, that his views will 'shock' other senior bureaucrats, and that the official body of the high-prestige government entity for which he works has already taken a public position against capital punishment. To quote the epigraph to this Part, Mr. Pataki, having relocated to Brussels and become a part of the EU bureaucracy, is urged, like Tolstoy's Stepan Arkadyevitch, to adopt views which are 'in closer accordance with his manner of life.'

The European Shift in Public Opinion

Thus far, we have seen how opposition to the death penalty became wide-spread among European elites, and how the political structure of EU member nations (as well as the EU itself) created the conditions under which the death penalty could be marginalized and then permanently abolished, despite the existence of residual popular support for it. David Garland has pointed out that public opinion on capital punishment rarely changes while the death penalty is still being actively used:

> That the death penalty appears to have massive popular support in the USA does not differentiate that nation from others, since virtually every other country has exhibited this kind of public opinion so long as the capital sanction is in place and usually for many years afterwards. Once governments have proceeded to abolish the death penalty – and abolition has always occurred in the face of majority popular opposition – then public opinion tends slowly to change accordingly, and to learn to regard other sanctions as the 'ultimate' measures available in civilized society. (1990:246)

Garland's observation holds true for all three countries at issue here. Support for capital punishment remained strong in Germany until approximately two decades after its abolition, and, as shown in Chapter 2, majority support for capital punishment could be elicited by 'priming' poll questions until well into the 1990s. In the United Kingdom, majorities supported capital punishment until the early 2000s, and many polls still show considerable support, although the individual results vary.

A look at European opinion polls reveals a highly intriguing trend in support for capital punishment. In both France and Germany, 'top-line' support for capital punishment began to slide precipitously in the late 1990s, and reached stable new lows by the early 2000s. Figure 7.1 shows public opinion

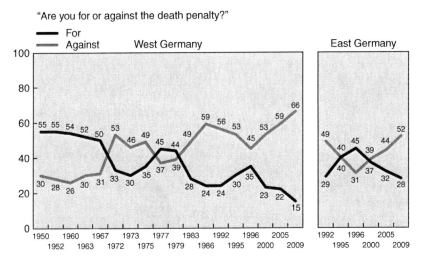

Figure 7.1 Public Opinion on Capital Punishment in West and East Germany, 1950–2009
source: Allensbacher Institute for Public Opinion Research, 2009

in West Germany and East Germany (the narrow graph on the right) from 1950–2009, with the black line indicating support and the gray line opposition. After a brief spike in the mid-1970s, support for capital punishment dropped again, before taking a precipitous plunge in the late 1990s. The trend in France (Figure 7.2) is even clearer – beginning in the mid-1990s, support for capital punishment plummets and opposition rises. The effect is apparently stable. One cause for this might be the continuing aggressive activism by EU officials against capital punishment. The slide in support does, after all, coincide with the adoption of abolition to capital punishment as a central theme in EU publications and global diplomacy. However, this theory would presuppose that European citizens (1) closely follow EU political initiatives; and (2) change their personal opinions in response to them. Neither of these hypotheses seems especially likely. Eurobarometer surveys indicate that most citizens in the European Union have only rudimentary information about that body's activities, and generally slightly less than half trust EU institutions (Ginsberg 2007:343–4).

The most likely explanation for the drop in support for capital punishment may instead be quite simple: George W. Bush. As we have seen, the European press has had a fascination with the death penalty reaching back at least to the 1950s. The 1990s saw blanket coverage of the fate of many citizens of EU countries who had ended up on death row in the United States. The 1995 execution of Nicholas Ingram, a Briton on death row in the U.S State of Georgia, was covered 'in minute detail' by the British press,

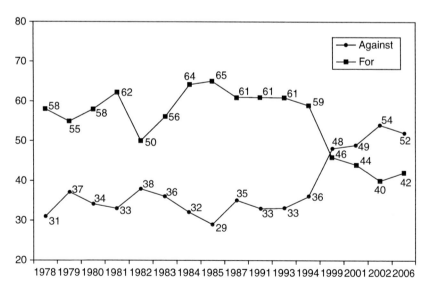

Figure 7.2　Public Opinion on Capital Punishment in France, 1978–2006
source: TNS/Sofres, 2006

which published interviews with the surviving victim and with Ingram's mother (Hodgkinson 1996:197). Germany fought the United States all the way to the World Court in the case of Walter and Karl LaGrand, Arizona death-row inmates who held German citizenship and who were executed in 1999. Before their executions, Germany launched a major legal effort on their behalf, claiming that the brothers had been denied their right to consular assistance under the Vienna Convention on Consular Relations. Germany's efforts resulted in published decisions from the International Court of Justice and the United States Supreme Court criticizing American criminal justice policies. The *Bild-Zeitung*, the mass-market tabloid which dominates the nationwide tabloid market in Germany and reaches some 10 million readers daily, has always been opposed to capital punishment, an exception in its otherwise right-wing orientation (Müller 1968; Ritzler 2009). The Italian press closely followed the case of Derek Barnabei, an American citizen of Italian heritage who was executed in Virginia in 2000. Barnabei's sentence 'prompted protests by the Italian Olympic team during the opening ceremonies of the Sydney Games in 2000, demonstrations in many Italian towns against the death penalty and calls for clemency by Italian politicians' (Girling 2005:122). The Italian press also 'adopted' Virginia death-row inmate Joseph Roger O'Dell, despite his lack of any links to Italy. After his execution, he was buried in Palermo, Sicily, where his headstone bears an inscription denouncing the 'merciless and brutal justice system' of the United States (Fleishman 2000).

Given the existing focus of the European press on the U.S. death penalty throughout the 1990s, the presidential campaign of George W. Bush was destined to hinge, in the eyes of the European press at least, on the issue of capital punishment. During Bush's Texas governorship (1994–2000), several inmates, such as Gary Graham and Odell Barnes (both were executed in 2000) were denied clemency by the Texas Board of Pardons and Paroles despite their claims of innocence. That board (which is technically independent, but whose members are appointed by the governor) also declined to extend clemency to Karla Faye Tucker (executed in 1998), despite an international campaign based on her apparent rehabilitation while on death row. Each of these dramas was followed intensely by the French press:

The life stories of American death-row inmates, such as Karla Faye Tucker, Betty Lou Beets, Gary Graham, Odell Barnes, or Mumia Abu-Jamal are thoroughly familiar to readers of French newspapers and some of the most famous French intellectuals, like Jacques Derrida, have been mobilized to denounce the injustice of the death penalty. Jack Lang, a former education minister, visited Texas to spend a few minutes with Odell Barnes in the hope of influencing the state's Board of Pardons. Robert Badinter, the former chief justice of the Constitutional Council, launched a press campaign against the U.S. death penalty, collecting close to a million signatures for a petition addressed to the newly elected American president, George W. Bush. Badinter found it deplorable that the 'oldest democracy in the world and the greatest power on earth ... has now joined the head pack of homicidal states, together with China, Iran, the Democratic Republic of the Congo and Saudi Arabia ... American society seems to be in the grip of a killing madness. And yet it has failed to rid itself of crime. All it has done is respond to killing with more killing.' (Lacorne 2005:44–5)

A similar attitude prevailed in the German press, which reported exhaustively on the Gary Graham and Karla Faye Tucker cases, among others. Even the British press, which tends to be more sympathetic to the United States than its German or French counterparts, featured many pieces on the more notorious executions that took place under Bush's watch.

With very few exceptions, this press coverage was critical of George W. Bush and the death penalty, and generally sympathetic to the inmate. In Great Britain, the tabloid press generally favors restoration of capital punishment, whereas the broadsheets are generally abolitionist (Hodgkinson 1996:197). Nevertheless, even British tabloids were often critical in their coverage of George W. Bush's use of capital punishment, and the broadsheets were even harsher in their assessment. The press coverage on the European Continent – as well as the reaction of European politicians – was even more uniformly hostile to Bush's record on capital punishment. The European press, of course, tends to have a sharper ideological profile than American press organs, and numerous studies confirm that European journalists have political opinions significantly left of the mainstream in their respective countries (Schulz 2008:100–1).

Even those few commentators who might favor capital punishment in the abstract could easily distinguish their support from the policies of George W. Bush, who was portrayed as reviewing clemency applications superficially, and allowing executions to proceed in the face of evidence of an inmate's mental impairment, rehabilitation, or possible innocence. Throughout Bush's presidency, capital punishment in the United States continued to receive sustained attention in the European press, even though the American president has extremely limited powers to intervene in executions. The fact that Americans elected, and then re-elected a President with perhaps the clearest pro-capital punishment record of any American politician was seen by many in the European press as somehow implicating the entire country in Bush's human rights policies.

If this analysis is correct, the European press helped drive a stake through the heart of support for capital punishment among the mass public in Western European countries. To understand why this might be so, it is important to understand the nature of European coverage of capital punishment in the United States. To frame its coverage, the European press looked to one of the tropes that had influenced European abolitionist discourse since the 19th century: the idea of the needless human suffering inflicted by capital punishment. European press coverage of U.S. executions remains within the tradition of intense focus on the condemned criminal which was such a prominent feature of Hans Hyan's reporting in early 20th-century Germany. A feature about an American death-row inmate almost invariably features extensive interviews with the inmate and his or her family members documenting the harsh and dehumanizing conditions on death row, the psychological anguish suffered by the condemned during the years of waiting, and the strain suffered by the death-row inmate's family.

Countless examples of this style of coverage in the European media could be cited, but one typical example may help illustrate the genre. In 2008, a German state-owned broadcasting company WRD (West German Broadcasting) broadcast a documentary in its series called 'The Story.' The episode was named 'A Death in Texas: The Execution of Frances Newton' (Giefer et al. 2006). Newton, an African-American woman, was sentenced to death in Houston, Texas in 1987 for shooting to death her husband and two children. According to the prosecution, Newton shot her family to collect insurance benefits. However, she maintains that her family was killed by rivals of her husband, an alleged drug dealer.

As the documentary begins, we see photographs of Newton, shown by her mother, Jewel Helms. Newton is shown in her wedding dress, with her family members, and in other pleasant settings. We then see an extensive interview with Newton, filmed on Texas' death row. Through a glass barrier, Newton (dubbed into German) explains her daily routine, the sources of strength she relies on to deal with her fate, and her attitude toward the justice system. She complains that the 'headline mentality' which prevails in the United States prevents people from looking 'deeper' into her story and her case. She is also asked about her favorite reading, and says it is the 'Sword of Truth' series by Terry Goodkind, which Newton calls 'an adult version of Harry Potter.' Newton is asked to describe her two children (whom she was convicted of murdering). While somber piano music plays over a photograph of the children and her former husband, she describes their personalities and habits at length. Interspersed with this interview are comments from Newton's appeals lawyer, who points out flaws in her trial and asserts his belief in her innocence. The filmmakers ask a Houston prosecutor what good will come out of executing a 40-year-old woman who seems so attractive and pleasant (*liebenswürdig*). He replies that the jury made a decision that Newton was guilty and deserved lethal injection, and that the death penalty would have no deterrent effect if society were to spare condemned murderers based on their appearance.

The documentary then broadens in scope. Carol Pickett, a former Texas death row chaplain turned death penalty critic, denounces the 'very aggressive' death penalty policies of prosecutors in Harris County, Texas (where

Houston is located). Prison officials take the documentary filmmakers on a tour of the execution chamber and the lethal injection gurney. The scene changes to the evening of the execution. Protesters and news crews stand outside the building in which the injection will take place. Family members emerge, followed by a speaker for the Texas Department of Criminal Justice, who announces, over somber string music, that Newton shook her head instead of giving a last statement, that the lethal chemicals began flowing into her veins at 6:09 p.m., that she was pronounced dead at 6:17, and that her execution was the 13th to be carried out in Texas in 2005. The documentary was nominated for an Adolf Grimme Prize, a prize for excellence in television (it did not win). The description on the prize website (Adolf Grimme Institut 2007) reads:

> [The film] is not about the innocence or guilt of Frances Newton, the death-sentenced African-American woman who was executed in Huntsville. The main theme of the film is, rather, the chronology of the execution itself. The well-thought-out and carefully planned procedure by which Frances Newton, at the behest of the state, was sent to her death. The routine of death is simultaneously banal and moving – even down to the plastic flowers on the visitors' table and the Kleenex dispenser for the last tears.

As this short description indicates, Newton's guilt or innocence is not the focus of the documentary.

American coverage of capital cases, by contrast, is frequently driven by a 'whodunit' mentality – inmates rarely attract attention unless they can put forward a plausible claim of innocence. The inmate's background and personality, if they play a role at all, take a distant second position to the question of guilt. European coverage of death-row cases differs in emphasis. European journalists, confronted with the complexity of the U.S. criminal justice system, tend to take a diffident tack when addressing issues of guilt or innocence. The inmate's guilt or innocence, of course, plays no role in the needless suffering/human rights argument against capital punishment. The main focus becomes the individual on death row – life before prison, tastes and quirks, political opinions, and relationships with family members. Thus are viewers thousands of miles away brought into direct contact with the needless suffering imposed by executions. This humanizing, emotional style of coverage, coupled with a tendency to downplay the facts of the crimes of which the inmates have been convicted, doubtless fosters the intense emotional identification with American death row inmates that so many European activists experience. Dozens of European women, for instance, have formed romantic relationships with, and sometimes even married, American death row inmates (Farwell 2007).

This style of European coverage may also be related to cultural difference between American and European elites relating to the concept of human dignity. As James Whitman notes, the concept of human dignity, while 'almost entirely missing' in American prisons, is 'pursued in Europe with an intensity unlike anything to be found in the United States' (Whitman 2003:84). The concept of human dignity – with its roots in natural-law doctrine, is a foundational concept in all Continental European legal orders (Whitman 2004:1164–71). In the penal context, dignity involves treating prisoners as social equals, as human beings worthy of respect in their own right. Since the dignity they possess is inherent and irreducible, the fact that they have been convicted of a serious crime – while perhaps justifying restrictions on their liberty – does not justify curtailing respect for their dignity. Indeed, the state's duty to ensure respect for human dignity can even stretch so far as to protect humans from their own voluntary conduct. In 1969, the German Penal Code was reformed to decriminalize sex with animals – but not before a lively debate about whether the law should be maintained as a deterrent against human beings violating *their own* dignity by having sex with animals (Busch 2005:66). While it is impossible to say how many ordinary European television viewers endorse this ideology of human dignity, there is no question that the media elites who obtain funding to direct documentaries for major broadcast outlets do, and it determines their approach to capital punishment.

It is this style of intensely personal reporting that the European media brought to the series of questionable executions during the 1990s mentioned above, and to the several controversial Texas executions that occurred during or shortly after George W. Bush's 2000 presidential campaign. European reporting closely associated the death penalty with the hugely unpopular figure of George W. Bush. This seems as likely as any other factor to have contributed to a lasting drop in support for capital punishment in many Western European countries, on the order of 15–20% in public opinion polls. The drop in support appears to have persisted throughout the Bush presidency. In some European countries – especially Spain and Italy – majority opposition to the death penalty appears to have solidified. Even the terrorist attack on the Madrid Atocha train station in 2004 does not seem to have significantly increased public support for capital punishment in Spain, which remains at around 25%. As David Garland notes, the extended absence of capital punishment itself seems to have a calming effect on public sentiment. The death penalty is no longer discussed by politicians, and the public gradually gets used to the idea of other punishments being the 'ultimate' sanction. Even the extreme-right parties who favor reintroduction of capital punishment do not suggest making it the norm for murder – they would reserve it only for child murderers or terrorists. The rhetoric from the extreme right is just that – rhetoric. Generalized pro-death-penalty sentiments are not transformed into campaigns to restore the death penalty. After all, if society seems to function reasonably well without executions, and if the institutional obstacles to their reintroduction are so formidable, what is the point of reopening this closed debate?

Conclusion

Seen from a local viewpoint, the abolition movements in France, Germany, and the United Kingdom may seem to be conditioned by national circumstances and priorities. This chapter has traced some of the common aspects of death penalty policy in these three nations. In the mid-to-late 18th century, Enlightenment philosophers began to question the sovereign's divine authority to take life, and articulated a critique of capital punishment based on the new ways of conceiving of social order which were introduced by the Enlightenment. Beccaria and Voltaire advocated complete abolition, whereas other thinkers (von Sonnenfels and Mably, for example) wished merely to narrow the application of capital punishment to cases in which it would achieve rational ends, and integrate it into a carefully considered overall system of proportional punishments. On the Continent, criminal law reformers enjoyed some success in persuading enlightened monarchs to implement their suggested reforms. Throughout the 19th century, reformers gained ground, further limiting the scope of the death penalty and banning public executions. Abolitionists begin developing new ways of arguing against capital punishment – highlighting the suffering of the offender, and linking the death penalty to a bygone era of absolutist rule. Each of these rhetorical tropes helped establish abolition's place within the emerging discourse of universal human rights.

Throughout the latter part of the 19th century and the beginning of the 20th century, opposition to the death penalty established itself as a key indicator of an enlightened world view. The most prominent abolitionists tended to come from the liberal professions – journalists, doctors, lawyers, and writers. In these social circles, abolition of capital punishment took its place alongside support for mandatory education, universal suffrage, workers' rights, and other 'progressive' issues. Center-left and left parties began adopting the abolition of the death penalty as one of their goals during the late 19th century, and generally continued on this course into the 20th century. The beginning of the 20th century saw the first serious efforts at abolishing capital punishment on a nationwide level in France (1908) and Germany (in the mid-1920s), each of which was narrowly defeated. In each case, the abolition efforts were spearheaded by progressive lawyers, who had adopted the issue as their own. The issue had also gained prominence in Great Britain, where two pressure groups – the Howard League for Penal Reform and the National Council for the Abolition of the Death Penalty – were especially active in the 1920s.

Progress on abolition was interrupted during the 1930s and 1940s, as the rise of fascism and World War II swept other issues aside. After the war, the issue returned to public prominence, with another abolition vote in Great Britain in 1948, and Germany's somewhat unexpected abolition of capital punishment in its 1949 Constitution. It was in the 1950s and 1960s that the decisive shifts in elite consciousness took place in all three countries. Prominent intellectuals took up the cause of abolition, producing detailed and passionate broadsides. In all three countries, a movement grew up to reform the penal code in line with the most recent insights in sociology and psychology, which seemed to promise reliable, scientific methods to prevent crime and rehabilitate offenders. Among the products of this consciousness were the influential British White Papers of the late 1950s and 1960s, Marc Ancel's 'Social Defence' school of criminology in France, and the lively debates surrounding the reform of the German Penal Code, which had far-reaching effects not only in Germany but also in neighboring European states. Support for abolition of capital punishment solidified in the left-of-center parties and civil-libertarian parties. Since executions had become so rare in Great Britain and France – and since abolition appeared to have no discernible effect on crime in Germany – the notion that capital punishment was a vital weapon in the state's repressive arsenal lost plausibility. Whether to keep it became an issue of conscience which was felt to be appropriate for 'free votes' (Great Britain) or '*votes de conscience*' (France). Center-right politicians felt free to, and in fact did vote against it.

Despite this permanent shift in elite consciousness, the views of average voters remained unstable. In France and Britain, public opinion remained solidly in favor of capital punishment in the 1950s. It dropped somewhat in France in the late 1960s, but then – coinciding with the increase in overall crime in the industrialized world in the 1970s – again became popular with a significant majority of the French. The enduring popularity of capital punishment posed a significant obstacle for abolitionists. Again and again, retentionist politicians in France and Great Britain tried to remove the issue from the public agenda, claiming public opinion was 'not ready' for abolition, or that abolition would have to wait until crime rates declined. At this crucial juncture, the political skills of abolitionists such as Sydney Silverman and Robert Badinter were called for. Both of them framed the issue as a matter of conscience, obviating the need for any party to enforce a particular position on the bill. Silverman was unable to convince the Labour party to officially support his abolition bill, so he arranged to sponsor it as a private members' bill, which only required the party to carve out some time for its consideration, not officially to support it. Badinter used the powerful institution of the French presidency, coupled with a tectonic political shift (called the *vague rose* or 'pink wave' in French) which guaranteed a large Socialist victory in upcoming elections. By convincing François Mitterrand to take a prominent and public stand for abolition during his presidential campaign, Badinter made the issue less controversial for Socialist candidates in the 1981 legislative elections called by Mitterrand shortly after his election. Mitterrand's public stand also furnished an argument for the institutional – if not popular – legitimacy for abolition: the people were clearly advised that a vote for the Socialists meant a vote for abolition, and they voted for the Socialists in overwhelming numbers.

Once abolition had been achieved at a national level in all of the larger EU member states as of 1981, the policy/bureaucratic elite immediately set to work institutionalizing abolition at a supra-national level. The issue was thus, imperceptibly but ineluctably, taken out of the hands of national political elites. At the same time as the legislative and diplomatic work, abolitionists also created a public relations framework in which the abolition of capital punishment in Europe was portrayed not just as a series of policy decisions by individual countries, but rather a profound affirmation of modern European values, stemming from a uniquely European intellectual heritage: '[T]he modern European view is adamant that no civilized state should be permitted the power to employ execution as a criminal punishment. In the European rhetoric, the absence of a death penalty is a defining political matter, a question of the proper constitution of a modern state, not a criminal justice policy choice' (Zimring 2003:45). This approach can clearly be seen in the Council of Europe's proselytizing message to new member states: 'A choice whether to abolish or retain the death penalty is also a choice about the kind of society we want to live in and the values it upholds. Abolishing the death penalty is part of a package of values marked human rights, democracy and the rule of law' (Directorate General of Human Rights 2001:10). With the official adoption of abolition as a rallying cry of Europe as a political entity, the anti-death-penalty movement became formally what it had long been informally: a truly international movement, in which national-level ideological configurations and currents were subsumed within a universal narrative of human progress.

8
Why the European Model Failed in the United States

The global death penalty abolition movement's most spectacular failure has been the United States. The U.S. is not the only industrialized democracy to retain capital punishment (Japan also has the death penalty), nor is it the largest retentionist country (India and China are both retentionist). Yet the perception remains that the United States – with its European roots and Western legal system – somehow 'should' have abolished capital punishment by now: '[America's] stubborn attachment to capital punishment puzzles Europeans, who see abolition as a logical outgrowth of democratic development and who are mystified about why a country so similar to themselves in so many ways can behave so differently' (Schabas 2003:21). Executions in China or the Arab world are one thing; those parts of the world, it is said, operate against dramatically different cultural backgrounds and expectations. Europeans do not directly address the Chinese population, urging it to abolish capital punishment based on 'shared values' but, in 2000, two French activists addressed to the 'people of the United States' a book-length open letter urging abolition. Its real audience may be guessed at by the fact that it was written in French (Menasce and Taube 2000). A recent study argued that much of the 'puzzlement' at America's failure to abolish capital punishment stems from a problem of perspective: 'this literature sees the United States as exceptional and seeks to explain its distinctiveness in terms of American political institutions and culture *without explaining abolition in Europe*' (Greenberg and West 2008:312, emphasis added). Having at least tried to remedy the methodological flaw identified by Greenberg and West, I am now in a position to analyze America's unsuccessful movement to abolish capital punishment by using the illuminating contrast with Europe's success.

Some commentators question the focus of abolition efforts on the United States. China executes many more people than the United States each year, and its death sentences are handed down after trials that do not begin to meet American or European standards of due process. Further, the abolition movement in the United States appears stalled; for decades now, at least 30 states have officially allowed capital punishment, American public opinion still consistently favors the penalty, and – despite some recent judicial restrictions on the practice – there has been no movement toward a complete ban on the death penalty. Thus, from a purely practical standpoint, the United States does not appear to be a particularly promising target for the activities of abolitionists.

The United States may, however, be of interest to groups other than committed abolitionists. It is a developed industrial nation with a sophisticated legal system, and one that has come close to enacting abolition before. The reason why it hasn't taken the ultimate step is of interest to sociologists, criminologists, and comparative lawyers. The comparison between American and European criminal justice policies has fascinated many leading comparative-law scholars, such as James Q. Whitman, David Garland, Franklin Zimring, Michael Tonry, and Carol Steiker. Greenberg and West's recent 193-nation study (2008) found a link between capital punishment and lower levels of education and political freedom. The U.S. obviously stands as an outlier to that generalization. In fact, there is a lively debate – which will be addressed later in this chapter – concerning the best explanation for America's death penalty 'exceptionalism.'

The United States is also important because American legal norms still exert considerable influence around the world. Scholars such as Máximo Langer (2004) and Ugo Mattei (2003) have documented the global influence of legal concepts, such as plea-bargaining, arbitration, discovery, and anti-discrimination legislation, which were developed in the United States. The reasons for American law's growing influence in foreign legal environments are complex. In some contexts, American law has simply been recognized as offering pragmatic solutions to problems that vex foreign legal cultures. Other scholars, especially Mattei, point to the enormous financial and diplomatic power United States corporations and law firms bring to bear in their attempts to pave the way for international capital flows.

The United States' retention of capital punishment also has international ramifications. Although the United States' reputation as a leader in human rights protection has been damaged by recent controversies over torture and detention, American law is still seen as providing sophisticated and robust protections for many human rights. If the death penalty can successfully be integrated into such a system, the argument goes, then the abolitionist position that capital punishment 'taints' the entire legal order does not hold water. Manfred Nowak, current United Nations Special Rapporteur on Torture, argued that U.S. policies had significantly hampered efforts to enforce international law prohibiting torture: '[Other countries] say "why are you criticising us if the US, the most democratic country with the oldest history of human rights [tortures]; if they are torturing, you should first go there." It has a negative effect because the US is a very powerful and important country and many other countries take the US as a model' (as quoted in Munro 2007). Anti-death-penalty activists report similar experiences:

> [W]hen you speak to government officials from other countries that still execute people, what they always answer is, 'Well, the U.S. leads the world, it is the truest democracy and they still have the death penalty, so as long as they do it, we will do it.' So if there is some major change in the United States, we can use it as leverage in the rest of the world. (Saunders 2001, quoting anti-death-penalty activist Anne-Charlotte Dommartin)

Finally, as Peter Hodgkinson has pointed out, the American death penalty has been more exhaustively documented and studied than the death penalty in most other nations. Its case law and academic research on capital punishment are 'incomparably sophisticated' compared to that available in many other retentionist nations and thus 'its data and debate tend to dominate the Western approach to capital punishment' (Hodgkinson 2004:29). In many retentionist nations, such as Saudi Arabia and China, death penalty trials, appeals, and executions are regarded as closely held state secrets, and little or no information is available about them, especially to foreign journalists. Compared to these countries, the United States offers an abundance of accessible information and scholarly analysis of capital punishment. This fact ensures that the American system of capital punishment – justifiably or not – exerts a disproportionate influence on the worldwide debate about capital punishment.

Explaining America's Death Penalty: Culturalists v. Anti-Exceptionalists

The American experience is thus worthy of study, not only for itself but also because of the important structural contrasts it will reveal. The explanations for America's death penalty 'exceptionalism' vary, but can be broadly separated into two general camps 'culturalists' (to borrow David Garland's phrase) and the 'anti-exceptionalists' (to coin an admittedly clumsy phrase). The culturalists see the United States as having an exceptional culture that stresses individual personal responsibility, recognizes stark black-and-white moral absolutes, downplays 'societal' explanations for crime, and is relatively unconcerned about the racial and class bias that affect its justice system. James Q. Whitman has also argued that a crucial distinction between the United States and Europe lies in different understandings of human dignity. As Whitman (2004) sees it, Europeans have developed a robust notion of human dignity that is easily intelligible to them, and judge the level of civilization of their legal orders (and, by extension, all legal orders) primarily in terms of whether the state safeguards 'dignity,' thus understood. Americans, on the other hand, are acculturated to understand and prize liberty and autonomy more than dignity, and expect the state, first and foremost, to guarantee the individual citizen's freedom, rather than provide social support.

Europe developed its notions of dignity and respect in the treatment of criminal offenders, Whitman argues (2003), over centuries of social development. At first, these societies enforced a rigid differentiation in treatment between well-born or well-educated prisoners and the common run of inmates. It was necessary to develop rules for high-status inmates in Europe because writers or members of the nobility might well be sentenced to prison for offenses such as dueling, insulting officials, or *lèse-majesté*. High-status inmates enjoyed many privileges behind bars, including the right to be addressed with their titles, to receive visitors, to wear their own clothing and arrange for private meals. 'Common' inmates, on the other hand, could be humiliated at will, and forced to work long hours at demeaning tasks. During the 20th century, Whitman argues, the increasing democratization of European societies and the influence of progressive thinking on rehabilitation spurred a desire to improve treatment of prisoners. According to Whitman, European penal reformers had a ready template: the dignified, respectful treatment formerly accorded to privileged prisoners. Many European penal reforms consisted of nothing but extending the treatment formerly accorded high-status prisoners to the entire prison population. In the United States, by contrast, prisoners had always been treated relatively equally, and equally badly. Since the United States had no tradition of imprisonment for political offenses, no culture had grown up to foster respectful treatment of the prison population. Criminals could be and were branded as antisocial and dangerous, and treated accordingly.

Joachim Savelsberg (2000), in an informative comparison of American and German penal policy called 'Cultures of State Punishment: Germany and the USA,' highlights other cultural differences between the United States and Europe. For the past several decades, he observes, the United States has, on average, inflicted much harsher penalties for comparable crimes than any nation in Europe. Further, penal policies in the United States have undergone dramatic shifts in the past several decades, whereas policy-making in Europe has remained relatively stable. Savelsberg acknowledges the explanatory power of many factors identified by previous writers, which include sensational reporting, different everyday experiences of crime, the prominent role of victims, and political exploitation of fear of crime. However, he argues, all of these explanations do not really answer the central question, which is why, in response to rising crime, the United States chose a 'punitive, rather than a therapeutic, social-reform, or restitutive' reaction (ibid.:198). Savelsberg highlights the effects of America's Protestant-Calvinistic heritage: 'We see in these old Puritan orientations several properties of the current wave of punitive sentiment: the interest in certainty of punishment, in tough punishment and the stigmatization of the convict, and corresponding disinterest in rehabilitation, situational explanations for criminal activity, or social reform' (ibid.:201). Although this view of criminals is not universal, it is shared by a large segment of the population. And, thanks to the fluidity of American society and the openness of penal policy to the influence of public opinion and pressure groups, this inflexible approach to lawbreaking has come to dominate American thinking about crime.

A final example of culturalist thinking about the differences between American and European penal policy can be found in a recent piece by Michael Tonry, 'Explanations of American Punishment Policies: A National History.' 'Four answers,' Tonry proposes, 'stand out: the "paranoid style" in American politics; a Manichean moralism associated with fundamentalist religious views; the obsolescence of the American constitution; and the history of race relations in the USA' (Tonry 2009:377). Tonry relies on Hofstadter's paradigm of the 'paranoid style' in American politics, arguing that it helps provide a framework for understanding the dramatic punitive turn of America's penal policies that began in the 1970s and continues to this day. Tonry's analysis of the religious influence on American punishment (individualistic and rigid) accords broadly with Savelsberg's. America's Constitution, Tonry claims, was designed to address centuries-old problems which included pervasive fear of an unaccountable, powerful remote government. This fear, in turn, led to the establishment of highly decentralized, federalist structures and an exaggerated responsiveness to local sentiment, as seen in the unique American practice of subjecting many judges and almost all prosecutors to popular election: 'If the public is anxious about crime or angry at criminals, or if particular cases become notorious, there is nothing to stop prosecutors from seeking personal political benefit by posturing before public opinion. Judges are elected in most states and know that highly unpopular decisions can lead to their defeat' (ibid.:385). Finally, America's history of race relations plays a prominent role. Citing work by Loïc Wacquant (Wacquant 2002) and others, Tonry argues that the punitive turn in American criminal justice policy has had a harshly disproportionate impact on black Americans, turning the criminal justice system into a mechanism for controlling and subjugating racial minorities. The fact that this transformation has been greeted with indifference by mainstream American society indicates that deep currents of racism continue to influence policy in the United States. William Schabas likewise points to 'the racism that is endemic in the United States' justice system' as a factor in American punitive policies (Schabas 2003:21).

Other commentators, however, suggest limits to arguments based on the cultural 'exceptionalism' of the United States. David Garland recently took issue with some of the arguments made by Whitman and Zimring. He defined the 'culturalist' approach as asserting 'that there is an essential relationship of some kind between the USA's culture and institutions on the one hand, and capital punishment on the other. The death penalty persists in the USA and nowhere else because the USA is different in some deep and continuing socio-cultural sense' (Garland 2005:349). Garland locates Whitman in this camp, thanks to the emphasis Whitman places, in his 2003 book *Harsh Justice*, on the distinctive European tradition of dignity and respect accorded to high-status prisoners. Zimring, in his 2003 book *The Contradictions of American Capital Punishment*, stresses the individualistic vigilante culture of the United States, especially in the racially segregated American South, which, as Zimring notes, continues to be the national leader in legal executions.

Garland does not completely reject either thesis, and is open to well-grounded cultural explanations for penal practice. However, Garland maintains that these cultural explanations do not sufficiently explain America's continuing use *of capital punishment*. If American capital punishment were 'kept in place by force of underlying and long-standing cultural commitments,' Garland asked, then one must ask 'why these determinants slackened their hold for most of the 20th century, ceased entirely for a decade after 1967 and then reasserted themselves with renewed and increasing vigour in the two decades after 1977' (ibid.:355). Garland instead argues that America's commitment to the death penalty is a recent phenomenon, contingent on a constellation of factors that, while they are unique to the United States, are hardly a reflection of deep-seated cultural norms unique to that nation:

> Widespread public support for capital punishment exists in nations that have long since abolished the death penalty, as do fear of crime, hatred of heinous criminals, racist attitudes and an uncaring contempt for marginalized groups and 'underclasses.' But governments in other nations have been willing and able to abolish capital punishment despite these circumstances. They could do so because in these nations, political elites who controlled the national legislature had the legal capacity and political opportunity to pass laws that abolished the practice once and for all. (Ibid.:362, citations omitted)

Garland argues that structural factors – the extraordinary federalism of the United States, along with a tradition of direct public influence over criminal justice policies and outcomes – are the deciding factors in America's retention of the death penalty. And, in any event, Garland argues, the death penalty in the United States is largely expressive and symbolic. Although enormous resources and press attention are devoted to capital cases, executions are increasingly selective in the United States, and increasingly rare. Although I believe Garland belongs in the camp of the 'anti-exceptionalists,' it should be stressed that he limits the strongest form of his arguments specifically to capital punishment, and even then admits that cultural factors do, in fact, play a role. His main concern is to show that, in broad historical overview, American attitudes toward capital punishment were actually not all that different than European ones, and that it may be political structures – and historical contingencies that operate on them – that do the best job of explaining why the United States has yet to abolish capital punishment.

Anti-Exceptionalism in Historical Context

Are America's death penalty attitudes exceptional? The follow-on question is: Exceptional compared to what? Certainly not compared to European public opinion throughout most of the 20th century. Garland notes that public opinion in the United States generally tracked public opinion in Western Europe for most of the 20th century. Based on the showing in Chapter 2, we can also say American public opinion is unexceptional when considered against the background of what we know about measures of popular opinion across the globe. From this global perspective, the only real exceptionalism appears in Western Europe, which – in 2009 – stands as a remarkable outlier in a landscape of general public approval of capital punishment. The United States appears exceptional only when the field of comparison is limited to other 'industrialized democracies' (or a similar formulation). Even among this cohort, though, Japan and South Korea also boast sizable majorities in favor of capital punishment, with little recent change in that state of affairs.

Expanding the historical frame of reference also requires tempering of claims of American exceptionalism. An analysis of the history of capital punishment in America shows that for all of the stages in the development of the abolition idea among European elites, there was a close analogy in the thinking of American elites. Capital punishment was practiced in all American colonies as of the mid-18th century, although the practice of individual colonies varied widely, and some colonial codes diverged markedly from English law (Banner 2002:6–8). Beccaria's *On Crimes and Punishments* was translated into English shortly after its publication, and was read widely in the United States:

> The first English edition appeared in London in 1767, and additional editions were advertised in New York in 1773, published in Charlestown in 1777, and in Philadelphia in 1778. In the 1780s most catalogues of books for sale in America included an edition of Beccaria's essay, and newspapers such as the *New-Haven Gazette* and *Connecticut Magazine* serialized Beccaria for their readers. (Masur 1989)

Beccaria's ideas landed on fertile soil in revolutionary and post-revolutionary United States. Perhaps their strongest proponent was Dr. Benjamin Rush, a physician and signer of the Declaration of Independence who fought tirelessly for the complete abolition of the gallows and for the introduction of a modern penitentiary system. Jefferson cited Beccaria as one of the most important thinkers on the subject of crime and punishment, and the influence of Beccaria and other Enlightenment reformers shows in Jefferson's own proposed sentencing reforms (never fully enacted), which sought to proportion punishments according to a rational scheme, and which eliminated capital punishment for all but the most severe crimes (Banner 2002:95–6).

As might be expected, a version of the 'liberal' critique of capital punishment was particularly influential in post-revolutionary America. Rush (1792:18) wrote:

> Capital punishments are the natural offspring of monarchical governments. Kings believe that they possess the crown by divine right; no wonder, therefore, they assume the divine power of taking away human life. Kings consider their subjects as their property: no wonder, therefore, they shed their blood with as little emotion as men shed the blood of their sheep or cattle. But the principles of republican government speak a very different language. They teach us the absurdity of the divine origin of kingly power ... They appreciate human life, and increase public obligations to preserve it.

Of course, forces favoring complete abolition of capital punishment in the United States did not prevail. Jefferson, though privately an abolitionist, did not believe public opinion in Virginia would tolerate outright abolition of capital punishment, which is why he did not make it a part of his otherwise ambitious 1776 'Bill for Proportioning Crimes and Punishments in Cases Heretofore Capital' (Masur 1989:72–3).

Few of the framers of the United States Constitution were outright opponents of capital punishment. The Constitution itself clearly contemplates that capital punishment would remain a feature on the American legal landscape. The Fifth Amendment requires all 'capital' crimes to be tried by indictment, and prohibits anyone being 'deprived of life' without due process of law. Despite the lack of clear victories for abolitionism, the amount of intellectual ferment on this issue, coupled with bold steps greatly to narrow the application of the death penalty, impressed some foreign observers. In 1796, a French nobleman remarked that 'the attempt at an almost entire abolition of the punishment of death, and the substitution of a system of reason and justice, to that of bonds, ill-treatment, and arbitrary punishment, was never made but in America,' although one historian notes that this exaggerated assessment may well have sprung from the author's desire to ingratiate himself to American readers (Masur 1989:71). Nevertheless, the wave of reforms to capital punishment laws undertaken in many American colonies and states in the late 18th century placed them far in advance of developments in contemporaneous England or France (which, at this precise time, was under the rule of the Directory).

The 19th century continued to see very similar developments in the attitudes of educated elites on both sides of the Atlantic: in both places, opposition to the death penalty established itself as a key stance of the 'progressive' segment of the educated elite, and abolitionist sentiment was concentrated particularly strongly in the liberal professions. As the United States increased in territory, however, it became less and less meaningful to talk about 'American' trends or the sentiments of the 'American' elite. America's enormous geographic size and cultural diversity was reflected in capital punishment practices. Generally speaking, the South pursued executions the most vigorously, and held on to public executions longer than most other regions of the country. In the north-east, most states preserved capital punishment, but were relatively quick to abolish public executions, and led the way in replacing hanging with methods thought to be more scientific and humane. New York State came extremely close to abolishing capital punishment altogether in the early 1840s, under the influence of the indefatigable anti-gallows legislator John L. O'Sullivan (Mackey 1982:ch. 4). In the Midwest, progressives rallied around the cause of abolishing capital punishment altogether, and achieved their goal in states such as Wisconsin, Michigan, and Minnesota, which remain abolitionist to this day (Galliher et al. 2002).

In contrast to the European movement against capital punishment, the American movement was often explicitly religious, reflecting a liberal Protestant theology which stressed reform and the offer of salvation to all who accepted Jesus Christ. Opposition to capital punishment was also often seen as a natural accompaniment to opposition to slavery and efforts to improve treatment of animals, which also became objects of progressive activism in the first half of the 19th century. As in Europe, emotional identification with the condemned offender became a significant driving factor in abolition. As historian Stuart Banner notes:

> [T]he earliest American critics of capital punishment for property crime spoke not of its inefficacy but of their own emotional identification with the condemned prisoners ... Spectators at executions had long sympathized with individuals who were executed without translating that sympathy into a general opposition to capital punishment, but that changed in the second half of the eighteenth century. More and more people felt that their moral responses to individual executions justified them in expressing dissatisfaction with the criminal law. (Banner 2002:108)

Despite being motivated in part by sympathy for the individual offender, American critics, like their European counterparts, were not above advocating that executions be replaced with a long term of hard labor under harsh conditions.

We have seen how sensibilities evolved in 19th-century Europe in a way that recalls Elias' 'civilizing process': elites began to project themselves imaginatively into the world of the condemned in the last hours of his suffering. Instead of neutral or positive events, executions began to seem disgusting and shameful; cruel spectacles that defiled those who viewed them. The more refined and exquisite the viewer's sensibility, the more disgust and shame he or she felt and expressed. By expressing this disgust and shame, members of the elite identified themselves as persons of cultivation and refined sensibility, superior to the vulgar masses who drank and chanted during the awful spectacle. Precisely the same change in sensibility occurred in the United States. As Stuart Banner puts it:

> Eighteenth-century Americans saw nothing unseemly about attending an execution. People from all walks of life watched hangings and described them without any hint of embarrassment about having been present. The experience was understood to be spiritually instructive, like attending a sermon, and for that reason parents took their children. In the first few decades of the nineteenth century, however, elite perceptions of mass gatherings shifted. The crowd came to be seen as an unruly, threatening mob. (2002:150)

Banner locates the growing aversion to public executions among the elite within a broader shift in sensibility among the middle classes. They began to 'see great differences in the realm of taste and manners between themselves and those they considered to be less refined [and] placed a new emphasis on etiquette and gentility, matters that had once been the province of the rich.' They arranged for death to be moved inside hospitals and for cemeteries to be relocated to garden-like settings outside the city limits. The middle class began to pride themselves on being 'humane and sensitive to the suffering of others,' as opposed to the crowd, which was 'callous to the sight of violence and enjoyed watching the infliction of pain' (153). Although Banner does not cite Elias by name, every one of these aspects of changing sensibility he identifies (feeling shame and revulsion at violence, moving death to the sidelines of society), dovetail precisely with Elias' framework of the civilizing process.

The historical parallels between Europe and the United States continued throughout the 19th century. As that century progressed, more and more states outlawed public executions, and brought the gallows inside the prison yard. One aspect in which the United States was even more forward-looking than Europe was in the technology of executions. Hanging had always been a gruesome affair, but as the 19th century progressed, unease mounted: '[Execution witnesses] in the 1870s were horrified at events that would not have horrified them as much in the 1840s or even the 1860s' (Banner 2002:173). Some states turned to the electric chair, touted as a more humane and 'medical' way to kill a convict. By the end of the 19th century, executions in the United States had become more infrequent, more medicalized, and almost completely non-public. Here again, however, it is essential to take into account dramatic geographic disparities: states in the former Confederacy were, in general, much slower finally to move to end officially sanctioned public executions. Lynching – a primarily if not exclusively Southern phenomenon – continued well into the 20th century.

However, by the late 19th century, the situation across most of the United States had stabilized. The death penalty for property crimes had been abolished, and was now only imposed for murder, rape, and other crimes involving serious personal violence. The late 1890s saw the birth of what Herbert Haines (1996:9–11) calls the 'second wave' of anti-death-penalty activism, based on the Progressive movement, liberal Christianity and the promise of new, 'scientific' means of correction. The movement, which led to the founding of single-issue abolitionist activist organizations, notched notable successes in the early 20th century, inducing ten states (most in the American Midwest) to abolish capital punishment. However, most of these states reversed course in the 1920s and 1930s, bringing back capital punishment, albeit often in a more limited form. Nevertheless, as the 20th century progressed, the number of annual executions in the United States gradually dwindled; from an average of 167 in the 1930s; to 128 in the 1940s; to 71 in the 1950s; and 19 in the 1960s (based on Haines 1996:12). In 1968, the number of annual executions dropped to 0, heralding an unofficial nationwide moratorium on capital punishment that would last a decade.

As the sharp decline in executions in the 1950s and 1960s might indicate, this period heralded a shift in elite thinking about capital punishment in the United States that corresponded with a very similar shift happening in France, Germany, and the United Kingdom at the same time. Koestler's and Camus' broadsides against capital punishment were each published in the United States shortly after they had appeared abroad. As both were anti-Communist intellectuals, their voices carried much more weight than those of more radical European philosophers. Given the close cultural ties between Great Britain and the United States, the report of the British Royal Commission on capital punishment also had a marked impact in the United States. Abolition enjoyed increasing relevance as a social reform issue, attracting the support of dozens of professors, researchers, and activists. Throughout the late 1950s and early 1960s, dozens of state-level abolitionist groups sprang up, hoping to convert what Haines calls the 'spontaneous decline' of capital punishment into permanent abolition (Haines 1996:12–13). Prominent law professors and activists began devising innovative constitutional arguments which would, they believed, force the Supreme Court to declare capital punishment unconstitutional. One professor began his contribution with the blunt observation: 'The season is presently open upon death as a penal sanction of a civilized society. The pattern of assault has been frontal'

(Oberer 1961:545). The professor then offered a technical argument against the death penalty's constitutionality, calling it a 'fifth column' approach.

The 1960s also saw an upsurge in progressive thinking about criminal justice policy similar to that which was occurring on the other side of the Atlantic. The parallels between the United States and Great Britain are especially close. Violent crime in both countries began increasing steadily in the early 1960s, causing increasing public concern and prompting a political response. In the UK, the Conservative government released a White Paper in 1964 entitled *The War on Crime in England and Wales 1959–64*. For all the combativeness of its title, the report argued that the 'war' on crime could and should be fought by means of improved administration of policing and parole programs, better focused rehabilitation programs, and improved social work with young offenders (Newburn, forthcoming). President Lyndon B. Johnson announced a similar 'war on crime' in a message to the United States House of Representatives in March of 1965 (Johnson 1965). Johnson then convened the President's Commission on Law Enforcement and the Administration of Justice, a 19-member blue ribbon commission under the leadership of Attorney General Nicholas Katzenbach. The Commission was composed of lawyers, judges, police officials, civil rights workers, and professors. After 18 months of intense effort, it released a report called *The Challenge of Crime in a Free Society*. The report first stressed the role of technology in combating crime: 'The Commission was extraordinarily prescient about technology. Its recommendations included separate radio bands for police communication, automated fingerprint systems, and investments in computing and information systems—this, at the very advent of the computer age' (Feucht and Zedlewski 2007:22).

More importantly, the report reflected anything but a 'law and order' approach to crime control. Writing in 2008, Robert Perkinson reflected on the report's optimistic tone:

> [T]he policy changes ultimately put forward by [the] panel in 1967 hail, seemingly, from another country. Nowhere among the Katzenbach commission's 200-plus recommendations were the sorts of punitive fixes presently in vogue. Rather than augmenting law-enforcement powers, the panelists urged greater respect for civil liberties and a national commitment to police fairness and professionalism, complete with in-service training courses like 'The civil rights movement and history of the Negro.' Instead of strengthening the hands of prosecutors, the commissioners recommended greater evidence sharing, eliminating most bail charges, and expanding legal services for low-income defendants. Instead of tougher criminal sentencing, they suggested rolling back mandatory minimum drug penalties passed in the 1950s and shifting resources from imprisonment to probation and parole. (Perkinson 2008)

The members of the Commission, which was split between abolitionists and retentionists, took a skeptical view of capital punishment. The report announced that the latest research indicated that the deterrent value of capital punishment was unproven, but that '[w]hatever views one may have on the efficacy of the death penalty as a deterrent, it clearly has an undesirable impact on the administration of criminal justice.' Not only were death penalty trials and appeals much longer and more expensive than other proceedings, but there was also disturbing evidence that 'the death sentence is disproportionately imposed and carried out on the poor, the Negro, and the members of unpopular groups,' a situation it deemed 'intolerable.' (President's Commission on Law Enforcement and Administration of Justice 1967:143). The report took no ultimate position on capital punishment, which it labeled as a matter for states to decide, but recommended that states which chose to retain capital punishment inflict it fairly, expeditiously, and selectively.

By the end of the 1960s, many members of the American legal elite were convinced that capital punishment was not only immoral, but doomed. To succeed Nicholas Katzenbach, President Johnson appointed Ramsey Clark as Attorney General of the United States. Clark served two years, and in 1970, shortly after leaving office, published a book called *Crime in America*. Clark's book closely mirrored the thinking of the liberal intelligentsia in the late 1960s. Crime, he argued, was a product of deprivation and social neglect, aggravated by the dislocations of modern urban life. The proper response to crime is a seamless network of guidance and assistance programs to address crime at its roots. Once a crime has been committed, the offender should be offered alcohol and drug abuse counseling, vocational training, work-release programs, and halfway houses to ease the transition back into regular society. Predictably, the death penalty had no place in Clark's recommendations. Its deterrent value has never been proved, it places enormous pressure on the criminal justice system, corrupts and warps those who must carry it out, and is applied in a discriminatory fashion. In short, Clark argued, '[c]apital punishment harms everything it touches' (Clark 1970:ch. 20). Clark ends the chapter with a grand peroration:

> A humane and generous concern for every individual, for his safety, his health and his fulfillment, will do more to soothe the savage heart than the fear of state-inflicted death, which chiefly serves to remind us how close we remain to the jungle ... Our greatest need is reverence for life – mere life, all life – life as an end in itself. (Ibid.:337)

Thorsten Sellin, Director of the Center of Criminological Research at the University of Pennsylvania and one of America's most renowned criminologists as of the late 1960s, titled his contribution to a 1967 essay collection on capital punishment 'The Inevitable End of Capital Punishment' and opined: 'It is an archaic custom of primitive origin that has disappeared in most civilized countries and is withering away in the rest' (Sellin 1967:253). Abolitionists such as Sellin and Clark had much ground for hope in the late 1960s: bureaucratic and policy-making elites in many parts of the country had come to disapprove of capital punishment, and a massive campaign of litigation by activist groups (coupled with institutional reluctance to carry out executions) had brought execution chambers across the country to a standstill. Perhaps most importantly, public opinion in the United States was almost evenly split on capital punishment, with over 40% of poll respondents saying they opposed the practice. In fact, 1965 and 1966 saw many American opinion polls registering a majority *against* the death penalty, even in the South (Banner 2002:240).

Furman and its Aftermath

The history of abolition in the United States so far seems to paint a very similar picture to its history in Europe. A 'liberal' political critique helps strip away the legitimacy of capital punishment in the late 18th century; the 19th century sees growing unease among elites with the practice, leading to the progressive limitation of capital punishment to the most serious crimes and reforms in its implementation; and the desirability of complete abolition grows among 20th century elites, especially among influential lawyers, professors, and government officials. What the history so far conceals, however, are profound differences in the political structure and in the world view of elites between the United States and Europe. These differences would, however, become extremely clear in the wake of the United States Supreme Court's landmark 1972 decision in *Furman* v. *Georgia*.

At first glance, the prospects of abolition through court decision might have appeared slim. Capital punishment was, after all, expressly mentioned in the United States Constitution, and the Court had never before indicated that it might be inclined to hold the death penalty, as such, unconstitutional. However the Supreme Court had sent out some promising signals in the 1950s and 1960s, during which time the Court had earned a reputation for courageous decision making and social progressivism under the leadership of Chief Justice Earl Warren. In the landmark case of *Trop* v. *Dulles* (1958), the Court found that stripping a U.S. Army deserter of American citizenship constituted 'cruel and unusual punishment' in violation of the U.S. Constitution's Eighth Amendment. In its first modern attempt to define more precisely the Cruel and Unusual Punishments Clause, the Court held that '[t]he basic concept underlying the [Clause] is nothing less than the dignity of man. While the State has the power to punish, the [Clause] stands to assure that this power be exercised within the limits of civilized standards.' Those standards, in turn, were to be determined by 'the evolving standards of decency that mark the progress of a maturing society' (ibid.:100–1). In his dissent, Justice Felix Frankfurter noted that desertion could be punished by the death penalty, yet the Court had never come close to declaring *that* punishment unconstitutional. He asked, rhetorically, 'Is constitutional dialectic so empty of reason that it can be seriously urged that loss of citizenship is a fate worse than death?' (125).

It was a reasonable question, and in the liberal environment of the early 1960s, it seemed that it might soon move from the rhetorical realm to the practical. In 1963, Supreme Court Justice Arthur Goldberg took the unusual step of having one of his law clerks, Alan Dershowitz, prepare a memorandum for the other members of the Court arguing that the death penalty, as such, was unconstitutional under the Eighth Amendment. The memorandum lays out a comprehensive (if lawyerly) case against capital punishment. Goldberg concedes that public opinion and state practice were still deeply divided on the death penalty, but made the case for judicial leadership:

> In certain matters – especially those relating to fair procedures in criminal trials – this Court traditionally has guided rather than followed public opinion in the process of articulating and establishing progressively civilized standards of decency. If only punishments already overwhelmingly condemned by public opinion came within the cruel and unusual punishment proscription, the Eighth Amendment would be a dead letter; for such punishments would presumably be abolished by the legislature. The Eighth Amendment, like the others in the Bill of Rights, was intended as a countermajoritarian limitation on government action; it should be applied to nurture rather than retard our 'evolving standards of decency.' (As reprinted in Schwartz 1985:403–4)

Goldberg's memo evoked a largely hostile response from his colleagues. Some of them simply favored the death penalty. Others, while sympathetic to Goldberg's arguments, thought it would be disastrous for the Supreme Court to wade into yet another controversial issue at a time when it was already issuing many unpopular decisions applying strict constitutional standards to state-level criminal procedure (Banner 2002:250).

Goldberg thus kept the memo confidential. However, he and two colleagues issued an unusual dissent from the Court's decision to hear a case of the death penalty for rape in *Rudolph* v. *Alabama* (1963), raising the issue of whether inflicting the death penalty for a non-lethal sexual assault could be justified under the Eighth Amendment. This dissent, which seemed to suggest the openness of one wing of the Court to challenges to capital punishment, rang like a shot across the bow among those familiar with the inside politics of the United States Supreme Court: 'The effect of Goldberg's dissent was to concentrate death penalty litigation in the hands of a few extremely intelligent and highly motivated lawyers with considerable experience in persuading courts to adopt novel legal positions' (Banner 2002:250).

These lawyers launched a coordinated nationwide legal attack on the death penalty which, less than a decade later, resulted in the Supreme Court's decision in *Furman*.

Furman was a consolidated appeal of three capital cases which presented the Supreme Court with the question of whether capital punishment violated the Cruel and Unusual Punishments Clause. Two of the three capital cases came from Georgia, one from Texas. In two of the cases, the defendants had been convicted of rape; the other involved a charge of murder. When *Furman* was finally handed down, the first reaction was confusion. The court had decided by a five-to-four margin to invalidate the death sentences, but each of the nine Justices had written his own separate opinion explaining his vote. The result was one of the longest opinions in Supreme Court history. The rationales of the five Justices in the majority varied widely. The most liberal, Brennan and Marshall, set out detailed and passionate cases for the categorical abolition of the death penalty once and for all. In addition to more prosaic arguments such as lack of deterrence and the possibility of error, Brennan (ibid.:272–73) invoked a recognizably European conception of human dignity:

> The true significance of [cruel] punishments is that they treat members of the human race as nonhumans, as objects to be toyed with and discarded. They are thus inconsistent with the fundamental premise of the [Cruel and Unusual Punishments] Clause that even the vilest criminal remains a human being possessed of common human dignity.

Marshall argued that public opinion appeared to be slowly coming around to the abolitionist side, but that in any event, the public *would* oppose the death penalty if it were only fully informed of the realities of capital punishment (the 'Marshall Hypothesis' discussed in Chapter 3).

The four Justices who voted to uphold capital punishment, on the other hand, invoked principles of federalism. Justice Powell (ibid.:418) argued:

> [T]he decision encroaches upon an area squarely within the historic prerogative of the legislative branch – both state and federal – to protect the citizenry through the designation of penalties for prohibitable conduct. It is the very sort of judgment that the legislative branch is competent to make and for which the judiciary is ill-equipped. Throughout our history, Justices of this Court have emphasized the gravity of decisions invalidating legislative judgments, admonishing the nine men who sit on this bench of the duty of self-restraint, especially when called upon to apply the expansive due process and cruel and unusual punishment rubrics. I can recall no case in which, in the name of deciding constitutional questions, this Court has subordinated national and local democratic processes to such an extent.

However, the key holdings turned out to be those of the Court's two centrists, Justices Stewart and White. They declined to hold that the death penalty, as such, was unconstitutional. However, they were concerned about its arbitrary application. In what turned out to be the most memorable and important passage of all nine opinions, Stewart (ibid.:309) argued:

> These death sentences are cruel and unusual in the same way that being struck by lightning is cruel and unusual. For, of all the people convicted of rapes and murders in 1967 and 1968, many just as reprehensible as these, the petitioners are among a capriciously selected random handful upon whom the sentence of death has in fact been imposed. My concurring Brothers have demonstrated that, if any basis can be discerned for the selection of these few to be sentenced to die, it is the constitutionally impermissible basis of race.

In the months after *Furman*, constitutional scholars struggled to derive a coherent position from the ruling. It appeared that the majority position that had gotten the most votes was not a sweeping condemnation of the death penalty, but rather a condemnation of the existing unreliable and arbitrary legal framework for imposing it.

Under this interpretation, all 40 of the state and federal death penalty statutes then in existence had indeed been struck down. However, nothing necessarily prevented states from enacting new statutes that promised a more fair and consistent application of capital punishment. And this is what happened. David Dow describes the result succinctly:

> [T]he court's decision in *Furman* did not usher in a new era. Instead, [it] inspired frenzied efforts to return to days of yore. Immediately after the Court declared the death penalty invalid, legislatures in more than thirty states began to draft new death penalty laws specifically designed to address the flaws the Court had identified in the earlier statutes. Popular support for the death penalty soared, with some surveys showing that more than 80 percent of Americans supported capital punishment. Legislatures passed new death penalty laws with uncharacteristic alacrity precisely because people overwhelmingly wanted them to. The Court's decision was promptly subverted, and its sense of popular opinion was exposed as an absurdity. (Dow 2005:xviii–xix)

In the face of the rise in violent crime that had been underway since the early 1960s, the Supreme Court liberals' sweeping statements of principle sounded untimely and presumptuous. *Furman* turned out to be one of the most broadly unpopular Supreme Court decisions in American history. The states not only enacted new death penalty statutes, but also quickly sentenced people to death under them. The restoration of capital punishment under new statutory regimes was so rapid that cases of inmates sentenced under the new, supposedly more reliable death penalty statutes had reached the Court by 1976. In another complex opinion (*Gregg* v. *Georgia*, 1976), the Supreme Court endorsed the more limited view of its earlier decision. The death penalty could still be inflicted in the United States, so long as the procedure for doing so met certain standards for reliability, transparency, and freedom from racial bias. In the following years, the Supreme Court followed what it saw as a compromise path: the Court would accept capital punishment as a part of the American penal landscape, but would attempt to create a kind of 'super due process' to ensure that it was inflicted in as fair a manner as possible. That attempt is now well into its fourth decade, and there is no sign of the United States Supreme Court coming any closer to outright abolition of the death penalty.

Europe and the United States: Comparative Analysis

The development of the anti-death-penalty movements in Europe and the United States can broadly be described as increasing convergence throughout the 1960s, followed by radical divergence in the course of the 1970s. The reasons for this divergence tell us a great deal about the approaches toward crime and justice on both sides of the Atlantic. While the rhetoric of politicians sharpened everywhere in response to increases in violent crime, the results could hardly have been more different. In the United States, the 1970s and 1980s saw the reintroduction of capital punishment, a wave of legislation dramatically sharpening criminal sentences leading to a four-fold increase in incarceration rates, and a judicial retrenchment resulting in reduced criminal procedure protections for defendants and limits on appeals. The reaction in European countries was much milder. Incarceration rates increased slightly in some European countries, but remained stable in many others. The death penalty was permanently removed from the legislative agenda despite its continuing popularity. Progressive reforms to criminal justice and criminal procedure codes passed in the 1970s were left largely untouched. European scholars often describe the climate in their societies in the last quarter of the 20th century as a time of 'penal populism' (Hörnle 2000:40–4; Salas 2005). However, the retrenchment in the United States was of an order of magnitude more dramatic than anywhere on the European continent. As Franklin Zimring aptly remarked: 'comparing increases in incarceration rates over the last three decades in Europe to those in the United States is like comparing a haircut to a beheading' (as quoted in Gottschalk 2009:466).

The death penalty stands as a clear and well-defined instance of this difference. I will argue below that the widely differing paths Europe and America took in relation to capital punishment in the 1980s and 1990s were a result of an interplay of cultural and social factors with the exceptional structural characteristics of the American justice system. The structural factors that led to the punitive turn in American policy starting in the 1970s were present long before that time, and were simply activated and brought into full prominence by a wave of crime and populism. We also see a genuine shift in the penal culture of the United States itself. The United States shared many aspects of a professionalized, expert-driven approach to criminal justice policy similar to that found in Europe. Prominent law professors, criminologists, and government commissions played important roles in shaping penal policy. The United States Supreme Court, the only branch of the federal government with nationwide 'rule-making' authority, imposed sweeping reforms designed to modernize the criminal justice system. Beginning in the 1970s, this system began to be dismantled: the influence of experts was attacked and undermined, and criminal justice policy began to be made from the ground up, by populist lawmakers and even by referenda. The rehabilitation-oriented program of criminal justice reformers was challenged both from within and without professional and academic ranks, and the public's desire for retribution was legitimized and adopted by official policy-making bodies.

The following analysis will be driven by the conceptual framework suggested by Dieter Reicher. In 2003, Reicher published a comparative sociological analysis of English and Austrian capital punishment policy in the 18th and 19th centuries. Austria, although it was an absolutist state for much of this period, sentenced far fewer criminals to death than England, which was a constitutional monarchy. Given that many commentators associate democracy with the abolition of capital punishment, Reicher decided to analyze the criminal justice policy process in both countries. Austria, he found, followed a more lenient course precisely *because* it was less democratic. To understand changes in criminal justice policy, Reicher suggests, one should focus on two questions. The first is *which social groups* influence criminal justice policy, and how much respective influence do they have? Of equal importance is the question what *expectations* do various social groups have of how much influence they, or others, should have on penal policy?

These questions may seem obvious, but it is remarkable how little literature there is that directly addresses them. Legal scholars often focus on laws that exist on the books, rather than the process that led to their creation. And even when they do broaden their focus 'backwards' to the time before legislation is passed, they rarely go so far as to contemplate steps in the process that occur long before the law is actually debated on the floor of the legislature. Many sociologists and criminologists, on the other hand, tend to focus either on the origins and nature of criminal behavior, or on the state's response – on the effect penal legislation has on disadvantaged groups. They also often assess changes in the public's mood about crime and criminals. However, the transition from public mood to public policy is rarely a primary focus of their work, with some notable exceptions (Zimring et al. 2001). In the remainder of this chapter, I will assess changes in death penalty policy through answers to the two questions noted above. I will begin by looking specifically at the legal system, and then later expand the analysis.

The Political Structure of American and European Criminal Justice

The fundamental structural difference between the United States and virtually every European nation is the unique quality of American federalism. As Ugo Mattei recently observed: 'No other legal system in the world has developed a full-fledged federal judicial system as complete and sophisticated as the United States has' (2003:391). Mattei refers here to the comprehensive system of state laws and state courts that is such a prominent feature of the American legal order. The constitutional framework of the United States government in fact 'presuppose[s] the existence of the states as entities independent of the federal government' (Tribe 2000:907). Many non-American commentators do not fully understand the extent of autonomy enjoyed by individual American states. An excellent German-language introduction to American private law, written for German-speaking law students, warns readers on page 1, under the heading 'The Problem of Diversity': 'One who wishes to explain the positive rules of private law in the United States immediately confronts a problem: *An* American private law, as such, does not exist at all, for the regulation of almost all private-law matters is reserved to each of the fifty states' (Riemann 2004:1). Riemann clearly expects this information to surprise readers in Germany. Further, every state in the United States has its own separate constitution, its own three-branch government, and its own court system ranging from courts of first instance to a state Supreme Court. Each state independently regulates virtually all fields of public and private law. Family law, corporate law, tort law, contract law, inheritance law, taxation law, commercial law – all are regulated by state legal codes and state court decisions that apply only within that particular state. Depending on the individual area of law under review, the differences can be considerable. Accordingly, all lawyers in the United States are licensed by individual states. If a licensed lawyer wishes to practice in another state, he or she must separately qualify in the destination state.

The same variety holds for criminal law and criminal procedure. All felonies and misdemeanors, from the smallest to the most serious, are defined and prosecuted under state law. States have their own criminal procedure codes and precedents which can and often do provide more protection than the federal Constitution. There is, as well, a parallel federal court system and criminal code in the United States, but federal jurisdiction is limited in many ways. First, the federal government does not have a general authorization to criminalize conduct; it must instead invoke one of a few forms of specific, limited jurisdiction. Further, federal government jurisdiction is complementary to the jurisdiction of state criminal codes. When the United States government makes a particular activity a federal crime, this does not supersede state laws making it a crime as well. The two jurisdictions – state and federal – are regarded legally as 'dual sovereigns,' which means that criminal suspects can be prosecuted by *both* the state and federal government for the same activity. The tremendous diversity is not lamented, but rather seen as a positive benefit of the American legal system. In 1932, Supreme Court Justice Louis Brandeis observed, in a phrase that has been much quoted by later courts and scholars: 'It is one of the happy incidents of the federal system that a single courageous state may, if its citizens choose, serve as a laboratory; and try novel social and economic experiments without risk to the rest of the country' (*New State Ice Co.* v. *Liebmann*, 1932:311, Brandeis J, dissenting).

All Western European legal systems are much more centralized than the United States. Lawyers admitted to the bar in all three countries discussed in this book are generally permitted to practice nationwide. In Germany and France, all serious crimes are defined by one binding code (in Germany the *Strafgesetzbuch*, in France the *Code pénal*) which governs the entire national territory. The situation is similar in the United Kingdom, although the statutory structure there is much looser than it is in civil-law systems, and Wales and Scotland enjoy increasing autonomy. The German constitution grants individual German states the jurisdiction to pass laws regulating minor crimes and local security issues under the rubric of so-called *Polizeirecht*, but this authority does not permit the states to deviate in any significant way from the national criminal code. France is, if anything, even more centralized than Germany, since French *régions* have less autonomy than German federal states, and French civil servants who are active on a local level are generally obliged to carry out federal law (Roché 2007:478–82).

This strongly centralized structure can be explained in many ways. First, European states are more geographically compact and ethnically uniform than the United States. However, there is also a legal-historical aspect to centralization in civil-law states. Civil-law legal orders place such a premium on legal security – roughly translated, consistency and predictability in the law – that one scholar has called it an 'unquestioned dogma' (Merryman 1985:48). In civilian legal orders, it is still accepted that legal disputes usually have one correct answer, and that that answer can be derived by locating the relevant sections of the legal code and applying them to the facts using the mode of legal reasoning called 'subsumption.' The link between 'legal security' and uniformity in the law is obvious. A legal order whose primary value is consistency and predictability in legal outcomes can hardly permit large regional variations in the applicable law. We can only expect judges in Brest and Nice to arrive at the same conclusions in similar cases if they are applying the same laws. The central place legal security has in European legal thinking explains the profound shock many European jurists experience in learning that an activity which is punishable by a prison sentence in one American state may not even be illegal in a neighboring state.

Another structural factor which differentiates the United States and Europe in criminal justice policy is the level of public involvement in criminal justice policy-making and adjudication. In the United States, the institution of the jury is so central to the criminal justice system that it is enshrined in the Sixth Amendment to the United States Constitution. As that Amendment has been interpreted by the United States Supreme Court, it guarantees all defendants charged with felonies and serious misdemeanors an absolute right to a jury trial. Every American state constitution contains a parallel state law guarantee of the right to a jury trial, and state courts sometimes interpret this local provision as providing a broader entitlement than is contained in the federal Constitution. Historically, the jury was seen as a vital bulwark against tyrannical magistrates and oppressive laws, and it continues to enjoy prestige: 'Americans hold much more favorable opinions of the jury system than of the courts more generally' and, compared to alternative decision-making bodies, 'the traditional jury structure [is] seen as fairer, more accurate, more thorough, and more representative of community viewpoints' (MacCoun 2001:8642). In a criminal jury trial, the jury alone possesses the right to make factual determinations relevant to the case. The law also protects jury verdicts from being overturned by judges unless the jury's decision was unreasonable.

Of course, the United Kingdom and France (and to a lesser degree, Germany) also permit the participation of laypersons in the adjudication of serious criminal cases, whether in the form of juries or lay judges. However, the American jury is seen as not just another criminal justice institution, but as a profound expression of American 'equalitarian' values, to use Seymour Martin Lipset's phrase (Lipset 2003:265). Further, the jury is only one institutional embodiment of the public's right to help shape criminal justice policy. The idea that the criminal justice system should be responsive to the will of the majority is woven deeply into many other American institutions as well. In 38 American states, for instance, state-level judges run for office in general elections, sometimes in partisan elections (Friedman 2009:451). Prosecutors are elected officials in almost all American states. Of course, they routinely promise strict enforcement of the laws to crime-weary citizens, and may be voted out of office if they are not perceived as being tough enough on crime. Because of America's first-past-the-post electoral system, politicians are not insulated from voter will by a strong party apparatus. They are thus highly responsive to voter concern about crime. The 1980s and 1990s brought wave after wave of legislative reform, including 'truth in sentencing' laws, restrictions on parole and work-release programs, mandatory sentencing laws, and sex-offender registries.

If voters do not see enough responsiveness from their politicians, they can influence criminal legislation directly, through popular referenda. In fact, citizens of a particular state will often use the mechanism of the referendum to 'fight back' against legislative or judicial decisions that thwart the popular will. Oregon voters, for instance, passed a referendum to abolish capital punishment in 1964. By 1978, however, violent crime had begun its steep increase, and voters passed a referendum to bring back capital punishment. The Oregon Supreme Court then struck down the resulting law. Pro-death-penalty forces then returned in 1984 with an updated referendum that not only addressed the court's concerns, but added a separate provision stripping the Oregon Supreme Court of the ability to strike down capital punishment by invoking the state constitution. The referendum passed, and the new law was then approved by the Oregon Supreme Court, adding Oregon to the list of death penalty states (Tack 1989:655–7). The Massachusetts Supreme Judicial Court struck down a death penalty statute passed by the state legislature in 1980, calling the penalty (in the words of one concurring judge) 'impermissibly cruel when judged by contemporary standards of decency' and 'antithetical to the spiritual freedom that underlies the democratic mind' (*Dist. Attorney for Suffolk Dist.* v. *Watson*, 1980:1289, 1294, Liacos, J, concurring). The Massachusetts legislature promptly passed another death penalty law, and the voters, for good measure, approved a 1982 referendum amending the state constitution to the effect that '[n]o provision of the Constitution ... shall be construed as prohibiting the imposition of the punishment of death' by any Massachusetts court. The court, now prohibited from ruling on the fundamental constitutionality of the death penalty, nevertheless held (in 1984) that the death penalty statute had other technical flaws, and invalidated it (Rogers 2002:351–3). Since that time, Massachusetts has several times come very close to reinstating capital punishment, but has yet to do so.

California provides perhaps the most remarkable example of citizen control over criminal justice policy. The famous California 'Three Strikes and You're Out' law (which requires long mandatory prison sentences for someone convicted of a third felony) was initially drafted by a photographer from Fresno, Mike Reynolds, after his daughter had been murdered by a man with a long criminal record. During a 1994 gubernatorial campaign in which crime rates were a key issue, both the legislature and the governor pledged to enact Reynolds' proposal word for word, and carried through on that promise. Thus, in California, a statute drafted by a man who had no legal training passed through the entire lawmaking bureaucracy and review process without being changed, and became the law of the land for some 20 million people (Zimring et al. 2001). The results of the referendum process go beyond direct changes in the law – lawmakers who fear being one-upped by citizens' initiatives are likely to try to get 'in front' of a well-publicized criminal justice issue by proposing tough laws themselves, before the referendum process can begin. Thus, the 1990s saw a string of state and federal laws named after children who had been criminally victimized, aiming to stiffen penalties and enhance investigative power in cases of crimes against children.

This level of permeability of the criminal justice system to the will of ordinary citizens would be utterly inconceivable anywhere in Europe. This is not to say that public opinion was irrelevant to government committees and parliamentary debates in Europe. Indeed, it was always one of the key and recurring topics of discussion. However, it was always invoked merely as a cultural or social backdrop to a legal or philosophical question. In other words, European lawmakers *themselves* had the autonomy to decide how much or little influence public opinion should have on their debate. Conservatives such as Lange (Germany), Peyrefitte (France), or Churchill (Great Britain) could argue that the death penalty's popularity should counsel in favor of its retention, but their point of view did not prevail. Their opponents decided to ignore the public will, as was their prerogative. The options of a pro-death-penalty activist in all of these countries to *directly* influence the decision makers who abolished capital punishment were minimal, for several reasons. First, the national legislature had exclusive control over the issue, and was thus the only organ that could reintroduce capital punishment. Even if voters ousted an member of parliament for voting against the death penalty, this would have little effect, because national parliaments have hundreds of members, and (even more importantly) because the grass-roots local constituency may have little influence over whom the local party chooses to nominate to replace a delegate who is voted out. In a proportional-representation system, seats in a national parliament are coveted posts reserved for those who have proven their loyalty by years of dedicated service to the party organization.

In any event, as of the mid-1960s, the elite consensus against capital punishment took shape, and it became increasingly difficult to find viable candidates of any major party who were willing to *forcefully advocate* the return of capital punishment. In Great Britain and France, there was a short period of uncertainty after final abolition of capital punishment, but then the new reality settled in, and an elite consensus quickly emerged that the abolition of capital punishment had been a wise step, and that no purpose would be served by reopening the controversy surrounding it. In Great Britain, leading figures in the Conservative party came to terms with the abolition of capital punishment, ensuring that the accession of Margaret Thatcher to power would have no effect on abolition. Abolition likewise survived shifting parliamentary majorities in France and Mitterrand's departure from office in 1995. Germany was the closest case among the three: had Germany's abolition of capital punishment taken the form of an ordinary law, it might well have been overturned in the early 1950s. However, its constitutional status shielded it long enough to permit an abolitionist consensus to take hold.

How satisfied are Europeans with this state of affairs? Some scholars have suggested that European publics appear to have more trust in expert control of institutions than do Americans. In an insightful 2004 analysis, Michael Tonry attempted to explain why German incarceration rates had remained relatively constant in the late 20th century, while they increased in the United Kingdom and skyrocketed in the United States. Tonry identified several factors, including less punitive attitudes among the German population in comparison with the American, and the professionalization of judges and prosecutors in Germany. Tonry also suggested that:

> German political and popular culture appear considerably more prepared than in the United States and England to defer to professional expertise, in relation both to policy making and policy implementation ... [A] number of bits of evidence document the hypothesis that Germany accords considerably higher status to elite opinion than do some other places. (Tonry 2004:1204–5)

Many Americans who live in Europe or who study European politics come away with the impression that Europeans must be more comfortable living in societies in which experts largely control criminal justice policy-making. One American journalist registered astonishment at what he called the 'condescension' of European elites:

> When a 1997 poll showed that 49 percent of Swedes wanted the death penalty reinstated, the country's justice minister told a reporter: 'They don't really want the death penalty; they are objecting to the increasing violence. I see this as a call to politicians and the justice system to do more.' An American attorney general – or any American politician, for that matter – could never get away with such condescension toward the public, at least not for attribution. (Marshall 2000:13)

An American writer who has lived in Europe for a decade likewise recently suggested that one of the most profound differences he had noted between Europeans and Americans is their attitude toward experts: 'Americans, it seemed to me, were more likely to think for themselves and trust their own judgments, and less easily cowed by authorities or bossed around by "experts"; they believed in their own ability to make things better' (Bawer 2004:20).

Yet these diagnoses may miss the mark. It is true that European political *systems* repose a great deal of trust in experts, but the situation among European citizens is different, at least when it comes to criminal justice policy. A recent review of French public opinion found:

> The French population believes that the judiciary is too lenient in general and increasingly perceives a lack of harshness regarding juveniles. The

turning point was probably between the mid-1980s and early 1990s. [Poll responses reflecting endorsement of] social explanations [for crime] lost ground as of 1993 (whereas lack of authority gained some), and ... more severity is believed required; even in 2001 a large majority of the population would welcome judging juveniles as adults. (Roché 2007:518)

Jean-Marie le Pen and the far-right *Front National* have always railed against the *laxisme* of French justice in their speeches and campaign platforms, and continue to be a prominent force on the French political landscape, although their performance varies considerably from year to year.

Dissatisfaction with the justice system is just as widespread in Germany. The Allensbacher Institute, Germany's leading polling firm, publishes a comprehensive handbook of German public opinion once every four years. The firm's use of standard questions over periods of decades sheds considerable light on the evolution of German attitudes toward criminal justice. In August 2001, for instance, 25% of respondents stated they had 'full trust' in the justice system, whereas 39% stated they did not trust the system, and 31% said they sometimes did and sometimes did not. An accompanying chart tracking responses since 1964 showed that the percentage of Germans who trusted the system peaked at 40% in the mid-1970s, but that since the mid-1980s, the number who did not trust the system exceeded the number who did, and the gap continued to grow throughout the 1990s (Noelle-Neumann and Köcher 2002:672). In 1998, 66% of Germans stated that the nation needed 'stronger laws against crime'; whereas 21% said the current laws were satisfactory, and 13% had no opinion (ibid.:674). In February 1995, 27% of respondents agreed with the statement that 'prosecutors and judges cannot be influenced/bribed (*bestochen*); whereas 58% said that some of them could be influenced; 15% were undecided (ibid.:748). In November 1996, only 22% of respondents felt themselves 'well-protected' by the state, whereas 51% felt 'not well-protected' (ibid.:759). In May 1993, the poll asked respondents whether they agreed with the following statement: 'In this country, not enough is being done to reduce the number of crimes. The police must absolutely be more aggressive in combating crime. It would also be a good idea to increase penalties, so that we can get control of crime.' The statement was agreed with by 71%. Only 17% agreed with the statement that stricter penalties would unacceptably infringe freedoms, and that the citizens of a free society must accept some level of crime (ibid.:760). A majority of respondents was also unsatisfied with some prison policies. *Hafturlaub*, (literally, 'vacation from prison') is the general name for various prison furlough programs designed to permit prisoners to learn job skills or visit the outside world. Asked whether prison authorities were too 'generous' with such programs, 64% of respondents agreed in 1995, and 75% agreed in 1996. When the respondents were broken down by political parties, even majorities of the smaller, more liberal parties such as the Greens (57%) and FDP (54%) thought too many furloughs were being granted (ibid.:765).

The data from Germany should be treated with some care. In Germany, the mid-1990s saw a wave of public concern about crime, especially sexual offenses against young victims (Hörnle 2000:642–3). The influx of East Germans into the overall German population also played an important role. Crime was relatively rare in East Germany, and thus East Germans perceived the years after Germany's 1990 reunification as heralding a decrease in personal safety. This explains why East Germans, when separated out among the respondents to the above questions, registered much more dissatisfaction with the justice system and a stronger desire for tougher sanctions than their West German counterparts. Nevertheless, even if one discounts these (possibly) transitory factors affecting public trust in the justice system, the numbers show that most Germans distrust their criminal justice system, and wish to see harsher criminal sanctions. However, they're not exactly sure what to do about this. One thing is clear: Germans do not seem to be eager to adopt features of the American criminal justice system. In January 1997, 87% disagreed that the 'American legal system, with its particularly strong role for the jury,' was superior to the German system, and 61% opposed televising important trials, as is done 'in America' (Noelle-Neumann and Köcher 1997:747, 750).

Thus, it would be inaccurate to depict Europeans as blindly accepting expert control of criminal justice policy. Put simply, it is not that Europeans *endorse* an expert-controlled criminal justice system – they simply have to accept it; since they have very little chance to change it, at least in the short or medium term. European countries are no different from other nations, in which the general population is rarely satisfied with the state's efforts to control crime, and desires speedier trials and tougher penalties. Most Americans, for that matter, also believe their own criminal justice system is too lenient toward offenders (MacCoun 2001:8642). The European world view is not particularly concerned about public dissatisfaction with the criminal justice system. Some level of dissatisfaction will likely *always* exist. Ordinary citizens experience crime primarily by following grisly and manipulative reports in the tabloid press and on television. Although the public may have some understanding of how the justice system works, they are not likely to be familiar with the details of its operation, and may not understand the rationale behind controversial rules which require the exclusion of evidence, for example, or the existence of prisoner furlough programs.

It is this world view which leads to comments such as that by the Swedish Justice Minister (Laila Freivalds), who chose not to interpret at face value a poll result stating that 49% of Swedes wished to see the death penalty reintroduced. Rather, she asserts, as an expert, the authority to interpret public opinion, and thus, to determine how much influence it will have on government policy. This expert 'push-back' against public opinion extends far beyond capital punishment. A report by the National Council for Crime Prevention Sweden, entitled *Our Collective Responsibility* (1997), acknowledged that lawbreaking had increased dramatically in Sweden, and with it public fear of crime. However, the report also noted that the fears of certain population groups, such as seniors, were wildly inflated compared to their actual risk of victimization (ibid.:10–11). The report sets out a comprehensive plan for crime prevention, stressing social work, intervention in troubled families and blighted areas, encouragement of citizen initiatives, and community policing strategies. The report explicitly dismisses longer prison sentences:

> Since imprisonment has not proved particularly effective as a deterrent, or as a means of preventing relapse into crime, it is important to review the feasibility of finding alternatives to imprisonment. The development work which has been initiated in this matter is therefore important in the light of current circumstances. A central theme of this work is the development of credible alternatives to imprisonment by moving away from locking up offenders in prisons towards less destructive and more cost-effective methods. (Ibid.:22)

The overall tone of the report is that crime is a complex problem whose solution requires an equally complex and multifaceted approach. Although the report does mention public opinion and calls for greater citizen involvement in crime prevention, there is no suggestion anywhere in its pages that crime-control priorities should be set by consulting the public mood.

The Swedish report also provides a neat example of the 'insulated delegation' (to use Franklin Zimring's phrase) that governs criminal justice policy-making in Europe. Attitudes toward crime in general have, in fact, become much harsher in Sweden, but that has not led to dramatic policy changes in a punitive direction. Much the same can be said of France. A recent survey by Sebastian Roché noted that French public opinion had become somewhat more punitive recently, and that crime was a constant issue in national politics. French politicians had taken to importing tough-sounding slogans from the Anglo-Saxon world, such as 'zero tolerance,' and denouncing the rise in violent crime among juveniles. After analyzing several different possible measures of actual policy change, however, Roché finds that none of them indicates a clear trend toward much harsher penalties (Roché 2007). Several factors account for the fact that severity in French penal policy remains an 'illusion,' to quote from the title of Roché's piece: a centralized and professionalized judiciary, broad cross-party consensus among political elites against punitive solutions to the crime problem, and the existence of 'veto players' (in the form of professional associations and unions of probation workers or social workers) who can and do undermine policies they feel to be unnecessarily punitive.

To sum up, then, it does not fully capture the situation to say that Germans, or other Europeans, 'trust' experts to make criminal justice policy. European voters can exercise only gradual influence over the broad outlines of criminal justice policy, by voting for different political parties. However, because mainstream parties largely agree on the outlines of criminal justice policy, a change in power at the top will have little effect on day-to-day policy implementation. European voters have no power to replace lower level actors in the criminal justice bureaucracy, such as judges, district attorneys, or probation officers. Unlike voters in many American states, they cannot use referenda to pass criminal laws. They certainly do not have the power to dictate to judges how to interpret the law; this power would violate conceptions of judicial independence that are elemental to the understanding of law in civil-law nations.

Elites and Political Representation in the United States

Thus far, we have been primarily addressing the structural aspects of criminal justice policy-making in Europe and the United States: who sets the overall strategic priorities, and who controls day-to-day operations. Before going further, I want to make a methodological point. Speaking of public opinion and the structure of the criminal justice system as if they were entirely separate is somewhat misleading. In Chapter 1, I quoted an observation by Max Weber which compared the 'world images' created by 'ideas' to railroad switchmen, who have the power to permanently shape the course of future development. The analogy aptly describes the relationship between public opinion, on the one hand, and the concrete structure of political institutions, on the other. For centuries, European criminal codes have been drafted and revised by assemblies of experts, and the majority opinion of the general public, to the extent it could be measured at all, played little role in legal codification. Even in Great Britain, where criminal legislation was not under expert control, it was still under the control of Parliament, a body which, before universal suffrage, was hardly representative of the population as a whole. Even after these countries became vastly more democratic during the course of the 19th century, few members of the elite felt the need to revise their previous understanding that experts should regulate criminal legislation, and that those experts should have the autonomy to decide how much influence the will of the public should have – if indeed it were to have any at all. In a sense, nobody 'decided' in Europe that criminal justice policy should be insulated from public opinion – that system was simply inherited from past political orders, and none of the actors perceived a reason to change it.

As I have attempted to argue, the United States followed a much more ambiguous path. Although there were some strains in American political culture that favored expert control over criminal justice policy, there were other, competing values – 'switchmen' who shunted the locomotive of institutional development along a different set of tracks. Thus, we see institutions – such as election of judges and prosecutors, state-level control of penal policy, a jury-trial right anchored in the Constitution, broad state-level referendum powers – which were designed to ensure that the local community would always have a say in formulating and carrying out the task of combating crime. These policies are expressions of the fundamentally different position of elites in American society. Social elites in the United States have a much more limited ability to push through progressive social change than they do in Continental Europe, for several reasons. First, as Stephen Mennell (2007:102–3) recently observed, the United States is simply too vast, diverse, and decentralized to have generated *one* unified class of elite policy-makers, such as exists in more centralized European societies. America does not have a genuine 'aristocracy of office,' to use Mennell's term, peopled by influential and respected civil servants. The elites that do exist have significantly less influence on public debate, given America's traditional anti-intellectualism and suspicion of expertise.

This distrust of elites reached a fever pitch in the United States in the mid-1970s, when criminal justice policy experts seemed to have no satisfactory response to rapidly rising crime rates, and when crusading lawyers seemed intent on continuing to expand defendants' rights. As David Garland (2001) and Jonathan Simon (2007) have recently documented, the political and social atmosphere in which criminal justice policy decisions were made in the United States changed enormously starting in the 1970s. Crime became a constant focus of political debate, the U.S. experienced 'moral panics' (about drugs, for instance) that crystallized public fears, crime victims organized themselves and began lobbying for tougher sanctions. Discourse concerning crime became much more emotional and fear driven. Distrust of experts and disgust at the seeming powerlessness of courts and police to protect the public undermined public confidence in expert control. Citizens began demanding reductions in crime by any means necessary, and by and large insisted that tougher punishments be used to achieve this end.

We saw earlier how the 'Burkean trusteeship' concept of representation played an influential role in the parliamentary debates to abolish capital punishment in Great Britain, France, and Germany. There, abolitionist politicians could fit capital punishment into a respectable and widely accepted conceptual framework within which men and women of sound judgment may occasionally – in the name of the greater good – place principle (advancing human rights) above expediency (satisfying their constituents). This model of representative 'trusteeship' is far less influential in the American political landscape. Noting Burke's idea that the representative should represent 'interests' rather than specific 'persons', Pitkin points out: 'In America, representation was clearly to be of persons, and interests became an inevitable evil, to be tamed by a well-constructed government' (Pitkin 1967:190). Commenting on James Madison's theory of representation, Pitkin observed:

> Unlike the Burkean representative, however, Madison's representative does not know his constituents' interests better than they do themselves; if anything, he is in this respect thoroughly their equal. His furtherance of their interests is conceived as fairly responsive; and when, in time, an enlarged and rational view prevails, it prevails both in the legislature and in the minds of the people. Politics is not a realm of knowledge and reason for Madison as it is for Burke. It is much more a realm of pressures and opinion. (Ibid.:197)

This is not, of course, to say that America is a paradigm of direct democracy – many features of the American constitutional order, such as the Electoral College, are meant to filter the popular will. Yet the overall character of representation in the United States is, comparatively, more responsive to public opinion – especially concerning issues that are relatively easy to grasp, and on which most voters have a strong opinion. As Chapters 2 and 3 demonstrate, capital punishment is definitely such an issue.

The pressure to satisfy constituents is particularly intense in state legislatures, which control the legislative framework governing capital punishment in the United States. Virtually all members of state legislatures are directly elected by voters in first-past-the-post elections; there are no 'lists.' The relatively loose structure of American political parties means representatives have fewer orders from above, and less insulation from unhappy constituents. Europeans who analyze American state legislatures come away struck by the differences in function between these bodies and analogous institutions in European countries. A German critic, after watching 'State Legislature,' a three-and-a-half hour documentary portrait of the state legislature of Idaho directed by filmmaker Frederick Wiseman, commented:

> 'State Legislature' documents both the idea and the praxis of politics in America, showing how even – or precisely – at the semi-professional state level, the two are inseparably linked. The politicians we watch are shown as embodiments of the indissoluble interweaving of praxis and idea … Even if you don't share many or even most of the often reactionary positions and attitudes expressed, 'State Legislature' shows what holds not only this state, but the whole of the United States together: the idea that procedures must exist that give people a hearing in matters that concern them. The grandeur of this idea shines through the nuts and bolts of political workings, and Europeans can only look on in astonishment. (Knörer 2007)

After analyzing French views of the American death penalty and comparing them with the political reality in the United States, French historian Denis Lacorne came to the following conclusion:

> In France, a simple majority vote in the National Assembly was all it took, in 1981, to abolish the death penalty, at a time when 62 percent of the French still favored the practice. In the United States, federalism and local democracy tilt the balance in favor of a practice that many jurists recognize as cruel and unjust, especially vis-à-vis ethnic minorities. The death penalty lives on simply because it is the will of the people! (Lacorne 2005)

To put it simply, state and local politicians in the United States are responsible for criminal justice policy; their constituents, knowing this, demanded tough responses to increasing crime; and their local representatives obliged. After legislators had toughened criminal sanctions, the remaining links in the chain of enforcement followed suit. Prosecutors did their best to address public fears. Those state-law judges who were subject to popular election knew that their continued employment depended on their doing the same – and often ruled accordingly (Bright and Keenan 1995). In 1995, Justice John Paul Stevens of the United States Supreme Court denounced 'a political climate in which judges who covet higher office or who merely wish to remain judges – must constantly profess their fealty to the death penalty' (*Harris* v. *Alabama*, 1995:519, Stevens J, dissenting).

Prison populations began increasing dramatically as sentences were lengthened and 'truth-in-sentencing' laws reduced opportunities for parole and probation. The result, as has been well-documented elsewhere, was a quadrupling of the American prison population; the expansion of a culture of generalized monitoring and control; and a significant increase in the powers of law enforcement. These policies had particularly severe effects on African-Americans, who were incarcerated and brought under the supervision of the justice system in staggering numbers. Glenn Loury, after mustering the sobering statistics of the disproportionate effect America's 'punitive turn' has had on black Americans, argues:

> The punitive turn in the nation's social policy – intimately connected with public rhetoric about responsibility, dependency, social hygiene, and the reclamation of public order – can be fully grasped only when viewed against the backdrop of America's often ugly and violent racial history … This historical resonance between the stigma of race and the stigma of imprisonment serves to keep alive in our public culture the subordinating social meanings that have always been associated with blackness. Race helps to explain why the United States is exceptional among the democratic industrial societies in the severity and extent of

its punitive policy and in the paucity of its social-welfare institutions. (Loury 2008:11)

What is perhaps most distressing about mass incarceration in the United States is that it is unquestionably the result of the normal and intended operation of American political institutions. Elected prosecutors and judges, referenda, state-level control over criminal justice: these institutional arrangements were intended to ensure that community sentiment would be reflected in penal legislation, prosecutorial charging decisions, and even judicial determinations.

What is more unexpected, however, is the reaction of those American institutions that are insulated from direct accountability to public opinion. One such institution is the legal academy. Of course, most American law professors are likely death penalty skeptics, although precise numbers are hard to come by. The overall tone of commentary on capital punishment in American law journals is critical, especially when it comes to the Supreme Court's rulings during the 1980s and 1990s, many of which restricted the appeal rights of death-row inmates. An example may suffice. In 1987, the United States Supreme Court decided the case of *McCleskey* v. *Kemp* (1987). In that case, the Court held, by a 5–4 vote, that general statistical evidence of racial discrimination in death penalty sentencing proceedings was insufficient to demonstrate that the death penalty sentencing process was unconstitutional, as long as the prisoner could not show that his individual sentencing proceeding was tainted by intentional racial discrimination. A search for law journal articles in the Westlaw online database with the word *McCleskey* in the title yields 27 results. Aside from short articles merely summarizing the decision, almost all of the articles are critical of the Supreme Court decision, and many propose legislative remedies for the problem of racial discrimination in capital sentencing.

However, this critical backlash within the legal academy had no effect on the legal system. This outcome is not unusual in the United States, where law professors have little influence on legislation or court decisions. This is in stark contrast with civil-law systems, in which 'the importance of ... academics' function in presenting analyses of cases and statutes to judges and lawyers is hard to overestimate' (Glendon et al. 1999:135–6). The reasons for American law professors' comparative lack of influence are complex, but one is simply stated: the 'complex federal structure' of the United States results in a massive and diffuse corpus of law that no one legal scholar can hope to master (ibid.:92). Further, scholarly influence in the area of criminal law and procedure is particularly small – the recommendations of left-leaning legal scholars were not likely to be accepted by a crime-weary public, or judges responsible to that public. In the late 1970s, the United States Supreme Court signaled decisively that it had accepted the constitutionality of the death penalty, and that this punishment was going to remain an established feature of the American legal landscape for the foreseeable future. Long, carefully reasoned academic protests against the Supreme Court's decisions had no effect on the fundamental issue – the constitutional acceptance of capital punishment. Scholars soon lost interest in propounding yet another argument against the death penalty which, they knew, would have no chance of influencing any court's approach to the issue. They turned from the lost cause of arguing about whether the death penalty was constitutional to critiquing the procedures used to implement capital punishment, or arguing that certain groups (minors, the mentally retarded) should be exempt from its reach. Here, scholars have enjoyed some success. Yet every article which suggests an improvement in the administration of the death penalty – such as my own contribution to the genre (Hammel 2002) – implicitly concedes the legitimacy of capital punishment.

As a result of this pragmatic orientation, the ideological spectrum of debates over capital punishment in the U.S. has shifted well to the right. Compared to Continental European debates on criminal justice and punishment, American ones look tame. Ideas that are consigned to the radical fringe in the United States are discussed openly in Europe. One example is the idea that prisons – as such – should be completely abolished. As David Downes notes, Dutch lawyers and policy-makers are, during their professional training, routinely exposed to arguments for the complete abolition of prisons (Downes 1988:81). An editorial in the September 5, 2009 edition of *Le Monde* also advocated abolition:

> The abolition of the death penalty therefore constituted less the symbolic accession of the left than the event that signified the defeat of its thought. Far from resolving a moral and political problem under the banner of the rights of Man, the abolition of the death penalty in 1981 sanctioned and sanctified punishment as incarceration. The left ratified a vast tendency in society in which squeamishness vies with hypocrisy. (Dalrymple 2009)

In Germany, the field of criminal law scholarship has always had a vigorous camp of left-leaning professors. An example of their thinking can be seen in an essay contributed by Karl-Ludwig Kunz, a prominent German and Swiss criminal law scholar, to a book entitled 'Must Punishment Exist?' (*Muss Strafe Sein?*). Taking as his starting point David Garland's (2001) *Culture of Control*, Kunz argues that criminal law scholars must resist the tide toward mindless retribution, and continue posing the most basic questions concerning the justification of punishment. After a brief historical review of theories of punishment, Kunz concludes:

> Realistically, we must accept the reality that in the foreseeable future, we will have to expect continued dominance of the idea that punishment is

necessary. However, the fact that there is no philosophical (*wissenschaftlich*) justification for preferring the concept of punishment is not meaningless – rather, it has a direct influence on the realization of punishment. (Kunz 2004:79)

Kunz concludes that, because punishment can only be justified by political realities, not by philosophical necessity, it must be kept to the bare minimum. Although Kunz concedes that his reasoning would be rejected by the dominant forces in criminal law, he holds it out as the 'only hope for creating a rationally-inspired science of sanctioning' (ibid.:81).

Needless to say, the Netherlands, France, and Germany still have prisons. However, the thinking of 'abolitionist' scholars still has an impact, by moving the goalposts of what is considered 'mainstream' in the debate over penal policy. When a prominent professor proposes a radical reform to criminal law, procedure, or sentencing, the rest of the policy-making community must, at the very least, take notice and prepare a response. Although the most radical ideas – such as abolishing prisons – are likely to remain thought experiments, this is not true of less ambitious reform proposals. In Continental Europe's expert-driven criminal justice policy process, professors can hope to see their suggested reforms enacted into law. The German experience of the 1960s shows this process clearly: the 'alternative' draft Penal Code drafted in 1965 exercised considerable worldwide influence in those nations (such as Brazil and Argentina) which also had expert-driven, civil-law policy structures. Further, in the late 1960s and early 1970s, many of the ideas first proposed in the 'alternative' criminal code became law in Germany.

As one might imagine, an intellectual landscape in which prominent professors debate whether punishment, as such, is necessary is not likely to host many supporters of capital punishment. American scholars are much more divided on the subject of punishment and retribution than their European counterparts. In the United States, the 1980s saw a resurgence in traditional theories of punishment:

[T]he three decades after *Furman* saw the idea of retribution return to intellectual respectability. Long rejected as a legitimate goal of punishment in academic and policymaking circles, retribution made an astonishingly fast comeback. Part of its rise was a reaction to the widespread loss of faith in the power of prisons and similar institutions to rehabilitate criminals. Part grew out of the resurgence of causal models of crime that rested on the free will of the criminal rather than on social or biological forces beyond the criminal's control. (Banner 2002:282)

Although many American states had passed laws during the 1970s which had excluded retribution as an acceptable ground for punishment by the state, courts reintroduced retribution in the 1970s and 1980s, partly because retribution was by far the most convincing justification for capital punishment (Cotton 2000). Motivated partly by the 'rehabilitation' of retribution, scholars in the United States have openly endorsed capital punishment, stricter sentencing laws, or 'shame sentencing' involving the public humiliation of offenders (Kahan 1996, endorsing shame sentencing).

U.S. Courts and Capital Punishment

We have seen that for all their independence, American legal scholars cannot serve as a bulwark against pro-death-penalty sentiment, because they (1) have almost no influence over the operations of the criminal justice system; and (2) are themselves deeply divided over such subjects as the desirability of public influence over the criminal justice system, the legitimacy of retribution as a goal of punishment, and even the legitimacy of capital punishment. But what of American federal courts? The Constitution grants American federal judges significant independence: they are appointed by the President (subject to the 'advice and consent' of the Senate), have life tenure, and their salaries cannot be reduced by Congress. Further, since the epochal 1803 decision of the United States Supreme Court in *Marbury* v. *Madison*, U.S. Supreme Court judges (and, by extension, all federal judges) have the power of judicial review: they may invalidate state laws and acts of Congress which they believe violate the Constitution. As a result, the United States Supreme Court is arguably the most powerful tribunal among the highest courts in the U.K., Germany, and France. It has the unquestioned power of judicial review, automatic authority over all lesser courts in the country, and broad jurisdiction to decide all questions of constitutional law.

Further, in America's deeply decentralized polity, the United States Supreme Court is the only organ of government that has the power to directly command nationwide uniformity on a matter of law. The United States Congress has no authority to interpret the Constitution, and has no ability to override state criminal laws. The Court, however, issues binding interpretations of the Constitution, and can override state criminal laws found constitutionally wanting. The Court, for instance, overruled capital punishment laws in 40 U.S. states in its 1972 *Furman* decision. The Court could have declared capital punishment to be fundamentally irreconcilable with the United States Constitution, and immediately consigned it to history forever. It still could take this step, at least theoretically.

Why has the Court not yet done so? The most obvious reason for this is that, since the mid-1970s, a consistent majority of Justices of the Supreme Court have belonged to two different camps: Justices who themselves personally have no qualms about capital punishment; and second, Justices who believe – regardless of their personal views on the practice – that capital punishment does not violate the U.S. Constitution. Justice Antonin Scalia, who has sat on the Court since 1986, serves as an example of the first group. He recently stated his opinion on capital punishment with characteristic directness:

> For me, therefore, the constitutionality of the death penalty is not a difficult, soul-wrenching question. It was clearly permitted when the Eighth Amendment was adopted (not merely for murder, by the way, but for all felonies – including, for example, horse-thieving, as anyone can verify by watching a western movie) ... And so it is clearly permitted today. That is not to say I favor the death penalty (I am judicially and judiciously neutral on that point); it is only to say that I do not find the death penalty immoral. (Scalia 2002)

Most American judges, like Scalia, choose – on grounds of 'judicial judiciousness' – not to reveal their personal opinion on the ultimate issue of the death penalty's desirability as a policy. However, the unmistakable tone of the opinions written by Justice Scalia and his like-minded colleagues leave little doubt where they stand. Consider Scalia's opinion in the 1994 case of *Callins* v. *Collins*. In response to his colleague Justice Blackmun's denunciation of the unfairness of capital punishment in that case, Scalia contrasted Blackmun's concern for procedural fairness with the brutality of the crimes for which the death sentence had been imposed:

> [Consider a case pending before the Court involving an] 11-year-old girl raped by four men and then killed by stuffing her panties down her throat ... How enviable a quiet death by lethal injection compared with that! If the people conclude that such more brutal deaths may be deterred by capital punishment; indeed, if they merely conclude that justice requires such brutal deaths to be avenged by capital punishment; the creation of false, untextual and unhistorical contradictions within 'the Court's Eighth Amendment jurisprudence' should not prevent them. (1994:1148, Scalia J, concurring in denial of certiorari)

Despite his prominence, Scalia is an outlier in the American judicial landscape, being decidedly more outspoken than the majority of American federal court judges. The majority of judges belong to the second category: those who subordinate their personal opinions about capital punishment to their judicial duty. Justice Harry Blackmun's opinion in the epochal *Furman* case (1972:406–11) is an unusually personal statement of this approach:

> Cases such as these provide for me an excruciating agony of the spirit. I yield to no one in the depth of my distaste, antipathy, and, indeed, abhorrence, for the death penalty, with all its aspects of physical distress and fear and of moral judgment exercised by finite minds. That distaste

is buttressed by a belief that capital punishment serves no useful purpose that can be demonstrated ... To [strike down the death penalty] in these cases is, of course, the easy choice. It is easier to strike the balance in favor of life and against death. It is comforting to relax in the thoughts – perhaps the rationalizations – that this is the compassionate decision for a maturing society; that this is the moral and the 'right' thing to do; that thereby we convince ourselves that we are moving down the road toward human decency; that we value life even though that life has taken another or others or has grievously scarred another or others and their families; and that we are less barbaric than we were [in decades past] ... Our task here [however], as must so frequently be emphasized and re-emphasized, is to pass upon the constitutionality of legislation that has been enacted and that is challenged. This is the sole task for judges. We should not allow our personal preferences as to the wisdom of legislative and congressional action, or our distaste for such action, to guide our judicial decision in cases such as these.

Thus, Blackmun joined the four-Justice minority who voted to uphold the death penalty against constitutional challenge. It is likely that dozens, if not hundreds, of federal judges occupy the same category as Blackmun, even if they do not state their views so bluntly.

Aside from the personal attitudes of the Justices, there are other – largely self-imposed – institutional constraints on the Court. The Court indeed has considerable power, but is also loath to be seen as exercising that power too promiscuously. Judicial review, as institutionalized in the United States, is 'the power to apply and construe the Constitution, in matters of the greatest moment, against the will of a legislative majority, which is, in turn, powerless to affect the judicial decision' (Bickel 1986:20). This extraordinary power gives rise to the 'countermajoritarian difficulty' (to use the term coined by Alexander Bickel in 1962). How much judicial interference with the legislature's will can be tolerated in a political system which prides itself on democratic legitimacy? The difficulty is not just felt by legislatures, who must see their laws overturned, it is felt by judges as well. Learned Hand, one of the most influential American federal judges of the 20th century, described his unease at the power entrusted to him as follows:

For myself, it would be most irksome to be ruled by a bevy of Platonic Guardians, even if I knew how to choose them, which I assuredly do not. If they were in charge, I should miss the stimulus of living in a society where I have, at least theoretically, some part in the direction of public affairs. Of course I know how illusory would be the belief that my vote determined anything; but nevertheless when I go to the polls I have a satisfaction in the sense that we are all engaged in a common venture. (As quoted in Bickel 1986:20)

Hand's quotation exemplifies the assumption, publicly subscribed to by virtually every American judge, that the will of the people – as identified by referendum or legislative enactment – should be respected, unless compelling reasons exist not to do so.

This assumption takes institutional form in various doctrines developed by the United States Supreme Court. One is the principle that 'courts should neither anticipate a question of constitutional law in advance of the necessity of deciding it nor formulate a rule of constitutional law broader than is required by the precise facts to which it is to be applied' (*Washington State Grange* v. *Washington State Republican Party*, 2008:447, quotation marks omitted). The Court has also established a number of different 'abstention doctrines' – usually articulated in the form of multi-pronged tests – which require it to abstain from ruling on questions of law until coordinate state-level courts have had a chance to interpret them. The 'political question' doctrine, in turn, requires the Court to decline to decide issues more suited to decision by other branches of government. It is important to note that these self-imposed restrictions on judicial review are quite malleable. Whenever a Supreme Court majority strikes down a law, there is almost inevitably a dissenting opinion accusing it of overreach and the converse is true as well. This seemingly endless debate over the technical aspects of jurisdiction and interpretation is a characteristic of Supreme Court jurisprudence. The Court, seemingly uncomfortable with its power to make law, has increasingly shied away from direct debate over the normative substance of Constitutional issues (such as: is capital punishment constitutional?), and instead developed a series of multi-pronged 'tests' designed to conceal the Court's normative rule-setting power behind a veil of apparent 'objectivity.' In comparative law scholar Mitchel Lasser's words: '[T]he American judiciary justifies and legitimates the exercise of its lawmaking powers by deploying a technical, wordy, and safe judicial discourse whose compromise mode of *formalizing the pragmatic* therefore dominates the American judicial landscape' (Lasser 2004:344).

We can thus see two distinct paradigms of 'judicial restraint' operating in American courts. The first paradigm consists of straightforward self-imposed limits on the power of the courts, driven by the judges' sincere desire to minimize interference in democratic processes. The second, more subtle paradigm is identified by Lasser – a tendency to conceal the Court's lawmaking, norm-establishing power behind an edifice of objective-sounding tests and standards. These standards enable the court to distance itself from the 'dirty work' of enforcing Constitutional norms directly, by presenting decisions as driven by a value-neutral, rationally constructed judicial 'test,' the outcome of which is determined by factors external to the court. Both of these paradigms of restraint influence the United States Supreme Court's jurisprudence on capital punishment. As we have seen, the Court is now dominated by Justices who, regardless of their personal stance on the death penalty, believe that the issue of capital punishment's fundamental legitimacy is simply not a matter for the Court to decide. The Justices courted the 'countermajoritarian difficulty' in 1972, when their apparent decision to declare capital punishment unconstitutional was swiftly rejected by an overwhelming majority of legislators and citizens. After this bruising defeat, they are unlikely to venture another frontal assault on capital punishment – assuming they believe the Constitution required them to do so, which is currently not the case.

Further, the Court's jurisprudence on capital punishment is now firmly governed by its second paradigm of restraint – the tendency to deflect responsibility for deciding a fundamental normative issue by the construction of various tests and standards which appear to yield an 'automatic' resolution of the case not influenced by any Justice's personal leanings. After yielding on the fundamental issue of capital punishment, the Court chose to compensate by handing down an intricate set of procedural rulings designed to create a form of 'super due process' exclusively for capital cases. However, beginning in the mid-1980s, the Court then changed direction, enacting a variety of complex exceptions and limitations to the framework of super due process, hoping to respond to the concerns of critics who bemoaned the length of capital appeals. The result, as documented by Jordan and Carol Steiker, was that the death penalty was 'perversely both over- and under-regulated' (Steiker and Steiker 1995:349): it was governed by an arcane jurisprudence that created an *illusion* of a searching review of death sentences, but – owing to various procedural obstacles – in fact often delivered nothing of the sort.

Many of these rules serve to deflect or delegate judicial responsibility for norm-creation, as well as for the outcome of any specific case. For instance, the Court judges the 'evolving standards of decency' enshrined in the Eighth Amendment prohibition of cruel and unusual punishment not solely by its own unaided reflection or constitutional analysis, but primarily by whether American society *as a whole* appears to have *already* concluded a certain punishment practice is 'cruel and unusual.' To make this determination, in turn, the Court relies on the 'clearest and most reliable objective evidence of contemporary values ... the legislation enacted by the country's [state and federal] legislatures' (*Atkins v. Virginia* 2002:378). Thus, the Court, in *Atkins*, overruled a 1989 decision permitting the execution of mentally retarded offenders principally because many American state legislatures had banned the practice in the 13 years since the Court had last addressed the issue. It would be difficult indeed to imagine this level of institutionalized deference to public opinion in any European constitutional court. Another example of the U.S. Supreme Court's reluctance to directly address normative questions is its continuing failure to answer the question whether executing an innocent inmate – regardless of whether there were any flaws at his trial – would violate the American Constitution. An inmate can have his claim of actual innocence of the crime which put him on death row heard, but only if he first proves that there was an independent constitutional weakness in his trial, *and* that he has not forfeited, on procedural grounds, the right to present that argument. As Justice Scalia recently observed:

> This Court has *never* held that the Constitution forbids the execution of a convicted defendant who has had a full and fair trial but is later able to convince [an appeals] court that he is 'actually' innocent. Quite to the contrary, we have repeatedly left that question unresolved, while expressing considerable doubt that any claim based on alleged 'actual innocence' is constitutionally cognizable. (In re *Troy Anthony Davis* 2009:5 Scalia J, dissenting (citations omitted))

Thus has the Supreme Court patiently, over a span of decades, obscured the fundamental normative questions raised by capital punishment in the United States. Many jurists are puzzled by the American Supreme Court's seeming inability to 'grasp the nettle' in the manner of the Constitutional Court of South Africa which, in the case of *State* v. *Makwanyanye and Mchunu* (1995), forthrightly declared capital punishment incompatible with the South African Constitution's ban on 'cruel, inhuman and degrading' punishment. The answer is that the United States Supreme Court, while unquestionably having the power to declare capital punishment unconstitutional, no longer has the will or desire to do so. The only body possessing a weapon strong enough to eliminate capital punishment in all 50 states overnight has, so to speak, unilaterally disarmed.

Conclusion

As I have argued in this chapter, the European model of death penalty abolition has foundered on the unique institutional and structural characteristics of United States criminal justice. The President of the United States has no power to influence American capital punishment policy, except by issuing pardons or giving speeches. The U.S. federal government will not sign international treaties calling for the abolition of capital punishment. Even if the Congress were dominated by abolitionists, which is certainly not the case, that body has no power to dictate criminal justice policy to the individual states. Individual state legislators, who ushered capital punishment back onto the American penal landscape, are extremely sensitive to the wishes of their constituents. The Burkean notion of legislators as members of an elite which must occasionally defy the public mood in the name of higher principle is, to put it mildly, not a prominent feature of day-to-day state-level politics in the United States. Finally, the long tradition of direct public involvement in criminal justice policy-making and implementation ensures that not only legislators, but also powerful actors in the criminal justice system, such as prosecutors and judges, must tack close to the wind of public opinion or risk losing their jobs.

These structural obstacles would be formidable enough on their own, but they must be considered in light of the different role and ideological make-up of the American bureaucratic and policy-making elite. First, unlike their European counterparts, American law professors have almost no institutional influence on legislation or court decisions. Nor, for that matter, do national expert panels or commissions, which played so important a role in abolition in Europe. The American Society of Criminology called for the abolition of capital punishment in 1989 (Bohm 2008:286). Outside of academic circles, the resolution was ignored. Eight years later, the American Bar Association House of Delegates (1997) passed a resolution calling for 'each jurisdiction that imposes capital punishment not to carry out the death penalty until the jurisdiction implements policies and procedures that ... ensure that death penalty cases are administered fairly and impartially, in accordance with due process, and ... minimize the risk that innocent persons may be executed.' Although the resolution generated some debate, it did not lead any American jurisdictions to suspend executions. 'Outside' experts from the profession and the academy have marginal influence on American penal policies. They are rarely consulted before those policies are adopted, and their criticism of existing policies goes largely unnoticed.

Finally, and perhaps even more significantly, the American bureaucratic and policy-making elites have not reached the anti-death-penalty consensus that their European counterparts have. There are many open supporters of capital punishment among American judges, prosecutors, law professors, and legislators, and these men and women need not fear being stigmatized as 'backward' or 'demagogic' for holding these views. American judges largely view the death penalty as a policy choice to be made by individual states, not a transcendent human-rights issue or test of society's moral fiber. The only institutional actor that actually possesses the authority to enforce a nationwide ban on capital punishment is the United States Supreme Court. The last open, committed death penalty abolitionists left that Court decades ago, and were replaced either by judges who appear comfortable with capital punishment, or who believe themselves bound to respect previous precedents establishing capital punishment's constitutionality.

Abolitionists will likely continue to achieve important piecemeal victories in the United States, but it is impossible to envision nationwide, permanent abolition, short of a massive cultural shift away from punitive approaches to crime control, coupled with fundamental structural reforms. As Franklin Zimring and his colleagues noted in their perceptive 2001 analysis of California penal policy, one way to change policy outcomes in the United States would be to introduce 'insulated delegation' – practices and procedures which 'delegate' penal policy authority to bodies or individuals who are 'insulated' from the public will (Zimring et al. 2001:184–5). Although this approach would require a considerable amount of structural reform, it has precedents in American history, as the authors show. However, what may prove promising for a diffuse, complex policy area such as criminal sentencing *in general* may not work for the single, specific issue of capital punishment. As this book has shown, the death penalty is (1) a high-profile, symbolically charged issue; (2) a matter on which most people already have a firm opinion; (3) based largely on social or moral intuitions that are impervious to 'rational' disputation. When it comes to such issues – issues people feel close to and strongly about – there is no way to make major changes in policy 'on the sly.' Americans simply do not care what 'experts' think about capital punishment, and will resist efforts to subject the issue to expert decision – if they believe that this move is a pretext for abolition.

Conclusion – Abolitionism beyond America and Europe

Despite its signal failure in the United States, versions of the European model of death penalty abolition have been successful in other Western European nations, as well as nations that more closely resemble Western European nations in terms of political structure and the influence of intellectual elites. In Belgium, the jurist Edouard Ducpétiaux published his first broadside against capital punishment in 1827 when he was just 23 years old. Entitled *On Capital Punishment*, the 396-page opus makes Beccarian arguments against the death penalty and other backward penal practices that 'all the world condemns, yet at the same time tolerates' (1827:xxi). Ducpétiaux would later become Inspector of Prisons in Belgium, and wrote many treatises and essays on crime prevention and penal reform. In 1863, Belgian authorities agreed on an informal ban on capital punishment. The law would remain on the books, but each person condemned to death would receive a guaranteed royal commutation (perhaps the ultimate form of elite-driven abolition). The agreement held, with exceptions for the execution of one soldier in 1918 and of 242 collaborators in the aftermath of World War II. Only in 1996 did Belgium finally officially repeal its capital punishment laws. That repeal set the stage for Belgium's later ratification of Additional Protocols 6 and 13 to the European Convention on Human Rights. In 2005, the formal abolition of capital punishment was enshrined in the Belgian constitution.

Canada abolished capital punishment in 1976, when the penalty was still quite popular among the population as a whole. Abolition was only possible after 'several dedicated MPs, teams of sociologists and criminologists, media pressure, popular abolitionist groups ... and prominent abolitionists with expertise in criminal justice ... convince[d] MPs to vote against the tide of public opinion by outlawing executions' (Strange 1992:8). Nevertheless, a majority of Canadians continued to favor capital punishment for decades after the vote, and this public support occasionally found expression in Parliament, where a 1987 campaign for the return of capital punishment was defeated by a margin of just 21 votes (ibid.:23). The periodic waves of public anger caused by notorious serial killers such as Clifford Olson and

Karla Homolka drive occasional spikes in support for capital punishment, but in Canada, as in many European countries, the early 2000s appear to have seen a noticeable drop in support.

Mexico's legal heritage was greatly influenced by a progressive legal class which was steeped in Enlightenment ideas. Following France, Mexico abolished capital punishment for political crimes in 1857. In 1929, following heated debate, capital punishment was finally eliminated for all ordinary crimes, first by the Federal government, and then by all the Mexican states. Public opinion was largely unaffected by this development. As historian Everard Kidder Meade (2004) notes, '[s]ensational newspaper coverage of heinous crimes has driven attempts to reinstate the death penalty in Mexico since it was first stricken from the penal code in 1929.' In the early 1940s, the focus of debate was Gregorio Cárdenas Hernández, a young chemist who had abducted and murdered four young women. His case prompted loud public calls for the reinstatement of capital punishment in the Mexican Chamber of Deputies. Opponents of capital punishment 'combin[ed] Enlightened notions of natural law with a hyper-modern vision of the state ... constructing the independence of personhood from the physical body as an inalienable "right to life" that the state would guarantee through therapeutic interventions.' They also argued the 'illegitimacy of popular opinion, affective and localized notions of justice, and purely biological or hereditarian constructions of Mexican people as legitimate loci of rights' (Meade 2004:17). Capital punishment was not reinstated, and Cárdenas was released from prison, rehabilitated, in the mid-1970s. Mexico continues to adhere to an abolitionist policy despite strong public support for capital punishment, and has launched a vigorous and high-profile legal assistance campaign to assist Mexican nationals on American death rows. Almost all of the nations in South and Central America, which by and large have civil law legal orders and multi-party parliamentary systems, are likewise abolitionist.

The question for the abolition movement going forward is where the next victories can be achieved. This book has argued for the importance of structural characteristics, including a relatively centralized state and uniform nationwide penal code; public intellectuals who can shape national debate; strong expert influence on criminal law legislation and policy-making; proportional or multi-party parliamentary systems which afford delegates some insulation from public opinion; and civil law legal orders with concomitant bureaucratic professionalization of the judiciary. The problem is that most of the relatively advanced countries in this category have already abolished capital punishment. The low-hanging fruit, so to speak, has mostly been picked.

This leaves two remaining fields of endeavor for international abolitionists. The first is to try to expand upon abolition by international agreement. One of the principal reasons for the spectacular successes of abolitionism in Europe was the policy developed in the late 1980s of requiring aspiring Council of Europe member states to abolish capital punishment. This linkage permitted national elites in countries as diverse as the Czech Republic, Lithuania, and Poland to deflect blame for a potentially unpopular policy move by shifting the responsibility to a relatively amorphous international body. Further, the Council's policy irremediably tied the abolition of capital punishment to a sought-after step in national development. The model of establishing 'death-penalty-free' regions – especially if the issue of capital punishment can be tied to economic integration – may hold promise elsewhere, such as Asia.

What of capital punishment in the world's two most populous nations? China would seem to be the abolitionists' white whale, since it carries out the vast majority of executions year-for-year, and apparently regards the death penalty as an essential element of state policy, given the large number of offenses which are punishable by death. Given China's size and economic might, it seems difficult to entice it into abandoning capital punishment by external inducements. China would also, at first glance, not seem to offer fertile grounds for a home-grown abolition movement on the European model. What information is available indicates that capital punishment enjoys considerable support not only among the general population but also among policy-making and bureaucratic elites. These superficial dissimilarities, however, may conceal trends in favor of abolition. One recent country study suggested the following reason for China's reliance on capital punishment:

> While the old value system of communitarian and collectivism was abandoned, a new value system associated with individualism and economic entrepreneurship along with its control mechanisms has not yet been fully established. This state of anomie in the post-reform era created both opportunities and confusions. With the increasing crime rates and the lack of internal control in many regulatory agencies (e.g., financial institutions in preventing financial fraud, government agencies in prohibiting corruption, and business bureaus in regulating fraudulent business practices and preventing hazardous products), stiff legal sanctions, including the use of the death penalty, were considered one of the only viable methods of social control. (Lu and Miethe 2007:57, footnotes omitted)

This thesis suggests that as China continues along its current path of developing reliable, modern regulatory institutions, the perceived need for exemplary executions of corrupt officials or manufacturers of tainted goods may dwindle.

China further exhibits two of the preconditions for the European model of death penalty abolition: it has one unified national penal code (adopted in 1979 and modified many times since), and a political structure which insulates ruling elites from popular opinion. Were China's ruling elites to be convinced that abolition was a desirable step, they would be able to implement it without fearing a formal political backlash. Even if Chinese leaders were not swayed by humanitarian concerns, there is a pragmatic case for the move: abolition of capital punishment by China would generate an avalanche of favorable coverage from the international media, and would be a potent weapon against critics of China's human rights policies. In particular, China could point to the continued use of capital punishment by the United States to parry American criticisms. Given the sensitivity of Chinese officialdom to critiques of its human rights policies, it would seem that abolishing capital punishment would be a low-cost way to project a more sympathetic image on the world stage.

Finally, there is the case of India. Although measuring public opinion in such a vast and diverse country is difficult, evidence points to strong support for capital punishment among the general population (Greenberg and West 2008:308). In particular, the rough justice of 'encounter killings,' in which police gun down notorious criminal suspects during violent 'encounters,' appears to enjoy some legitimacy as a response to a notoriously inefficient criminal justice system (Eckert 2005). Nevertheless, officially sanctioned executions are rare in India. A 2008 Amnesty International Report summarizes the conflicting situation:

> Continuously refusing to enter into any form of debate or discussion with national or international bodies over abolition, the Indian state has shown an apparent disdain for world opinion by retaining a 'wall of silence', signaling its intention by failing to respond to the quinquennial UN surveys on the death penalty and more worryingly passing new laws that provide for the death penalty ... [T]he Indian state has assumed a moralistic and conservative tone, arguing that the death penalty is required to instill fear as a means of deterring future criminals, and to safeguard society against rising crime and acts of terrorism. (Amnesty International India and People's Union for Civil Liberties 2008:14)

Nevertheless, the report continues, the Indian government's current hiatus on executions seems to indicate a 'lack of official enthusiasm' for capital punishment. Despite being a common-law country, India has one unified criminal code, the Indian Penal Code. Section 1 of that Code specifies that it 'shall extend to the whole of India.' The punishment for murder could, thus, be abolished by an act of Parliament revising the Code. Unlike Chinese officials, Indian MPs would face a public backlash after such an unpopular step. However, as the Amnesty International report suggests, the idea of abolition seems to be slowly gaining in support among Indian legal elites.

Conclusion

A common defensive response from Americans, Chinese, and Indians to European critics of the death penalty is 'if you had our social problems, you would have capital punishment, too.' This is too superficial. A more interesting thought experiment is as follows: hold the history, culture, and state of public opinion constant, and simply swap the structure of criminal justice policy formation: France stays France, say, but suddenly has American institutions: capital punishment is decided on a *région-by-région* basis, prosecutors and judges are elected. America stays America, but is governed by one uniform American Penal Code, drafted by a committee of renowned scholars from the leading American law faculties, and implemented by appointed, civil-servant judges. I hope to have convinced readers that the results of this thought experiment might be quite intriguing. Further, the results might well hold *regardless* of public opinion. As I have argued, public opinion on capital punishment is subject to mysterious shifts and is resistant to abolitionists' attempts to change it. However, this hardly need concern abolitionists if, as I have maintained, the straightest road to abolition involves bypassing public opinion entirely.

This analysis leads to the seemingly counterintuitive suggestion that China is a better candidate for abolition than the United States precisely *because* it is less democratic. This reflects a confusion which plagues transatlantic debates about capital punishment – two very different uses of the word 'democratic'. On the one hand, we have the capital-D concept of Democracy articulated by European abolitionists in the past and the European Union in the present. In this understanding, abolishing capital punishment expresses values that are central to the peaceful order constructed in post-war Europe: respect for human rights and rehabilitative sanctioning; a definitive rejection of dictatorship and state terror; and the creation of a zone of protection around human life which can never be breached by the state. How can a reform which permanently deprives the state of the power to kill its own citizens be anything *but* democratic?

On the other hand, we have the traditional, homely concept of small-d democracy: a government that follows the clear and expressed will of the people. These two conceptions of 'democracy' are anything but coextensive. As this study has shown, a government action can be Democratic without being democratic, and vice versa. Briefly put, European activists and legal elites have made a passionate case that there are certain issues, such as capital punishment, which require a government to ignore democracy to realize the promise of Democracy. The argument has succeeded among legal elites across the world, but has often received mixed reactions among ordinary citizens. Only time can tell whether it can bring about worldwide abolition – or whether a novel strategy is needed to achieve that goal.

Bibliography

Cases

Marbury v. *Madison*, 5 U.S. (1 Cranch) 137 (1803).

New State Ice Co. v. *Liebmann*. (1932). *U.S. Reports*, United States Supreme Court. **285**:262.

Trop v. *Dulles*. (1958). *U.S. Reports*, United States Supreme Court. **356**:86.

Rudolph v. *Alabama*. (1963). *U.S. Reports*, United States Supreme Court. **375**:889.

Auslieferung I. (1964). *Entscheidungen des Bundesverfassungsgerichts*, Federal Constitutional Court of Germany. **18**:112.

Furman v. *Georgia*. (1972). *United States Supreme Court Reports*, United States Supreme Court. **408**:238.

Gregg v. *Georgia*. (1976). *U.S. Reports*, United States Supreme Court. **428**:153.

Dist. Attorney for Suffolk Dist. v. *Watson*. (1980). *Northeastern Reporter, 2nd Series*, Supreme Judicial Court of Massachusetts. **411**:1274.

Decision No. 85–188 DC (1985). *Conseil Constitutionnel de France. Journal Officiel*.

McCleskey v. *Kemp*. (1987). *United States Reports*, United States Supreme Court. **481**:279.

Soering v. *United Kingdom*. (1989). *European Human Rights Reporter*, European Court of Human Rights. **11**:439.

Callins v. *Collins*. (1994). *United States Reports*, United States Supreme Court. **510**:1141.

Harris v. *Alabama*. (1995). *United States Supreme Court Reports*, United States Supreme Court. **513**:504.

S. v. *Makwanyane and Mchunu*. (1995). *South African Law Reports*, Constitutional Court of South Africa. **3**:391.

Atkins v. *Virginia*. (2002). *United States Reports*, United States Supreme Court. **536**:304.

Roper v. *Simmons*. (2005). *Supreme Court Reports*, U.S. Supreme Court. **543**:551.

Washington State Grange v. *Washington State Republican Party*. (2008). *United States Reports*, United States Supreme Court. **552**:442.

In re Troy Anthony Davis. (2009). *Supreme Court Reports*, United States Supreme Court. No. 08-1443, August 17 2009.

Other Sources

Adolf Grimme Institut (2007). 'Nominierte 2007: Information & Kultur.' Retrieved September 7 2009, from http://www.grimme-institut.de/html/index.php?id=309=c15.

Alford, J. R., C. L. Funk and J. R. Hibbing. (2005). 'Are Political Orientations Genetically Transmitted?' *American Political Science Review* **99**(2): 153–67.

American Bar Association House of Delegates (1997). Report with Recommendations No. 107 (Death Penalty Moratorium).

Amnesty International India and People's Union for Civil Liberties (2008). *Lethal Lottery: The Death Penalty in India*. London, Amnesty International.

Ancel, M. (1965). *Social Defence*. London, Routledge.

Ancel, M. (1967). 'The Problem of the Death Penalty.' In T. Sellin (ed.) *Capital Punishment*. New York, Evanston and London, Harper & Row, pp. 3–22.

Andre, M. (2007). 'Democratic Consciousness.' *Commission en Directe*. **450**.

Assemblée Nationale de France (1981). Journal officiel – Débats parlementaires – Assemblée nationale – 1ère séance du jeudi 17 septembre 1981.

Assemblée Nationale de France (2008). 'Constitution of 4 October 1958 (Official English Version, current as of 2008).' Retrieved 1 July 2009, from http://www.assemblee-nationale.fr/english/8ab.asp.

Ataner, A. (2006). 'Kant on Capital Punishment and Suicide.' *Kant-Studien* **97**: 452–82.

Badinter, R. (1973). *L'exécution*. Paris, Grasset & Fasquelle.

Badinter, R. (2000). *L'abolition*. Paris, Fayard.

Badinter, R. (2008). *Abolition: One Man's Battle Against the Death Penalty*. Boston, MA, Northeastern University Press.

Bae, S. (2007). *When the State No Longer Kills: International Human Rights Norms and Abolition of Capital Punishment*. Albany, NY, State University of New York Press.

Bagehot, W. (1872). *The English Constitution*, Henry S. King.

Bailey, V. (2000). 'The Shadow of the Gallows: The Death Penalty and the British Labour Government, 1945–51.' *Law and History Review* **18**(2): 305–49.

Bandes, S. (2007). 'The Heart Has Its Reasons: Examining the Strange Persistence of the American Death Penalty.' *Studies in Law, Politics & Society* **42**: 21–52.

Banner, S. (2002). *The Death Penalty: An American History*. Cambridge, MA, Harvard University Press.

Barron, J. (1998). *Judgment Misguided: Intuition and Error in Public Decision Making*. New York, Oxford University Press.

Bawer, B. (2004). 'Hating America.' *The Hudson Review* **LVII**, Spring (1).

BBC (British Broadcasting Corporation) (2002). 'Death Penalty Call Renewed.' Retrieved July 20 2009 from http://news.bbc.co.uk/2/hi/uk_news/politics/2204738.stm.

Beccaria, C. (2008). *On Crimes and Punishments*. Toronto, CA, University of Toronto Press.

Bedau, H. A. (1983). 'Bentham's Utilitarian Critique of the Death Penalty.' *Journal of Criminal Law and Criminology* **74**(3): 1033–65.

Bedford, S. (1961). *The Faces of Justice: A Traveller's Report*. New York, NY, Simon & Schuster.

Benn, P. (2002). 'Soham, Widdecombe and the Death Penalty.' Retrieved July 20 2009 from http://www.royalinstitutephilosophy.org/think/article.php?num=15.

Berman, D. A. and S. Bibas (2008). 'Engaging Capital Emotions.' *Northwestern University Law Review* **102**: 355–64.

Berman, H. J. (1983). *Law and Revolution: The Formation of the Western Legal Tradition*. Cambridge, MA, Harvard University Press.

Berman, M. (1982). *All that is Solid Melts into Air: The Experience of Modernity*. New York, NY, Simon & Schuster.

Bickel, A. M. (1986). *The Least Dangerous Branch: The Supreme Court at the Bar of Politics*. New Haven and London, Yale University Press.

Blackstone, W. (1884). *Commentaries on the Laws of England, In Four Books*. Chicago, Callaghan and Company.

Bloch-Michel, J. (ed.) (2002). *Réflexions sur la peine capitale*. Paris, Editions Gallimard.

Block, B. P. and J. Hostettler (1997). *Hanging in the Balance: A History of the Abolition of Capital Punishment in Britain*. Hook, Waterside Press.

Bohm, R. M. (2008). 'Karl Marx and the Death Penalty.' *Critical Criminology* **16**: 285–91.

Bohm, R. M. and B. Vogel (2004). 'More than Ten Years After: The Long-Term Stability of Informed Death Penalty Opinions.' *Journal of Criminal Justice* **32**: 307–27.

Boswell, J. (1881). *The Life of Dr. Johnson, Including a Journal of a Tour to the Hebrides*. London, John Murray.

Bourdieu, P. (1998). *On Television*. New York, The New Press.

Bourdieu, P. (2007). *Distinction: A Social Critique of the Judgement of Taste* (11th edn, trans. Richard Nice). Cambridge, MA, Harvard University Press.

Bright, S. and P. J. Keenan (1995). 'Judges and the Politics of Death: Deciding between the Bill of Rights and the Next Election in Capital Cases.' *Boston University Law Review* **73**: 759–835.

British National Party (2008). *Thinking of Voting CONservative?* Bracknell, Andy McBride.

Brubaker, R. (1992). *Citizen and Nationhood in France and Germany*. Cambridge, MA, Harvard University Press.

Buller, D. (2005). *Adapting Minds: Evolutionary Psychology and the Persistent Quest for Human Nature*. Cambridge, MA, MIT University Press.

Bundesminister der Justiz (1989). *Im Namen des Deutschen Volkes. Justiz und Nationalsozialismus*. Katalog zur Ausstellung des Bundesministers der Justiz. Köln, Wissenschaft und Politik.

Busch, T. (2005). *Die deutsche Strafrechtsreform: Ein Rückblick auf die sechs Reformen des deutschen Strafrechts (1969–1998)*. Kiel, Kieler Rechtswissenschaftliche Abhandlungen.

Campbell, J. L. C. (1899). *The Lives of the Chief Justices of England, from the Norman Conquest till the Death of Lord Tenterden*. Northport, Long Island, Edward Thompson Co.

Camus, A. (1960). *Resistance, Rebellion, and Death*. New York, Alfred A. Knopf.

Caplan, B. (2007). *The Myth of the Rational Voter: Why Democracies Choose Bad Policies*. Princeton, NJ, Princeton University Press.

Carlsmith, K. M., J. M. Darley and P. H. Robinson (2002). 'Why Do We Punish? Deterrence and Just Deserts as Motives for Punishment.' *Journal of Personality and Social Psychology* **83**: 284–99.

Center for the Study of the American Electorate (2006). 'Registration Percentage Unchanged From 2002 – Record Percentage Eschew Major Parties.' Retrieved August 10 2009 from http://www.american.edu/ia/cdem/csae.

Cesarani, D. (1998). *Arthur Kotstler: The Homeless Mind*. London, Vintage.

Christoph, J. B. (1962). *Capital Punishment and British Politics: The British Movement to Abolish the Death Penalty 1945–57*. Chicago, University of Chicago Press.

Clark, R. (1970). *Crime in America: Observations on its Nature, Causes, Prevention and Control*. New York, NY, Simon and Schuster.

Cohen, J. (1989). 'Deliberation and Democratic Legitimacy.' In A. Hamlin and P. Pettit (eds) *The Good Polity: Normative Analysis of the State*. Oxford, UK, Blackwell.

Conrad, H. (1967/68). 'Joseph von Sonnenfels (1733–1817): Zum 150. Todestag eines Vorkämpfers gegen die Folter.' *Juristen-Jahrbuch* **8**: 1–16.

Converse, P. A. (2006). 'The Nature Of Belief Systems In Mass Publics', (Originally published 1964) *Critical Review* **18**(1–3): 1–74.

Cosmides, L., J. Tooby and J. H. Barkow (1992). 'Introduction: Evolutionary Psychology and Conceptual Integration.' In Barkow, J. H., L. Cosmides and J. Tooby (eds) *The Adapted Mind*. New York, Oxford University Press, pp. 3–15.

Costa, S. (2001). *La Peine de Mort: de Voltaire à Badinter*. Paris, Flammarion.

Cotton, M. (2000). 'Back with a Vengeance: The Resilience of Retribution as an Articulated Purpose of Criminal Punishment.' *American Criminal Law Review* **37**: 1313–62.

Crozier, M. (1984). *The Trouble with America*. Berkeley and Los Angeles, University of California Press.

Dalrymple, T. (2009). 'The Cult of Insincerity.' *New English Review*. Nashville, TN.

Daly, M. and M. Wilson (1988). *Homicide*. New York, Aldine de Gruyter.

Dann, P. (2006). 'The Gubernative in Presidential and Parliamentary Systems. Comparing Organizational Structures of Federal Governments in the USA and Germany.' *Zeitschrift für ausländisches öffentliches Recht und Völkerrecht* 66(1): 1–40.

Dawkins, R. (2006). *The Selfish Gene.* Oxford, UK, Oxford University Press.

Death Penalty Information Center (2007). *A Crisis of Confidence: Americans' Doubts about the Death Penalty,* Washington, DC, Death Penalty Information Center.

Dehler, T. (1969). *Thomas Dehler: Reden und Aufsätze.* Köln and Opladen, Westdeutscher Verlag.

Dell'Agnola, R., O. Dassault, J. Auclair et al. (2004). 'Proposition de Loi No. 1521, tendant à rétablir la peine de mort pour les auteurs d'actes de terrorisme' (M. Richard Dell'Agnola). Paris, Assemblée Nationale de France.

Delli Carpini, M. X. and S. Keeter (1996). *What Americans Know about Politics and Why it Matters.* New Haven and London, Yale University Press.

Dieter, R. (2007). *The Death Penalty in the United States: Strategies for Change.* Roundtable of the World Congress Against the Death Penalty, Paris, France.

Directorate General of Communications (2007). 'Press Release Launching the European Day against the Death Penalty,' No. IP/07/850, European Union.

Directorate General of Human Rights (2001). *Death is not Justice: The Council of Europe and the Death Penalty.* Brussels, Council of Europe.

Donovan, J. M. (1999). 'Magistrates and Juries in France, 1791–1952.' *French Historical Studies* 22(3): 379–420.

Dorey, P. (2006). 'The Social Background of Labour MPs Elected in 1964 and 1966.' In P. Dorey (ed.) *The Labour Governments, 1964–70.* London, Routledge.

Dostoevsky, F. (2004). *The Idiot.* New York, Barnes & Noble Classics.

Dow, D. (2005). *Executed on a Technicality: Lethal Injustice on America's Death Row.* Boston, MA, Beacon Press.

Downes, D. (1988). *Contrasts in Tolerance: Post-war Penal Policy in The Netherlands and England and Wales.* Oxford, UK, Clarendon Press.

Dreier, H. (ed.) (2000). *Grundgesetz: Kommentar.* Tübingen, Mohr Siebeck.

Ducpétiaux, É. (1827). *De la peine de mort.* Bruxelles, H. Tarlier.

Düsing, B. (1952). *Die Geschichte der Abschaffung der Todesstrafe in der Bundesrepublik Deutschland.* Offenbach, Bollwerk-Verlag.

Eckert, J. (2005). 'Death and the Nation: State Killing in India.' In A. Sarat and C. Boulanger (eds) *The Cultural Lives of Capital Punishment: Comparative Perspectives.* Stanford, CA, Stanford University Press, pp.195–218.

Eddowes, M. (1955). *The Man on Your Conscience: An Investigation of the Evans Murder Trial.* London, Cassel and Co.

Eisner, M. (2001). 'Modernization, Self-control, and Lethal Violence: The Long-Term Dynamics of European Homicide Rates in Theoretical Perspective.' *British Journal of Criminology* 41: 618–38.

Elias, N. (2000). *The Civilizing Process: Sociogenetic and Psychogenetic Investigations.* Oxford, UK, Wiley-Blackwell.

Ellsworth, P. C. and L. Ross (1983). 'Public Opinion and Capital Punishment: A Close Examination of the Views of Abolitionists and Retentionists.' *Crime and Delinquency* 29: 116–69.

Emsley, C. (2005). *Hard Men: The English and Violence Since 1750.* London, Continuum.

Enders, U. and C. Schawe, (eds) (2002). *Die Kabinettsprotokolle der Bundesregierung 1958.* Munich, Oldenbourg Wissenschaftsverlag.

Evans, R. J. (1996). *Rituals of Retribution: Capital Punishment in Germany 1600–1987.* Oxford, UK, Oxford University Press.

Farwell, S. (2007). 'European Women Looking for Love on Texas' Death Row.' *Dallas Morning News*. Dallas.

Fehr, E. and S. Gächter (2000). 'Cooperation and Punishment in Public Goods Experiments.' *American Economic Review* **90**: 980–94.

Ferejohn, J. A. (1990). 'Information and the Electoral Process.' In J. A. Ferejohn and J. H. Kuklinski (eds) *Information and Democratic Processes*. Urbana and Chicago, University of Illinois Press.

Feucht, T. E. and E. Zedlewski (2007). 'The 40th Anniversary of the Crime Report.' *NIJ Journal* **257**: 20–3.

Fijalkowski, A. (2005). 'Capital Punishment in Poland: An Aspect of the "Cultural Life" of Death Penalty Discourse.' In A. Sarat and C. Boulanger (eds) *The Cultural Lives of Capital Punishment: Comparative Perspectives*. Stanford, CA, Stanford University Press, pp. 147–68.

Flaubert, G. (1954). *The Dictionary of Accepted Ideas*. New York, New Directions.

Fleishman, J. (2000). 'Italians Fight U.S. Use of Death Penalty.' *Philadelphia Inquirer*.

Foucault, M. (1995). *Discipline and Punish: The Birth of the Prison*. New York, Vintage Books.

Frady, M. (1993). 'Death in Arkansas.' *New Yorker*.

Friedman, L. (2009). 'Benchmarks: Judges on Trial: Judicial Selection and Election.' *DePaul Law Review* **58**: 451–71.

Fussell, P. (1983). *Class: A Guide Through the American Status System*. New York, NY, Touchstone.

Galliher, J. F., L. W. Koch, D. P. Keys and T. J. Guess (2002). *America Without the Death Penalty: States Leading the Way*. Boston, MA, Northeastern University Press.

Garland, D. (1984). *Punishment and Welfare: A History of Penal Strategies*. Brookfield, VT, Gower Publishing Co.

Garland, D. (1990). *Punishment and Modern Society: A Study in Social Theory*. Chicago, IL, University of Chicago Press.

Garland, D. (2001). *The Culture of Control: Crime and Social Order in Contemporary Society*. Oxford, UK, Oxford University Press.

Garland, D. (2005). 'Capital Punishment and American Culture.' *Punishment & Society* **7**: 347–76.

Garland, D. (2006). 'Concepts of Culture in the Sociology of Punishment.' *Theoretical Criminology* **10**(4): 419–47.

Gatrell, V. A. C. (1996). *The Hanging Tree: Execution and the English People, 1770–1868*. Oxford, UK, Oxford University Press.

German Parliament Reporting Service (1950). Drucksache Nr. 619. Bonn, Bonner Universitäts-Buchdruckerei.

German Parliament Reporting Service (1952). Drucksache Nr. 3679. Deutscher Bundestag Druckerei.

Giefer, T., R. Giefer et al. (2006). 'Ein Tod in Texas: Die Hinrichtung von Frances Newton.' Cologne, WDR/ARTE.

Gillis, A. R. (1994). 'Literacy and the Civilization of Violence in 19th-Century France.' *Sociological Forum* **9**(3): 371–401.

Ginsberg, R. H. (2007). *Demystifying the European Union: The Enduring Logic of Regional Integration*. Lanham, MD, Rowman & Littlefield.

Girling, E. (2005). 'European Identity and the Mission Against the Death Penalty in the United States.' In A. Sarat and C. Boulanger (eds) *The Cultural Lives of Capital Punishment: Comparative Perspectives*. Stanford, CA, Stanford University Press, pp. 147–68.

Glendon, M. A., M. W. Gordon and P. Wright-Carozza (1999). *Comparative Legal Traditions*. St. Paul, MN, West Group.

Goethe, J. W. von (1976). *Faust: A Tragedy (An Authoritative Translation, Interpretive Notes, Contexts, Modern Criticism)*. New York, W. W. Norton & Co.

Gordon, S. (1964). *Our Parliament*. London, The Hansard Society.

Gottschalk, M. (2009). 'The Long Reach of the Carceral State.' *Law & Social Inquiry* 34: 439–72.

Green, W. M. (1967). 'An Ancient Debate on Capital Punishment.' In T. Sellin (ed) *Capital Punishment*. New York, Evanston and London, Harper & Row, pp. 46–54.

Greenberg, D. F. and V. West (2008). 'Siting the Death Penalty Internationally.' *Law & Social Inquiry* 33: 295–343.

Greene, J. D. (2007). 'The Secret Joke of Kant's Soul.' *Moral Psychology, Vol. 3: The Neuroscience of Morality: Emotion, Disease, and Development*. W. Sinnott-Armstrong. Cambridge, MA, MIT Press, pp. 35–79.

Grosse Strafrechtskommission (1959). *Niederschrift über die Beratungen zur Todesstrafe am 17. Oktober 1958*. Bonn, Bundesdruckerei (Federal Printing Office). 11.

Grossman, K. M. (1986). *The Early Novels of Victor Hugo: Towards a Poetics of Harmony*. Geneva, Libraire Droz S.A.

Gurr, T. R. (1981). 'Historical Trends in Violent Crime: A Critical Review of the Evidence.' *Crime and Justice* 3: 295–353.

Habermas, J. (2007). 'Keine Demokratie Kann Sich das Leisten.' *Süddeutsche Zeitung*. Munich.

Haidt, J. (2001). 'The Emotional Dog and its Rational Tail: A Social Intuitionist Approach to Moral Judgment.' *Psychological Review* 108: 814–34.

Haines, H. H. (1996). *Against Capital Punishment: The Anti-Death Penalty Movement in America, 1972–1994*. Oxford, UK, Oxford University Press.

Hammel, A. (2002). 'Diabolical Federalism: A Functional Critique and Proposed Reconstruction of Federal Death Penalty Habeas.' *American Criminal Law Review* 39: 1–99.

Hammel, A. (2006). 'Preventive Detention in Comparative Perspective.' *Annual of German & European Law* II & III: 89–115. New York and Oxford, Berghahn Books.

Hansard (Commons) (1810) Speech of Samuel Romilly.

Hansard (Commons) (1955). Capital Punishment (Royal Commission's Report).

Hansard (House) (1956a). Death Penalty (Abolition) Bill.

Hansard (House) (1956b). Queen's Speech, 6 November 1956.

Hansard (House) (1965). Murder (Abolition of Death Penalty) Act 1965.

Hansard (House) (1969). Murder (Abolition of Death Penalty) Act 1969.

Hart, H. L. A. (1968). *Punishment and Responsibility*. Oxford, UK, Clarendon Press.

Haubtmann, P. (1982). *Pierre-Joseph Proudhon: Sa vie et sa pensée 1809–1849*. Paris, Beauchesne.

Henke, J. and U. Rössel (eds) (2003). *Die Kabinettsprotokolle der Bundesregierung 1959*. Munich, Oldenbourg Wissenschaftsverlag.

Herbert, Z. (1985). *Barbarian in the Garden*. Manchester, Carcanet.

Ho, V. K. Y. (2005). 'What is Wrong with Capital Punishment? Official and Unofficial Attitudes Toward Capital Punishment in Modern and Contemporary China.' In A. Sarat and C. Boulanger (eds) *The Cultural Lives of Capital Punishment: Comparative Perspectives*. Stanford, CA, Stanford University Press, pp. 274–90.

Hodgkinson, P. (1996). 'The United Kingdom and the European Union.' In P. Hodgkinson and A. Rutherford (eds) *Capital Punishment: Global Issues and Prospects*. Winchester, Waterside Press.

Hodgkinson, P. (2004). 'Preface.' In P. Hodgkinson and W. Schabas (eds) *Capital Punishment: Strategies for Abolition*. Cambridge, UK, Cambridge University Press.

Hogan, B. (1974). 'Crime and the Criminal Law.' In *Then and Now 1799–1974: Commemorating 175 Years of Law Bookselling and Publishing.* London, Sweet & Maxwell.

Hohmann, O. (2002). 'Die Geschichte der Todesstrafe in Deutschland.' In C. Boulanger, V. Heyes and P. Hanfling (eds) *Zur Aktualität der Todesstrafe Interdisziplinäre und globale Perspektiven.* Berlin, Berlin Verlag, pp. 247–68.

Hood, R. (2002). *The Death Penalty: A Worldwide Perspective.* Oxford, UK, Oxford University Press.

Hörnle, T. (2000). 'Penal Law and Sexuality: Recent Reforms in German Criminal Law.' *Buffalo Criminal Law Review* 3: 639–85.

Hornum, F. (1967). 'Two Debates: France, 1791; England, 1956.' In T. Sellin (ed) *Capital Punishment.* New York, Evanston and London, Harper & Row, pp. 56–75.

Hughes, E. (1969). *Sydney Silverman: Rebel in Parliament.* London and Edinburgh, Charles Skilton Ltd.

Hugo, V. (1840). *The Last Days of a Condemned Man.* London, Smith, Elder & Co.

IFOP/France Soir. (1998). 'Le rétablissement de la peine de mort.' Retrieved June 5 2009, from http://www.ifop.com/europe/sondages/opinionf/peinemor.asp.

Ipsos/Public Affairs & Associated Press. (2007). 'International Death Penalty Opinion Poll.' Retrieved October 15 2008, from http://surveys.ap.org/data/Ipsos/international/2007-04%20AP%20Globus%20topline_042507.pdf.

Jarvis, M. (2005). *Conservative Governments, Morality and Social Change in Affluent Britain, 1957–64.* Manchester, UK, Manchester University Press.

Jenkins, R. (1959) *The Labour Case.* Harmondsworth, Penguin.

Johnson, D. T. (2005). 'The Death Penalty in Japan: Secrecy, Silence, and Salience.' In A. Sarat and C. Boulanger (eds) *The Cultural Lives of Capital Punishment: Comparative Perspectives.* Stanford, CA, Stanford University Press, pp. 252–73.

Johnson, E. and A. Heijder (1983). 'The Dutch Deemphasize Imprisonment: Sociocultural and Structural Explanations.' *International Journal of Comparative and Applied Criminal Justice* 7(1): 3–19.

Johnson, L. B. (1965). *Crime, its Prevalence, and Measures of Prevention.* United States House of Representatives. Washington, D.C.

Jowell, J. and D. Oliver (2004). *The Changing Constitution.* Oxford, UK, Oxford University Press.

Judt, T. (1998). *The Burden of Responsibility: Blum, Camus, Aron, and the French Twentieth Century.* Chicago, The University of Chicago Press.

Judt, T. (2007). *Postwar: A History of Europe Since 1945.* London, Pimlico.

Kahan, D. M. (1996). 'What do Alternative Sanctions Mean?' *University of Chicago Law Review* 63: 591–653.

Kann, R. A. (1960). *Kanzel und Katheder: Studien zur Österreichischen Geistesgeschichte vom Spätbarock zur Frühromantik.* Vienna, Herder.

Kennedy, L. (1961) *10 Rillington Place.* Worthing, UK, Littlehampton Book Services.

Klein, S. and S. Fowler. (2000). 'How can we protect our children if these monsters are allowed to live? There is no cure for them ... they MUST HANG.' *People.* London.

Knörer, E. (2007). 'Politics American Style: Frederick Wiseman's Documentary "State Legislature" (Forum).' *Signandsight.com.*

Köcher, R. (2009). Allensbacher Jahrbuch der Demoskopie Band 12, 2003–2009 (Die Berliner Republik). Berlin, De Gruyter-Saur.

Koestler, A. (1957). *Reflections on Hanging.* New York, The Macmillan Company.

Kuhn, D. (1991). *The Skills of Argument.* Cambridge, Cambridge University Press.

Kunz, K.-L. (2004). 'Muss Strafe Wirklich Sein? Einige Überlegungen zur Beantwortbarkeit der Frage un zu der Konsequenzen daraus.' In E. Müller (ed.) *Muss Strafe Sein?* Baden-Baden, Nomos Verlagsgesellschaft, pp. 71–84.

La Porta, R., F. Lopez-de-Silanes, A. Shleifer and R. W. Vishny (1998). 'Law and Finance.' *Journal of Political Economy* **106**(6): 1113–55.

Lacorne, D. (2005). 'Anti-Americanism and Americanophobia: A French Perspective.' In D. Lacorne and T. Judt (eds) *With Us or Against Us: Studies in Global Anti-Americanism*. New York, Palgrave MacMillan, pp. 35–59.

Lakoff, G. (2006). *Thinking Points*. New York, Farrar, Straus & Giroux.

Lambert, E. and A. Clarke (2001). 'The Impact of Information on an Individual's Support of the Death Penalty: A Partial Test of the Marshall Hypothesis among College Students.' *Criminal Justice Policy Review* **12**(3): 215–34.

Lane, C. (2005). 'Why Japan Still Has the Death Penalty.' *Washington Post*.

Langbein, J. (2003). *The Origins of the Adversary Criminal Trial*. Oxford, UK, Oxford University Press.

Langer, M. (2004). 'From Legal Transplants to Legal Translations: The Globalization of Plea Bargaining and the Americanization Thesis in Criminal Procedure.' *Harvard International Law Journal* **45**(1): 1–64.

Lasser, M. E. (2004). *Judicial Deliberations: A Comparative Analysis of Judicial Transparency and Legitimacy*. Oxford, UK, Oxford University Press.

Le Quang Sang, J. (2001). *La Loi et la Bourreau : La Peine de Mort in Débats, 1870–1985*. Paris, Editions L'Harmattan.

Le Quang Sang, J. (2002). 'L'abolition de la peine de mort en France: le rendez-vous manqué de 1906–1908.' *Crime, Histoire & Societé /Crime, History & Society* **6**(1): 57–83.

Lee, A. and J. Twomey (2005). 'Police Killers Must Hang.' *Daily Express*. London, pp. 6–7.

Lehmann, L. (1975). *Mably und Rousseau: Eine Studie über die Grenzen der Emanzipation im Ancien Régime*. Bern, Herbert Lang.

Lensu, M. (2007). DG RELEX reply to Mr Pataki 'Death Penalty.' *Commission en Directe*. No. **450**.

Linebaugh, P. (2003). *The London Hanged: Crime and Civil Society in the Eighteenth Century*. London, Verso.

Lipset, S. M. (2003). *The First New Nation: The United States in Historical and Comparative Perspective*. New Brunswick, Transaction Publishers.

Lord, C. G., L. Ross and M. R. Lepper (1979). 'Biased Assimilation and Attitude Polarization: The Effects of Prior Theories on Subsequently Considered Evidence.' *Journal of Personality and Social Psychology* **37**(11): 2098–109.

Loury, G. C. (2008). *Race, Incarceration and American Values*. Cambridge, MA and London, MIT Press.

Lu, H. and T. D. Miethe (2007). *China's Death Penalty: History, Law, and Contemporary Practices*. New York, NY and Oxford, UK, Routledge.

Lustgarten, L. (2003). '"A Distorted Image of Ourselves": Nazism, "Liberal" Societies and the Qualities of Difference.' In C. Joerges and N. S. Ghaleigh (eds) *Darker Legacies of Law in Europe: The Shadow of National Socialism and Fascism over Europe and its Legal Traditions*. Oxford, UK, Hart Publishing.

Lüttger, H. (ed.) (1979). *Strafrechtsreform und Rechtsvergleichung: Berliner Gastvorträge*. Berlin and New York, Walter de Gruyter.

Mably, G. B. de (1776). *De la Législation, ou principes des lois*. Amsterdam.

MacCoun, R. (2001). 'Legal Issues: Public Opinion.' In N. J. Smelser and P. B. Baltes (eds) *International Encyclopedia of the Social and Behavioral Sciences*. Amsterdam, Elsevier, pp. 8641–6.

Mackey, P. E. (1982). *Hanging in the Balance: The Anti-Capital Punishment Movement in New York State, 1776–1861*. New York and London, Garland Publishing, Inc.

Mackie, J. L. (1985). 'Morality and Retributive Emotions.' In *Persons and Values: Selected Papers, Volume II*. Oxford, UK, Oxford University Press.

MacKuen, M. (1990). 'Speaking of Politics: Individual Conversational Choice, Public Opinion, and the Prospects for Deliberative Democracy.' In J. A. Ferejohn and J. H. Kuklinski (eds) *Information and Democratic Processes*. Urbana and Chicago, University of Illinois Press.

Marshall, J. M. (2000). 'Death in Venice: Europe's Death-Penalty Elitism.' *The New Republic* **223**(5): 1–.

Marx, K. (1853). 'Capital Punishment – Mr. Cobden's Pamphlet – Regulations of the Bank of England.' *New York Tribune*. New York, NY.

Masur, L. P. (1989). *Rites of Execution: Capital Punishment and the Transformation of American Culture, 1776–1865*. New York and Oxford, Oxford University Press.

Mattei, U. (2003). 'A Theory of Imperial Law: A Study on U.S. Hegemony and the Latin Resistance.' *Indiana Journal of Global Legal Studies* **10**: 383–448.

McCullough, M. (2008). *Beyond Revenge: The Evolution of the Forgiveness Instinct*, San Francisco, CA, Jossey-Bass.

Meade, E. K. (2004). 'From Sex Strangler to Model Citizen: Gregorio Cárdenas Hernández and the Death Penalty Debate in Mexico, 1942–45.' *The Death Penalty and Mexico–U.S. Relations Historical Continuities, Present Dilemmas*, Austin, Texas.

Megivern, J. J. (1997). *The Death Penalty: An Historical and Theological Survey*. Mahwah, NJ, Paulist Press.

Menasce, B. and M. Taube (2000). *Lettre ouvert aux Américains pour l'abolition de la peine de mort*. Paris, L'Ecart.

Mennell, S. (2007). *The American Civilizing Process*. Cambridge, UK, Polity Press.

Merryman, J. H. (1985). *The Civil Law Tradition: An Introduction to the Legal Systems of Western Europe and Latin America*. Stanford, CA, Stanford University Press.

Mill, J. S. (1988). *Collected Works of John Stuart Mill, vol. XXVIII: Public and Parliamentary Speeches*. Toronto, University of Toronto Press.

Miller, W. I. (2006). *Eye for an Eye*. Cambridge, UK, Cambridge University Press.

Mittermaier, C. J. A. (1862). *Die Todesstrafe, nach den Wissenschaftlichen Forschungen, der Fortschritte, der Gesetzgebung, und der Erfahrungen*. Heidelberg, Akademische Verlagshandlung von J.C.B. Mohr.

Moir, J. M. (1865). *Capital Punishment, based on Professor Mittermaier's Todesstrafe*. London, Smith, Elder & Co.

Müller, H.-D. (1968). *Der Springer-Konzern: Eine kritische Studie*. München, R. Piper & Co. Verlag.

Munro, I. (2007). US Accused of Torture. *The Sydney Morning Herald*. Sydney October 31 2007.

Musil, R. (1995). *The Man Without Qualities*. New York, Vintage International.

National Council for Crime Prevention Sweden (1997). *Our Collective Responsibility: A National Programme for Crime Prevention*. Stockholm, Swedish Dept. of Justice.

Newburn, T. (forthcoming). 'The Abolition of Capital Punishment in Britain: Political, Cultural and Penal Change in the Mid-Twentieth Century.'

Noelle-Neumann, E. and R. Köcher (1997). *Allensbacher Jahrbuch der Demoskopie 1993–1997*. Allensbach, Allensbacher Institut für Demoskopie.

Noelle-Neumann, E. and R. Köcher (2002). *Allensbacher Jahrbuch der Demoskopie 1998–2002*. Munich, K.G. Saur.

Noyes, H. (1969). 'How Peers Divided to Reject Delay.' *The Times*. London, December 19, 1969.

Nye, R. (2003). 'Two Capital Punishment Debates in France: 1908 and 1981.' *Historical Reflections/Reflexions Historiques* **29**(2): 211–28.

Oberer, W. (1961). 'Does Disqualification of Jurors for Scruples Against Capital Punishment Constitute Denial of Fair Trial on Issue of Guilt?' *Texas Law Review* **39**: 545–67.

OECD (2008). *Education at a Glance 2008: OECD Indicators*, Organization for Economic Cooperation and Development.

Osterloh, K.-H. (1970). *Joseph von Sonnenfels und die österreichische Reformbewegung im Zeitalter des aufgeklärten Absolutismus*. Lübeck and Hamburg, Matthiesen Verlag.

Paley, W. (1825). *The Principles of Moral and Political Philosophy*. Boston, Richardson and Lord.

Pataki, Z. B. (2007). 'Death Penalty.' *Commission en Directe*. **448**.

Perkinson, R. (2008). 'Guarded Hope: Lessons from the History of the Prison Boom.' *Boston Review*. July/August.

Peyrefitte, A. (1977). *Réponses à la violence: Rapport à M. Le Président de la République présenté par le comité d'études sur la violence la criminalité et la Déliquance*. Paris.

Pitkin, H. F. (1967). *The Concept of Representation*. Berkeley and Los Angeles, CA, University of California Press.

President's Commission on Law Enforcement and Administration of Justice (1967). *The Challenge of Crime in a Free Society*. Washington, D.C., United States Government Printing Office.

Prevezer, S. (1957). 'The English Homicide Act: A New Attempt to Revise the Law of Murder.' *Columbia Law Review* **57**: 624–52.

Prévost, M.-L. (2002). *Victor Hugo: l'homme océan*. Bibiothèque Nationale de France. Paris, Le Seuil.

Price, M. E., L. Cosmides and J. Tooby (2002). 'Punitive Sentiment as an Anti-Free Rider Psychological Device.' *Evolution and Human Behavior* **23**: 203–31.

Radbruch, G. (2002). *Gesetzliches Unrecht und übergesetzliches Recht (1946)*. Berlin, Berliner Wissenschafts-Verlag.

Radzinowicz, L. (1999). *Adventures in Criminology*. London, Routledge.

Reicher, D. (2003). *Staat, Schafott, and Schuldgefühl: Was Staatsaufbau und Todesstrafe Miteinander zu Tun Haben*. Opladen, Leske & Buderich.

Reicher, D. (forthcoming). 'Bureaucracy, "Domesticated" Elites, and the Abolition of Capital Punishment. Processes of State-Formation and Numbers of Executions in England and Habsburg Austria between 1700 and 1914.' *Crime, Law and Social Change*.

Reuband, K.-H. (1980). 'Sanktionsverlangen im Wandel.' *Kölner Zeitshcrift fuer Soziologie und Sozialpsychologie* **32**: 508–34.

Riemann, M. (2004). *Einführung in das US-amerikanische Privatrecht*. Munich, C. H. Beck.

Ritzler, C. (2009). Email: Kontaktformular Antwort von Bild.de. Springer Verlag. Hamburg.

Robinson, P. H., Kurzban, R. and Jones, O. D. (2007) 'The Origins of Shared Intuitions of Justice.' *Vanderbilt Law Review* **60**:1633–88.

Roché, S. (2007). 'Criminal Justice Policy in France: Illusions of Severity.' *Crime and Justice* **36**: 471–550.

Rogers, A. (2002). '"Success – At Long Last": The Abolition of the Death Penalty in Massachusetts, 1928–1984.' *Boston College Third World Law Journal* **22**: 281–353.

Rötzsch, R. (2007). 'Aumenta apoio à pena de morte entre os brasileiros.' *Folha de São Paulo*. São Paulo, April 8 2007.

Rousseau, J.-J. (1762). *The Social Contract*. Mineola, NY, Dover.

Rückert, S. (2003). 'Kriminalität, Medien, und Kriminalpolitik.' *Neues in der Kriminalpolitik: Konzepte, Modelle, Evaluation*. E. Minthe. Wiesbaden, Kriminologie und Praxis, pp. 39–48.

Rusche, G. and O. Kirchheimer. (1939) *Punishment and Social Structure*, New York, Russell & Russell.

Rush, B. (1792). *Consideration on the Injustice and Impolicy of Punishing Murder by Death.* Philadelphia, PA, Mathew Carey.

Salas, D. (2005). *La volonté de punir. Essai sur le populisme pénal.* Paris, Hachette Littérature.

Saunders, J. (2001). 'International Perspectives on the Death Penalty: Interview with Staff from Together against the Death Penalty.' February 27 2001. Retrieved September 3 2009, from http://www.cceia.org/resources/transcripts/184.html/:pf_printable?

Savelsberg, J. J. (2000). 'Kulturen staatlichen Strafens: USA und Deutschland.' In J. Gerhards (ed.) *Die Vermessung kultureller Unterschiede. USA und Deutschland im Vergleich.* Opladen, Westdeutscher Verlag, pp. 189–209.

Scalia, A. (2002). 'God's Justice and Ours.' *First Things.* New York, NY, Institute on Religion and Public Life, May.

Schabas, W. (2002). *The Abolition of the Death Penalty in International Law.* Cambridge, UK, Cambridge University Press.

Schabas, W. (2003). 'American Exceptionalism?' In W. Schabas (ed.) *The Barbaric Punishment: Abolishing the Death Penalty.* The Hague, Kluwer Law International.

Schama, S. (1989). *Citizens: A Chronicle of the French Revolution.* New York, Alfred A. Knopf.

Schmidt, E. (1948). 'Goethe und das Problem der Todesstrafe.' *Schweizerische Zeitschrift für Strafrecht* **63**: 444–64.

Schmidt, E. (1995). *Einführung in die Geschichte der deutschen Strafrechtspflege.* Göttingen, Vandenhoeck & Ruprecht.

Schubert, G. (2005) 'Umfrage: Zwei Drittel sagen Ja zur Todesstrafe.' *Tagesecho*, February 24.

Schulz, W. (2008). *Politische Kommunikation: Theoretische Ansätze und Ergebnisse empirischer Forschung.* Wiesbaden, Verlag für Sozialwissenschaften.

Schulze, H. (1998). *Germany: A New History.* Cambridge, MA, Harvard University Press.

Schwartz, B. (1985). *The Unpublished Opinions of the Warren Court.* Oxford, UK, Oxford University Press.

Sellin, T. (1959). *The Death Penalty.* Philadelphia, PA, American Law Institute.

Sellin, T. (1967). 'The Inevitable End of Capital Punishment.' In T. Sellin (ed.) *Capital Punishment.* New York, Evanston and London, Harper & Row, pp. 239–56.

Silverman, S. and R. Paget (1953). *Hanged – And Innocent?* London, Victor Gollancz Ltd.

Simon, J. (2007). *Governing Through Crime: How the War on Crime Transformed American Democracy and Created a Culture of Fear.* Oxford, UK, Oxford University Press.

Simpson, W. and M. Jones (2000). *Europe, 1783–1914.* London, Routledge.

Smets, P.-F. (2003). *Le combat pour l'abolition de la peine de mort : Hugo, Koestler, Camus, d'autres Textes, prétextes et paratextes.* Brussels, Academie Royale de Belgique.

Smith, K. J. M. (2002). *James Fitzjames Stephen: Portrait of a Victorian Rationalist.* Cambridge, UK, Cambridge University Press.

Smith, P. (2003). 'Narrating the Guillotine: Punishment Technology as Myth and Symbol.' *Theory, Culture and Society* **20**(5): 27–51.

Somin, I. (2004). 'Political Ignorance and the Countermajoritarian Difficulty: A New Perspective on the Central Obsession of Constitutional Theory.' *Iowa Law Review* **89**: 1290–371.

Somin, I. (2006). 'Knowledge About Ignorance: New Directions in the Study of Political Information.' *Critical Review* **18**(1–3): 255–78.

Spierenburg, P. (1984). *The Spectacle of Suffering: Executions and the Evolution of Repression.* Cambridge, UK, Cambridge University Press.

Steiker, C. (2002). 'Capital Punishment and American Exceptionalism.' *Oregon Law Review* **81**: 97–125.

Steiker, C. S. and J. Steiker (1995). 'Sober Second Thoughts: Reflections on Two Decades of Constitutional Regulation of Capital Punishment.' *Harvard Law Review* **109**: 355–438.

Stein, M. (2007). *Victor Hugo, orateur politique (1846–1880)*. Paris, Honoré Champion.

Strange, C. (1992). The Politics of Punishment: The Death Penalty in Canada, 1867–1976, Manitoba, University of Manitoba Canadian Legal History Project.

Sundby, S. E. (2005). *A Life and Death Decision: A Jury Weighs the Death Penalty*. New York, Palgrave MacMillan.

Sundby, S. E. (2006). 'The Death Penalty's Future: Charting the Crosscurrents of Declining Death Sentences and the McVeigh Factor.' *Texas Law Review* **84**: 1929–72.

Tack, T. N. (1989). 'Oregon Joins Texas at the Constitutional Outpost: The Oregon Supreme Court Upholds the Death Penalty Statutes in *State* v. *Wagner*.' *Willamette Law Review* **25**: 653–95.

Taylor, C. (1989). *Sources of the Self: The Making of the Modern Identity*. Cambridge, UK, Cambridge University Press.

Taylor, C. (1994). *Multiculturalism: Examining the Politics of Recognition*. Princeton, Princeton University Press.

Taylor, I., P. Walton and J. Young (1974). *The New Criminology: For a Social Theory of Deviance*. New York, NY, Harper & Row.

Thackeray, W. M. (1946). *The Letters and Private Papers of William Makepeace Thackeray*. Cambridge, MA, Harvard University Press.

The Times (1967). 'Calls to Restore Death Penalty.' *The Times*. London, April 19 1967.

Thomas, A. (2008). 'Preface.' In A. Thomas (ed.) *On Crimes and Punishments and Other Writings*. Toronto, CA, University of Toronto Press.

Times Political Editor (1969). 'Marplan Survey of Opinion on Three Political Issues: Common Market Loses Favour.' *The Times of London*. London, October 24 1969.

Tonry, M. (2004). 'Why Aren't German Penal Policies Harsher and Imprisonment Rates Higher?' *German Law Journal* **5**: 1187–206.

Tonry, M. (2009). 'Explanations of American Punishment Policies: A National History.' *Punishment & Society* **11**(3): 377–94.

Toulat, J. (1977). *La Peine de Mort en Question*. Pygmalion, Editions Pygmalion.

Tribe, L. (2000). *American Constitutional Law*. New York, NY, Foundation Press.

Twitchell, N. (2006). 'Abolition of the Death Penalty.' In P. Dorey (ed.) *The Labour Governments, 1964–70*. London, Routledge.

Tyler, T. R. and R. Weber (1982). 'Support for the Death Penalty: Instrumental Response to Crime, or Symbolic Attitude?' *Law & Society Review* **17**(1): 21–46.

Verfassungsausschuss der Ministerpräsidenten-Konferenz der Westlichen Besatzungszonen (1948). *Bericht über den Verfassungskonvent auf Herrenchiemsee vom 10. bis 23. August 1948*. Munich, Richard Pflaum Verlag.

Verri, P. and A. Verri (2008). 'From "Response to a Writing Entitled 'Notes and Observations on the Book *On Crimes and Punishments*'"' In A. Thomas (ed.) *On Crimes and Punishments and Other Writings*. Toronto, CA, University of Toronto Press.

Voltaire (1999). *Prix de la Justice et la Humanité*. Paris, L'Arche Éditeur.

Voltaire (2008). 'Commentary on the Book *On Crimes and Punishments* by a Provincial Lawyer.' In A. Thomas (ed.) *On Crimes and Punishments and Other Writings*. Toronto, CA, University of Toronto Press.

von Sonnenfels, J. (1769–76). *Grundsätze der Polizey*. Munich, C. H. Beck.

Vopel, R. (2007). 'Chop Their Heads Off?' *Commission en Directe.* **449.**

Wacquant, L. (2002). 'Deadly Symbiosis: Rethinking Race and Imprisonment in Twenty-First Century America.' *Boston Review* **27**(2).

Wehler, H.-U. (2006). *Deutsche Gesellschaftsgeschichte 1849–1914.* Munich, C. H. Beck.

Wengst, U. (1997). *Thomas Dehler, 1897–1967: Eine politische Biographie.* Munich, R. Oldenbourg Verlag.

Werner, W. (ed.) (1996). *Der Parlamentarische Rat 1948–49: Akten und Protokolle, Band 9 (Plenum).* Munich, Haraldt Boldt Verlag.

Westen, D., C. Kilts, P. S. Blagov, K. Harenski and S. Hamman (2006). 'The neural basis of motivated reasoning: An fMRI study of emotional constraints on political judgment during the U.S. Presidential election of 2004.' *Journal of Cognitive Neuroscience* **18**(11): 1947–58.

Whitman, J. Q. (2003). *Harsh Justice: Criminal Punishment and the Widening Divide between America and Europe.* Oxford, UK, Oxford University Press.

Whitman, J. Q. (2004). 'The Two Western Cultures of Privacy: Dignity versus Liberty.' *Yale Law Journal* **113**: 1151–221.

Whitman, J. Q. (2007). 'Consumerism Versus Producerism: A Study in Comparative Law.' *Yale Law Journal* **117**: 340–406.

Windlesham, L. (1993). *Responses to Crime.* Oxford, UK, Oxford University Press.

Zimring, F. E. (2003). *The Contradictions of American Capital Punishment.* Oxford, UK, Oxford University Press.

Zimring, F. E. and G. Hawkins (1997). *Crime is Not the Problem: Lethal Violence in America.* Oxford, UK, Oxford University Press.

Zimring, F. E. and D. T. Johnson (2008). 'Law, Society, and Capital Punishment in Asia.' *Punishment & Society* **10**(2): 103–15.

Zimring, F. E., G. Hawkins and S. Kamin (2001). *Punishment and Democracy: Three Strikes and You're Out in California.* Oxford, UK, Oxford University Press.

Index

WITHDRAWN